FINDING THE
WAY HOME

Kenly – Good to see
you last weekend. Peace –

Locke Rush

Finding The Way Home

Locke Rush, Ph.D

Ilm House-LLC
Unionville, PA

*T*hose who come to the world will

one by one drink the juice of death.

This world is just a bridge

although the young wouldn't guess it.

—Yunus Emre, **The Drop
That Became the Sea**

CONTENTS

INTRODUCTION i

1. LOSING EVERYTHING 1

2. CONQUEST AND FEAR OF COMMITMENT 7

3. THE LIFE I PLANNED 21

4. I CANNOT TELL YOU WHAT IT IS 27

5. FOR I WAS AFRAID THOU WOULDST HEAR ME TOO SOON....... 35

6. I ALL BUT DID IT 49

7. SUBTRACTING DAY BY DAY 61

8. NO PIOUS PRACTICE IS PERFECT 83

9. NOT THE TEACHING OF THE BUDDHA 95

10. HOW DO I LOVE? 103

11. EXPERIMENTING WITH TRUTH 121

12. POTENTIAL FORMS OF CONSCIOUSNESS 127

13. YOU WILL KNOW THEM BY THEIR FRUITS 141

14. THE WALK OF AN ENLIGHTENED MAN 151

15. WHO CAN CORRECT WHOM? 163

16. WASHING MY OWN GARMENTS 173

17. OPENING THE DOOR, LOOKING INSIDE 183

18. NOW YOU HAVE TO DO SOME WORK 197

19. WHAT IS WILL ALWAYS BE 211

20. WISDOM PSYCHOLOGY 219

21. COME TO PRAYER 233

22. TIME IS MOVING FAST 241

23. I KNOW I HAVE TO DIE 257

ACKNOWLEDGEMENTS 281

INTRODUCTION

For years, I had a recurring dream in which I found myself in a room with 99 doors. Every time I had the dream, I opened another door. Once I walked into an empty closet. Another time I opened a door into a passageway that looped around and led me back out the same door. One door led to a bottomless pit, another to a tiger. Every door presented a different distraction, sometimes dangerous, and none of the doors led me to anything I wanted. In the 99 doors dream, I was always aware of one particular door, one I had not opened, and I always wondered what was behind that one door.

The journey I have described in this book led me to explore many wonders and mysteries. It was also full of paths that led to nowhere and paths that led me around in circles. I opened and closed many doors and found behind each one an opportunity to confront my own issues, extract the wisdom to be found, and then move on. Finally I found the key to the one door that showed me the way home to my original connection with God. Behind that one door, I found the path of the 99 beautiful qualities of God. This book describes how I found my way to that path, and what it has been like to walk it.

My teacher, Sufi Master M.R. Bawa Muhaiyaddeen, spoke of the 99 beautiful qualities of God as the birthright of a true human being. He also spoke of the hundredth quality, which belongs to God alone. In another sense, the 99 divine qualities may also be seen as 99 steps on the path to God. Each step confronts us with issues related to a particular quality. Sometimes we say that God is testing us. However, Bawa taught that God does not test us. Instead, each step is an opportunity to deal with a particular issue and move up to the next level.

I was born in 1932, and though I suffered intensely from the disruptive effects that World War II caused in my family, I came of age during a period of prosperity and relative peace. Perhaps because of the war, my generation and the next felt a need to make sense of the world and our lives. Bohemianism, Woodstock, psychedelics, yoga, gurus, LSD, Zen, psychic stimuli, New Age techniques—our society was flooded with hundreds of responses to the deepest questions about the meaning of life.

I had the benefit of living in a privileged strata of our society: prep school, Ivy League college, and an inherited view that one should marry well, work for an established company, have children and grandchildren, go on European vacations, and accumulate wealth to leave to one's heirs. Until I was thirty years old, I assumed that eventually this scenario would unfold as expected. My career was off to a promising start, and my New York City life was fast-paced, involving lots of alcohol, women, parties, and what I perceived as fun. Pursuing this course had led me into a serious relationship with a woman that lasted for several years and dissolved, leaving me alone, unfulfilled, and acutely aware of the unsatisfactory nature of my existence. My life was a black and white movie and I was longing for living color.

My search took me to Europe and the Far East for eight years. It involved intensive Jungian analysis, a year as a Zen monk in Japan, and many other exotic experiences. Upon returning to the States, I explored psychedelic drugs, the death process, and transpersonal psychology, and I got to know a host of people who were then and are now considered the leaders of transpersonal psychology.

The list of people I knew and worked with is long. I gathered some knowledge along the way, but it took me years to find the goal I was seeking—the pure, precious gold of truth that needed no adornment. There were, of course, titillating experiences, sensual and emotional pleasures, and *Aha!* experiences, but no teacher, philosophy, or technique that truly made me a better or more compassionate human being. Many teachers I met and came to know were decent people who believed in their way or method, but I was put off by their worldliness and faults. I had heard or read that any teaching is only as high as the teacher and any therapy is only as high as the therapist, so I wandered from teacher to teacher and therapy to therapy, always seeking completion and never finding it.

After thirteen years of opening and closing doors, I found what I had been looking for—a real teacher, a true father, a saint, an enlightened being. He was the kind of person I had read about in hundreds of spiritual books but never before encountered. His name was M. R. Bawa Muhaiyaddeen. He was a tiny, small-boned, dark-skinned man with a white beard and eyes that radiated compassion and understanding. His eyes saw into me, and I sensed that they saw everything about me—past, present, and future. Bawa means Father in Tamil, and he was both the nurturing father I had always longed for and a father of a more divine nature. This good and wise man was truly 'in this world but not of it.'

I spent eleven years with Bawa. Without having to ask, I received answers to my most important questions. I did not discover what had happened to me in New York City, but it doesn't concern me anymore. It is not important to have a name for my experience or to know how and why it happened. It was simply a gift from God.

When I first met Bawa, he told me that everything I had experienced was only half of what exists and that I needed to look at the other half if I wanted to find the peace, understanding, and joy I was seeking. He called these halves left and right, referring to the left as the realm of illusion and to the right as the realm of God. I had been gamboling in the field of the left for years, and he showed me that it was time to cross over to the field of the right.

The moment he spoke the words, I knew he was right, and I understood why it had taken so long to find the truth. I had relegated God to the abstract. All my seeking had been world-oriented. The states and stages espoused by New Age gurus were pleasing and sometimes sublime, but they all enhanced the ego and cultivated a sense of 'I-ness.' Bawa's work focused on seeing through the identification with the ego and practicing the qualities of God. The veils covering our essential, pure being must be lifted, and this lifting is hard work, requiring more than periodic meditation retreats or courses in mind-body techniques. Lifting the veils requires determination and moment-by-moment awareness of our struggle with the darker side of our nature. Although most of the teachers I met acknowledged the necessity to struggle with worldly desires, they either minimized the struggle or placed the focus of their teaching somewhere else.

The path Bawa revealed leads back to the inherently pure nature that is our true being. He spoke of the world of the souls. For seventy thousand years, Bawa explained, God tried to tell the souls what the nature of paradise was and what evil was, but the souls could not understand what they had not experienced. God saw this and commanded them to go to earth so they could comprehend their true nature and the difference between good and evil. The souls cried out that they did not want to leave the place they were in. But God in His wisdom persisted, saying that when they had separated right from wrong and walked the path to understanding, they would find their way back home.

We all can see how beautiful, clear, and close to God a newborn baby is. Time passes, the child grows, and countless veils obscure awareness of the soul: ego, karma, illusion, anger, lust, racial prejudice, jealousy, greed, fear of death, and many more. When finally the Angel of Death comes to take him away, the same soul who many years before begged to stay in the world of the souls begs God, "No, please don't make me go. I don't want to leave this place. I want to stay."

We didn't want to come here, and when it is time to die, we don't want to leave. This is the irony of our lives, but also the catalyst for our progress as souls. This life on earth is a brief stay in a university of higher knowledge. We are here to experience, to learn, to make our choices, and to act according to our developing wisdom. If we make the effort and pass our final examination, we will return to our rightful place with God.

This is the path that spread out before me when I opened that one door I had been unable to open in my dreams. The work I did with Bawa did not require a monastery. It stressed the holy place inside and showed me how I could proceed inward to that place. The path to the inner heart does not require intellectual calisthenics or complex spiritual technologies. There are, however, many side roads and detours, and what is needed and is essential is a map in the form of the teachings and the example of a truly wise person, an enlightened being.

I am forever grateful for knowing Bawa and for the wisdom he imparted to me and to all people who care to seek it out. It is with this gratitude in my heart that I wrote this book. It tells of my journey toward that inner goal, and I hope it will be of some benefit to you.

Locke Rush
December 2001

To gain that which is worth having, it may be necessary to lose everything.

—Bernadette Devlin

-1-

LOSING EVERYTHING

I was born in December of 1932, the second of three sons. My brother Richard Stockton Rush, Jr., known as Tock, was two years older than I. When I was four, my brother John was born. My friends and I soon nicknamed him Barrel, and we were sometimes referred to humorously as Lock, Stock, and Barrel.

My father also had a nickname—Sticky. I never did find out how he got the name because the only time I called him that, egged on by Tock, my father picked me up by the seat of my pants and deposited me in my room for the night, where I dined on bread and water and memorized Bible verses.

During my first few years, I was attended to by a series of nannies, and I don't think I experienced much trauma. My mother was a lady, beautiful and kind, though I probably received more attention from my nannies. It is hard for me to extricate early memories of my mother from memories of my nannies. I do remember that the nannies looked after me, fed me, and trotted me out for parties and other special occasions, dressed in knee pants and white socks, but my mother always put me to bed with a story.

My life was ideal in many ways. I remember running through our house and playing with our dog, both house and dog huge to my small eyes. I romped through the fields, rode bareback, skated at the local ice skating club, tobogganed, and got into innocent mischief with my brothers.

My father was an insurance company executive who also ran

our sixty-acre farm. Every night he came home from work, put on his overalls, and went to work at what he loved best. Ours was a real working farm, located twenty miles west of Philadelphia. My father grew hay and alfalfa. Before the war changed our lives, we had two horses, twenty-eight Guernsey cows, fifteen pigs, and probably a thousand chickens. I earned pocket money by milking the cows and doing various other farm chores. Eventually, I raised my own chickens and learned how to castrate them, and I also learned how to castrate the pigs.

Although my father was a strict disciplinarian, usually his punishments were just and quite in keeping with the child rearing views of the 1930s. I knew the rules, and I knew what to expect when I broke them. If I swore, my mouth was washed out with green soap. If I didn't finish all the food on my plate, I was sent to my room and had to eat the leftover food cold at breakfast the next day. If I disobeyed my elders, I was given solitary confinement with nothing but bread and water, a Bible, and a list of verses to memorize. Extreme disobedience met with the razor strap on my bare backside. I bore my father's discipline well, probably because I learned quickly and was clever.

My father was a perfectionist. He had a thing about neatness, cleanliness, and order. He corrected any task I did and made me persist until it was perfect. Whether or not this was the motivating force, I grew up wanting to do everything perfectly. I don't think I was obsessive, but I strove to do my very best in everything—schoolwork, farm chores, special projects, athletics, everything. My early challenges never seemed too great to tackle or to master. At Haverford School, which I attended from first through ninth grades, I excelled at everything for the first few years. I won races in swimming and running. I enjoyed my schoolwork, and I earned top grades with moderate effort. A grade of B or even an A-minus felt like a failure and prompted me to work harder.

I was considered the most appealing and attractive brother. Whereas Tock was dark and brooding, I was a sunny child, with white blond hair and loads of self-confidence. I was optimistic and interested in everything. To me, life was a big circus. I had a good sense of humor, and I was a born mimic. I could imitate animals and birds and people. I taught myself the piano. Everything I touched turned to gold.

In December of 1941, when I was just nine years old, everything changed. War came, and my father left home. My hero had vanished, throwing my life off balance. As the months went by and he didn't return, I learned to cope, but the wonderful confidence I had taken for granted was badly shaken. I had lost my anchor, the reassurance that came from the presence of a strong father.

I was no longer the best. My grades and my athletic prowess had slipped along with my confidence. I had enjoyed being on the diving team, and suddenly I was afraid of difficult dives. During a wrestling match, I was pinned flat on my back while my antagonist shouted down at me, "Your father's a bastard!" Such taunts are common among young boys, but this time something snapped inside. I felt utterly hopeless, defeated, and incompetent. The last of my courage drained away.

What was left of my family collapsed during the summer of 1945, when my father was mustering out of the Navy. Instead of my life returning to normal, which I had been eagerly anticipating, my parents decided to divorce. I remember a lot of drinking and shouting. I remember seeing my father come into our house, very awkward and stiff and not saying anything to my mother as he packed some of his things. Children aren't stupid; I knew something bad was happening. I'm sure my mother must have told us that our father was going away for a while, but in those days people didn't sit their kids down and say, *Mother and Dad are going to separate and this is what will happen.* They broke the news piecemeal, hoping the kids wouldn't notice. I noticed. Despite losing my father to the war, I had trusted that, ultimately, both of my parents would be there for me, together. The dissension between them destroyed my trust. The security of my family had failed me, so how could I trust that I wouldn't fail myself? Everywhere I looked I saw evidence of my failure. I failed subjects for the first time. I wasn't good enough to make the teams in any sport.

I can vividly remember sitting in my classroom in eighth grade trying to do a fairly simple geometry problem. I thought I knew the answer but I didn't want to write it down because I might be wrong. The more I thought about it, the more convoluted my thoughts became.

A true ignominy came after ninth grade when I failed my entrance examinations to Phillips Academy in Andover, Massachusetts. The prestigious boarding prep school finally allowed me to enroll, but only on the condition that I repeat the ninth grade. I didn't want to go away to school. It certainly would have been much better for my self-image and my sense of security if I had been permitted to stay at home. But I was expected to go, along with most of the other children my age. In Main Line Philadelphia society in those days, children traditionally were sent off to boarding school after ninth grade to get the best education possible. I'm fairly certain, however, that the real reason was to give our parents some breathing room.

I resented being sent away. I felt further alienated from my family. With Father gone forever, I felt keenly the need for security and a home life, and instead I had been shipped off to boarding school. My world was dismal. After the freedom of the farm, it was a tremendous strain to spend so much time indoors with 750 boys, all of whom were extremely smart. During the first year, I regularly wrote and implored my mother, "Take me out of this awful place. I hate it!" My life felt like an automobile engine that was beginning to give out. Suddenly, it was hard to start, it sputtered, it made odd noises, and it backfired. I didn't know how to fix it. I knew I was running at seventy-five percent efficiency, and it really got to me.

Growing up on a farm had accustomed me to the realities of life and death, but I had never been tested the way I was being tested in boarding school. I went through a premature toughening which I have spent the rest of my life gradually undoing. Just to get through it, to meet the expectations set for me, and to get on to the next grade required that I work harder than I ever had. The worst of it was, the harder I worked, the worse my grades were. Fortunately, the housemaster during my tenth grade was a wonderful man who understood where I was emotionally. I could talk to him. He filled in the missing places left by my father.

By then, however, perfection was out of the question, replaced by a more modest desire to be 'good enough.' I was miserable not only because Phillips Academy was a tough school and my parents had divorced, but also because I was still hairless at fourteen! My delayed puberty was a further blow to my confidence. I'd make sure the shower was empty before I went in, and I'd make sure to face the wall. Not only that, but I was tiny, only five foot three. I was a hairless, five-foot-three wimp in a crowd of hairy giants, many of whom were younger than I. My late puberty mortified me. The die was cast—my fallibility had become a fact, and it lent a deep fear to my life.

I got through it. I was very relieved when I started shooting up. I grew nearly six inches in my sophomore and junior years. Gradually, my grades crept up to low honors, B-minus. I learned escape mechanisms. Since I could no longer excel at scholastics or even sports, unconsciously I looked for something else I could be really good at. I found it in the social arena: girls.

Although I went to an all boys' school, I had plenty of opportunity to hone my skills. Five hundred yards away was a sister school, Abbott Academy, and I kept in close touch with girls from home as well. I cultivated a modus operandi in place of my real work, which at that time should have been schoolwork. I knew I was good at charming people because I always had been the most outgoing of my brothers, the one who made everyone laugh and say, "How cute!" As a teenager, I grabbed hold of that strength and blew it up like a balloon. Charming people, especially girls, became a way of life for many years.

I remember tea dances with the girls from Abbott, dancing close, flirting. When I was a little older, I went to debutante parties. I could tell when a girl liked me, and I played on that. This is certainly a natural part of being a teenager and young adult, but my flirting and conquests didn't end after high school and college. They became a way of life that went on for years. And when I discovered alcohol, the pace of the game became much more frenetic.

Sex offered me great satisfaction at several levels: ego and sense gratification; revenge for the wrongs Mother had done to me through divorce; and, unconsciously, fulfillment of the desire for Oedipal union. To gain the upper hand, I played 'personality games' to woo girls who didn't know I would lose interest the minute I had made my conquest and satisfied my curiosity. The whole game was loaded emotionally because the areas of affection and need were highly charged. Women symbolized love, mother, peace, security, joy, and acceptance. At the same time, the slightest rejection aroused feelings of my mother's rejection and my own worthlessness, leaving me angry, frustrated, and afraid.

To succeed at the game and thereby avoid these potentially self-destructive feelings, I carefully constructed a desirable ego image, and this image was all-important. It was my mainstay, my emotional credit card. Since I was not unattractive physically and emotionally, and since I was quite well tuned to others' needs and appetites, I did it well. My social expertise soon became a unique defense mechanism that kept out a hostile world and any true feelings.

In love, there are two things important to a man: the conquest of a proud soul and the possession of a tender one.

—*Stendhal, De L'amour*

–2–

CONQUEST AND FEAR OF COMMITMENT

Somehow I survived and got into Princeton. My extracurricular activities helped a great deal, and I had very good recommendations from my teachers. Princeton was my father's alma mater, and my brother was already there. I'm sure my determination to make it into Princeton was helped by a great desire to live up to their achievements. Like many young men my age who didn't know what they wanted to do, I decided I would be another Ernest Hemingway. I dreamed of traveling the world and writing about life.

After my sophomore year, I went off to Europe for the summer with two friends. We pooled our money and bought a little car. That summer made a big impression on me. I was fascinated with being in a foreign country and learning to speak another language. I understood French because I had studied it at school, but I was unable to speak it until one day when I was standing near the altar at Chartres Cathedral. The light was filtering through the stained glass windows. The cathedral was beautiful and peaceful. A man spoke to me in French. He was a small man, French, with an un-lit cigarette dangling from his mouth. I asked him if he would speak more slowly. He did, and two hours later, I was flying. I had learned to express myself in another language! It didn't matter to me that I did it poorly. I could understand him and he could understand me. When I got back to Princeton, I changed my major to French literature in a special program on European civilization.

I did not graduate cum laude from Princeton, but I received

accolades I thought equal in prestige: *Parlor Athlete, Playboy,* and *Most Witty of the Class of 1955.*

I followed my older brother into the United States Marine Corps. In those days, military service was obligatory. I had attended three months of boot camp during the summer between my junior and senior years, so the next step was to complete six months of intensive officer training.

Boot camp was the toughest challenge I had ever faced. My drill instructor was a highly decorated war hero who had a plate of steel in his head from a wound he had received in battle. He worked our asses off. He let us know right in the beginning what was in store for us. "You guys are going to hate me. But when you get out of here, you will know what to do. You will have no question about how to survive. You will have no doubt or hesitation. What you are going to learn in these three months will save your life, and I'm not going to cut any corners. I care enough about you guys to make it tough for you. When it is over, you will thank me, but you won't be thanking me while you are here."

We sure didn't thank him while we were there. A third of the people dropped out, and in the entire training battalion, one died of heat exhaustion. On one occasion, we marched for hours in full sun, 105 degrees, up and down hills, wearing and carrying over a hundred pounds of equipment. After marching several miles, we stopped. "Break out your canteens," he ordered. I was relieved, because I had begun to think I wasn't going to make it.

We broke out our canteens.

"Hold your canteen up to your lips."

We raised our canteens and waited for the command that would allow us to relieve our thirst before starting back to camp.

"Tip your canteen, men, and pour the water on the ground."

We poured the precious water on the ground and resumed our march.

I received my lieutenant's bars and was stationed in Camp Pendleton, Oceanside, California, for my two years of service. I received command of my own communications platoon in an

Amtrak battalion. Putting me in charge of the platoon was like calling a green apple red. Fortunately, two of the men under me were highly decorated, battle-scarred veterans. They ran my platoon. Both were full-blooded American Indians. One, Tsoodle, was a Pima Indian, and the other, Choate, was Cherokee. These guys had fought in the Korean War; they had killed people and had been wounded. They took me under their wing like fathers, but it was always, *Yes, Sir. What would you like, Sir?*

Once, as we prepared for a general's inspection, I questioned them several times about something I thought had not been done according to regulations. "No, Sir." Tsoodle assured me repeatedly, brushing away my concerns as youthful inexperience. "We'll get a good grade on that, Sir." Well, he was wrong. We got a lousy grade. I was furious. I reamed Tsoodle up one side and down the other. It's funny, he could have run the platoon fifteen times better than I, but he bowed his head and took his medicine.

I gained a little respect then, but I noted that it had been gained through showing my anger. Even so, I had no desire to cross those guys because they made the platoon work. If they had not liked and respected me, my life would have been a nightmare; I saw it happen to others. I loved those men.

My experience in the Corps left me with a great respect for the tradition of people who have given their lives for a cause. The Marine Corps is a great outfit. Sloppy, dirty punks with no self-respect got their asses kicked around until they realized they were worth something and didn't have to be slovenly and wise-ass. I saw a number of lives get turned completely around for the better. That is what discipline with a purpose, enforced fairly, can do. Whenever I meet someone who was in the Corps, I feel an instant bond. Even if I have never met the person before, I know what he has been through because I have been through the same thing. Just making it through boot camp is an achievement.

On the personal front, nothing much changed except that my East Coast life moved west and intensified. My pattern of womanizing and other excesses continued. On the West Coast there were no debutante parties or chaperones or exams to pass or rules to adhere to. For the first time I was out in the wide world, an adult. My life was my own and I could do with it what I pleased, as long as I did not discredit the Corps.

There was, however, a rising uneasiness in me. The germ of disillusionment that had begun when my father left home was growing. Amidst all the drama and fun of life, I sensed that all was not best in this best of all possible worlds. I couldn't define my malaise. I knew my overdeveloped appetite for sex was unhealthy, but it seemed more a result than a cause.

I also knew I was drinking a lot, but I had always considered drinking a normal part of adult life. My parents had enjoyed their cocktails when I was growing up. They rarely drank to the point of drunkenness, but they became inebriated daily, beginning at five o'clock in the evening. Too young to engage, my two brothers and I watched with great interest and amusement as our parents consumed glass after glass of their magic potions. Humor, laughter, joking, and a feeling of all's-well-with-the-world soon filled the library. The big people did it, so we concluded it must be okay, especially since once in a while we were given a bit of sherry or sips of wine and champagne as previews and promises of better things to come.

By the time I was stationed in Laguna Beach, I was drinking so much that I was having blackouts. On Saturday and Sunday mornings, sometimes it took me over an hour to discover where I had parked my car the night before. I see now that I was already an alcoholic, although I certainly didn't think of it that way. In my circle, drinking to excess was no big deal. If you didn't, you were a wimp. At debutante parties, the person who drank the most and was the most outrageous without being harmful or obscene was considered the most entertaining. I knew how to hold my liquor. I learned to monitor my behavior and control my speech. A doctor friend of mine gave me some eye drops that shrank the blood vessels in my eyes, and I sprayed stuff in my mouth to mask my breath. I learned many gimmicks like this as my drinking increased.

At first, I drank to free my inhibitions so that I could express my feelings and opinions more openly, but soon I needed two or three shots of whiskey before I could even begin to relax. To complement the drinking and the womanizing and the worldly-wise image, I was smoking two or three packs of cigarettes a day.

I have since learned that an alcoholic is not determined by what or how much he or she drinks, or by when or where. The issue is whether the drinking causes a problem in the social, physical, emotional, spiritual, or legal realms. My blackouts were a sign of a physical problem, and soon a serious incident erupted in my social life that also affected my physical well-being. It was a wake-up call, and I still carry the scar to remind me of it.

While in Laguna Beach, I was dating a divorcee, Elaine. She was the ex-wife of a large Philippine-American professional boxer who was a bouncer in one of the local bars I frequented. More than once he warned me to stay away from his ex-wife. Since I was inevitably full of liquor during these encounters, I joked around with him and disregarded his warnings.

One evening after a long night of drinking and partying, Elaine and I returned to my apartment. We were already in bed when we were startled to hear someone pounding on the door. It was Emilio, roaring obscenities and threats. He weighed at least two hundred thirty pounds, and he was breaking the door down. To put a stop to the damage, I opened the door. He burst in. Wild-eyed and red with fury, he picked me up with one arm, held me against the wall, and battered my face. When he had finished with me, he began on his ex-wife. Eventually Emilio's rampage wound down and he left, slamming the broken door after him.

I drove Elaine to a nearby hospital emergency room for treatment. Emilio had broken her jaw. Elaine got her jaw wired and was given a glass straw, and I got ten stitches over my eye. As a Marine Corps lieutenant in charge of a platoon, I dared not press charges for fear of incurring a dishonorable discharge.

I knew I had no one to blame but myself for Emilio's brutality. All the danger signs had been there and I had ignored them. Alcohol had led me directly into the path of a buzz saw. Any sensitivity or intelligence I could have used to avert the situation had been blunted by alcohol. I was afraid Emilio would come after me again. I just wanted to get out of there, so I moved to San Diego to finish out my time with the Marine Corps.

There I moved in with an eighty-year-old spinster, my mother's cousin Sarah. She lived alone in a Spanish house on a hill overlooking Mission Bay, where I came and went pretty much at my leisure. She was a strong and independent soul who communed with God regularly and who attended six o'clock Mass every morning. She was grateful to have me stay with her. She said it kept her young.

Although I didn't realize it at the time, Sarah had a profound and subtle effect on my life. The things that influence us often are not loud and brassy. They are quiet, and they penetrate. And that was Sarah. For the first time, I saw the older side of life and what happens when you reach your seventies and eighties. Sarah knew the life I was leading and where it would take me. She also had the wisdom not to try to change me. I was too young to listen to sermons, and she was too wise to deliver them. Her character did the speaking and later the changing.

In the last few weeks before my discharge from the military, we regularly went for long rides in her car. We sat in the backseat while her driver took us to lovely places around the valley. Sarah had begun to suffer episodes of losing her sensory equilibrium, and sometimes during these drives she fell into unconsciousness for a few moments. She knew and I knew that these episodes were the forerunners of her death. Still, she took them as they came, more embarrassed for me than fearful of her passing.

After I left San Diego, Sarah corresponded frequently with me, opening her heart to me and expressing her religious convictions much more than she ever had done while I was living with her.

My last stop before returning to the East Coast was San Francisco, where I visited my older brother. Although Tock was married, he was eager to join me in my escapades. I had saved three or four thousand dollars, and I spent it all in three or four weeks. Once toward the end of my stay, I spent an evening drinking and came home with a woman I had singled out as attractive and accessible. When I woke up next to her in the morning, I saw that she was much older than I had realized; worse, she was the mother of one of the young women at the party. She could have been my own mother!

I left my car in San Francisco, borrowed plane fare from my brother, and arrived in Pennsylvania flat broke. I moved back into my old room at home and got a job selling Fuller Brushes in South Philadelphia.

I had the worst time selling Fuller brushes. My Fuller Brush mentor was Jimmy Stewart. He looked like Jimmy Stewart. He was tall and had a soft, smooth manner. On the first day, he showed me the ropes. The houses were very close together in South Philadelphia, a plus for any door-to-door salesman. We went to the first house. A woman opened the door. Jimmy said, "Madam, I'm Jimmy Stewart." He stuck out his hand and they shook hands. "I have a free gift for you."

"Oh, you do!" the woman said, interested.

"Yes, if I could come in, I'll get it for you. It's in the bag here." That was the gimmick, of course. The free gift was always at the bottom of the bag.

He sat down and pretended to search through his bag, laying out his wares on her carpet. By the time he worked his way down to the free gift, she had already found two or three things she wanted to buy.

The same thing happened at the second house and the third. "Do you get the idea?" he asked.

"Yeah! I got it." It certainly looked easy enough.

"Okay. You're on your own. Good luck."

I went up to the next house and knocked on the door. A woman answered. "Hi," I said cheerfully. "I'm Locke Rush. I'm a Fuller Brush salesman." The door slammed.

What did I do wrong? I wondered. I went to the next house and the next, and the same thing happened. Out of half a dozen houses that day, I got in the door only twice, and I didn't make a sale.

It was an enlightening experience. Jimmy Stewart was an expert at the subtle arts of salesmanship: the way he looked, the tone of his voice, his exact words, his body language, how much he leaned forward or kept back. All the work is done in the first few seconds, because that's what determines whether you will get into the house. It took me a while to learn that.

So for a few months I sold Fuller Brushes and managed to make a living. When I was having a bad day, my one recourse was to visit a woman who lived at the end of a narrow street. I could count on her to ask me in. She dressed a bit provocatively, usually smelled of alcohol, and loved to buy things from me, sometimes two hundred dollars worth. She seemed to want other things, but I never stayed long enough to find out for certain.

One day when I called on her, she said, "I'm sorry. I can't let you in. My husband says I'm not allowed to spend any more money."

I learned what a bad salesman I was, how much work it takes to be a good salesman, and how much patience and perseverance it takes. The days were hot, and I sweated in my obligatory tie and jacket. Most of all, it is not fun to get rejected, particularly when it happens several times a day.

Although I didn't recognize it then, I was also given a hint about the years of living that stretched out before me: my prize was at the bottom of the bag and I was going to go through a lot of other things before I found it.

In 1959, I landed a good job with a large and prestigious pharmaceutical company, SmithKline, which was staffed by members of some of the oldest families in Philadelphia society. It was a formal, suit-and-tie company, very hierarchical. I was accepted as part of a yearlong executive training program. I spent two months in each section of the company, learning the ropes. At the end of the program, I was slotted into Retail Relations as the assistant manager. I went to trade shows and the like.

Meanwhile, back in my childhood home, I found myself in a classic conflict with my mother. My mother had been overjoyed at my return from the Corps. I was twenty-five and an ex-Marine, but I was still her baby, and she was determined to take care of me. She'd get up at six to make my breakfast. I was accustomed to being independent, so I started getting up at quarter to six to make my own breakfast. Still determined, she set her alarm for five-thirty so she could beat me to the kitchen. It was ridiculous.

I had to leave. It was time for me to be on my own again. I realized then that the umbilical cord has to be cut more than once. It felt like a cruel thing to do. My mother was a loving and wonderful woman, but I felt her claws in me. She didn't mean to hurt me, but I couldn't move freely. She'd ask if I would be home for dinner. When I said no, she was upset. When I said yes, I wasn't free to live my own life. And so, once I was receiving a regular paycheck from SmithKline, I took an apartment in Haverford.

I struggled to fit in at SmithKline. I didn't feel comfortable there. At lunch, for instance, I wanted to go out alone and have a beer and a sandwich somewhere, but I was told that it was frowned upon, that I should hang around with the people in the office. As far as I was concerned, it was *my* free time; I continued to do what I wanted, but I could tell that people didn't like it when I went my own way. It felt like an echo of what I had experienced with my mother, as if they wanted to own my body and soul.

I also was disillusioned. I don't know how, but I had gotten the mistaken impression that pharmaceutical companies were altruistic, that their goal was to end suffering and serve the poor. I had dreamed of going to South America, finding new drugs in the jungles, and bringing them back to ease the suffering of humanity. Instead, I found that SmithKline was very much into making money.

While I was there, I was introduced to amphetamines. It was the late fifties and, like most of the people I worked with, I drank quite a bit and stayed up late, so I needed something stronger than coffee to get me going in the morning. Taken alone, amphetamines made me shaky and caused my heart to pound. But a friend introduced me to Dexamil, 'the feel good pill.' Pharmaceutical magic produced an upper that also left me feeling quite mellow. Dexamil was a major moneymaker for SmithKline.

I got in the habit of setting out two Dexamils and a glass of water next to the radio by my bed every night. I took the pills as soon as my alarm went off and lay back down. Only ten minutes later, I was so full of energy that I couldn't stay in bed.

I poured my newfound energy and my desire to make a difference into revamping the executive training program. Certainly I had learned a lot by working in the different areas of the company, but I thought the program was not properly structured or supervised and was lacking in many ways. Since many of my fellow trainees agreed with my assessment, I convened a meeting and asked for their suggestions on how to improve the program. Optimistically, and with some sense of self-importance, I combined and organized our ideas and forwarded them to our supervisor, who was in charge of the program.

He was furious. I had failed to realize that my reforming zeal would reflect badly on him. Indirectly, he let it be known that my career at SmithKline was finished. Undaunted, I plowed ahead on my proposal, and my colleagues seemed to share my enthusiasm. I was very naive in the ways of corporate America. When we took a vote on the final version, I discovered that my supervisor had gotten to everyone. Only one person voted for it.

That was the clincher. I didn't want to work for a company that didn't want good ideas. I left. I received many phone calls in the subsequent weeks from friends at SmithKline who applauded me and said they were going to leave, too.

Meanwhile, my personal life had taken a serious turn. Soon after I started at SmithKline, I met Mary.

Mary was my first love. We suited one another beautifully. She was somewhat prim and proper, but after a couple of drinks, her sense of humor came to the fore, and she was vibrant. She loved to sing and dance, and we spent many evenings in our favorite quiet bar, heads together, exchanging confidences. I learned to trust another human being.

Even though I had been promiscuous and often uncritical in my earlier choices, I cared deeply for Mary. I spent two years in Philadelphia with this lovely woman, and during that time I had no other interests. Mary was a unique person. She idealized all that

I sought in a woman. She was physically very attractive, with deep brown hair and blue eyes and the delicate hands and bones of a dancer. I photographed her constantly, trying to capture the grace and allure in her movements and her face.

Mary was a real prize. She was gifted not only physically but also intellectually. She was my age, but she was much more mature in her relationships than I. My philosophy had always been to woo them, bed them, and move on. She let me know right away that she expected more of me, and it was months before we consummated our relationship. Meanwhile, I suspected she was seeing other people. I rushed to pick her up from work early, worrying that she would go off with someone else, then sometimes waited for an hour or more until she could get away.

Although my need for independence had prompted me to move out on my own, I soon became dependent on Mary. Switching emotional dependency from mother to 'other' is a natural part of maturing, and I was now confronting my dependency issues with someone on my level.

Mary was independent. One day she announced that she was going skiing in Vermont over the weekend. "Are you coming?" she asked.

"I don't ski," I said, hoping that would be that.

Mary was matter-of-fact. "Okay, then. See you after the weekend."

I went. I fell down again and again. It was awful, but after several such trips, I learned to ski well enough to enjoy it.

I was going through a questioning period, wondering what to do with my life. I was emotionally needy and intense. Mary understood me. She started me on the path to self-understanding, introducing me to the writings of Kahlil Gibran and Erich Fromm. I was deeply infatuated with her. She was my life.

As our relationship progressed, I remained content with the situation as it was. Mary, however, was eager to get married and have a family. No matter how much I wanted her in my life, I had no intention of settling down or having a family. Two wills collided—I wanted romance, adventure, sex, travel, and partying, while she was looking for security, commitment, maturity, growth, and stability. I could not accept her domestic aspirations. Responsibility, accountability, and seeing life in a mature way were not only well beyond my ken, they were threatening and fear-provoking. I had seen my mother and father fight and separate, and I wanted no part of anything that might provoke such pain.

The situation reached crisis point. Mary, knowing that I was not interested in a serious commitment, had begun to date other men, one in particular. I was devastated, but I would not give in to marriage. On one terrible evening while I was still spending most of my time at her house, she insisted I park my car somewhere else and not make my presence known so that she could invite her date in for a nightcap. So there I was, listening and suffering upstairs when she came home with her date, laughing and joking, her mood buoyant. When he left and she came upstairs, I could say nothing—there was nothing to say. I knew I had painted myself into a corner.

"If you really want me," she said, "you can have me. Not just this but the whole package—marriage, kids, and all." I knew I could not do it. I sat on the floor, sobbing.

In one sense, my life began at that point. I saw myself clearly. All the elements of happiness were there for the taking but so also was the work. I could not taste the fruits in their fullness unless I was willing to invest myself in the work involved in a mature relationship. I would not do it. I was a gardener who was unwilling to pull weeds and carry water.

Mary was wise, much wiser than I. She let me cry out my longing for oneness, security, togetherness, and unity, and then she told me, "You need to let me go."

I had to let her go, even if I was not ready.

I was not my own man. My world was increasingly outer-directed. I had no feeling of center or self-worth. I sought approval in women, family, and professional life. I was so aware of jeopardizing my image that whatever sensitivity I had was covered over by a heavy shellac of role-playing and enforced habits.

I thought about two doctors I had consulted after returning home from military service. One told me I should be ashamed of myself. I was forty pounds overweight, he informed me, I drank and smoked excessively, and I was ruining my health and psyche. I agreed and lit a cigarette on my way out the door.

The second doctor, Dr. Bond, was a psychoanalyst and a fine old man. When I complained about my worthless life, he assured me that my life did indeed have value. This old gentleman was the first person who tried to help me see my positive side. He pointed out that, even if I hadn't been tops in my class, I still had the distinction of being a Princeton graduate. I also had been honorably discharged from the Marine Corps and was about to begin an excellent job at SmithKline.

"You don't need psychoanalysis," he told me. "You just need to go out and live your life."

I tried to see myself in the same light as Dr. Bond saw me, but I could not. When I looked at my life, I saw and felt waste, degradation, fear, and, worst of all, meaninglessness. Three years had passed since then, and my life felt more meaningless than ever. I was not willing to make a lasting commitment to Mary, I was drinking heavily, and I had no sense of direction. On the other hand, although I was out of a job, I was relieved to be free of the rigid formality of SmithKline. I thought about Dr. Bond's advice. I was twenty-seven. I had a college education. I could do anything I wanted. What did I want to do?

I got drunk and made a list of everything I had ever dreamed of doing. Next morning when I was sober, I crossed off things like playing bongo drums on the beach and traveling around on a schooner. Gradually a pattern emerged. Four or five things on my list called out to me: travel, teaching, helping people, music, and photography. I wondered if there might be a way to pull all those things together. One day I woke up and said, "Documentary films!"

To learn what it was like on a sound stage, I took a part-time job as a production assistant for the local film company that was making the sci-fi classic, *The Blob*. I liked the film business, and I had a knack for it. I decided it was time to plunge into documentary film-making wholeheartedly. When I looked around and found that there wasn't much documentary film production in Philadelphia, I set off for New York City.

We must be willing to get rid of the life we've planned, so as to have the life that's waiting for us.

—Joseph Campbell

-3-

THE LIFE I PLANNED

When I got to New York, I looked up an old college roommate who lived on the Upper East Side. He said I could stay at his place for free if I kept the apartment clean and if I got up and left when he brought a girlfriend home.

I made a list of the fifty top documentary film companies in the city, wrote a resume, and walked the streets of New York City in the middle of the summer, making my rounds. No one wanted to hire me. It was an awful experience. On weekends I went out to Long Island and recuperated at a friend's house on the beach, but on Mondays I was back for another round of rejection. When I had made it through my list, I started again at the top.

One day, when I went back to one of the first companies I had visited, the owner, Frank Thayer, said, "Where the hell have you been! I lost your resume. Do you want a job?"

"Sure!"

"Okay. You're a production manager. Now go clean up all those films, patch them up, whatever they need. There's a lot of work in there and I need it all done in ten days."

I moved a cot in, brought a few necessities, and stayed there until the job was finished. I did so well that Frank took me on full-time. I had a real New York job as production manager for United States Productions. I ordered the equipment, learned to operate it, and stayed there for a year, getting my feet wet in the business.

Frank was such a nice man that even when business dropped off, he continued to pay me. I saw what was happening and told him I was resigning. "You can't afford to keep paying me like this."

Shortly afterward, I met an old friend from college, Bob McCarty, who was starting a little company, Seneca Productions. His partner in the venture was Bob Gaffney, a superb cameraman and a very dear friend of Stanley Kubrick. In fact, Gaffney had been the cameraman on several of Kubrick's first films. The three of us had a lot of fun working on our own projects while doing training films for Grumman Aircraft, our bread-and-butter client. I was a camera assistant and production manager. My career was solidly underway.

I look back now and see that even during this period, I was fundamentally unhappy. I had started a new life and a new career in an exciting city, but I still was mired in unrest, womanizing, alcohol, loneliness, and misdirection. Even worse, I was still painfully attached to Mary. Although Mary and I had put some physical distance between us, we had not been able to let go of one another completely. So I drank to forget, to forget the little ego, to forget the shame, to forget the fears. I drank to ease the pain as Mary slipped further and further away. Whiskey was the grass of the early sixties, a way to forget the 'downer' side of life. Whiskey helped me crowd out unpleasant thoughts and embrace a larger flow of life where enemies became friends and doormen philosophers, where money was no object and everything separate flowed together in a haze.

While I was drinking, I was positive and happy, but the depressive action of alcohol went to work on me after the initial stimulus. Unless I kept drinking, the secondary depressive action would take over. Several years later I read some of the dialogues of Sri Ramana Maharshi, an Indian sage who summed up man's plight in one apt statement, "Misery is due to multifarious thoughts." The attempt of all schools of meditation is to still the mind, and, to the extent that this is done, one feels true peace. The alcoholic's efforts, though misguided, are intuitively directed at the same target. Unfortunately he chooses a weapon that inevitably backfires.

As I had found, larger doses of alcohol slowed down my mental machinery and made me ebullient, but they also led to dangerous blackouts and irresponsible social behavior.

Sex had been a release, yet even the thrill of orgasm began to diminish. I sometimes tried to avoid sex when I felt I was being used as a 'male whore.' Even in these cases, however, I feared confrontation and rejection as a lover, so I told myself not to be hasty because this woman or that might be the only one around on a cold weekend. I was using women, and they were using me. I craved assurance that I was attractive to women as much as I craved their comfort.

One incident brought the drinking and womanizing to a head. I came home from work one night and, as usual, had a few stiff drinks as I dressed so that I would be nice and mellow for my evening on the town. This particular evening I was going to a party at a West Side apartment attended by many chic New Yorkers and Europeans. As I entered the room full of laughing and drinking people, I saw through the crowd a woman with a beautiful face. She was standing near a window. I watched her, fascinated by something I could not name. At times, it seemed she acknowledged me with a glance. I felt a strange connection between us. Eventually I had consumed enough alcohol to risk approaching her. She was very friendly. I asked her to dinner. She said she had a date. I asked her to meet me after dinner and, strangely, she agreed.

It was late when we met in a small candlelit bar. We held hands and talked as if we were old friends. She was lovely. I went back to her apartment and spent the night with her. The next morning, I awoke in a strange room that seemed hauntingly familiar, as if I had seen it in a movie. She was lying on her side watching me. I told her my feeling about the room. She was wide-eyed. "Don't you remember, Locke?" she asked, incredulous. "You were here six months ago!"

I was surprised, then embarrassed, and later deeply disturbed. I had totally forgotten my prior meeting with this woman. I had experienced a 'blackout.' I had no recognition of the former evening or of her. One whole evening of my life had been lost. How many others had been lost without my knowledge? Frequently, friends reminded me how funny I had been the night before or how rude, and I could only accept these remarks with a guilty grin, not knowing how true they might be. I had become oblivious to others' feelings as well as to my own.

Some spiritual force seemed to lean over and tap me on the shoulder. I could see that I was wasting my life and that, despite my budding career, I was not on track in a wholesome and productive sense. Something was missing. Something was missing.

What is going on? I asked myself. Something was hidden under the surface, something missing that would remedy all the things that were wrong in my life. I thought there must be more to life than getting drunk and getting laid and going to work and keeping the social gears oiled. Alcohol no longer eased my problems; rather, it complicated them. My hangovers were much more memorable than the 'highs' that preceded them. And still I went to parties at night to get drunk and find someone to go to bed with, then dragged myself out of bed in the mornings to go to work.

Even so, something had shifted. Cousin Sarah had shown me that there was much more to life than worldly pursuits, and my relationship with Mary had pointed out my dependencies and insecurities. I became more aware of my life. I asked myself what I was doing. I questioned the meaning of my life and why I had been born.

If the life I was leading was wrong, I pondered, what should I be doing instead? By then I was fifty pounds overweight, not forty. I was smoking three packs a day instead of two, and I was depressed. Something was wrong.

Mary was never far from my mind. She was always there to turn to, by phone or by train. We were still closely bound emotionally and spiritually, and we deeply respected one another. But the situation hadn't changed. She still wanted to get married. I didn't. I hadn't changed. I still wanted to keep her near without committing myself. I could not bear to part with her, yet I knew it was time to let her go completely so that both of us could grow.

After a particularly difficult weekend visit, we decided again that we must go our separate ways. It felt permanent, and it was. I still longed for another relationship, but I began to spend more and more time alone. I sensed that what I had been seeking in a sexual relationship was symbolic of something else. The ecstasy, relaxation, and release obtained through orgasm pointed at another more permanent state inside.

Many evenings I walked the streets of New York, seeking an answer to my unhappiness. Friends helped somewhat to ease my feelings of loneliness and despair, but my life was out of joint and felt very wrong. I could see no meaning to my existence. Every day was gray. My childlike sense of surprise and wonder was gone. There was no joy. Sense gratification was odious. Although I sought a deep and meaningful answer, I saw no avenue of escape from myself. My self-value was at its lowest ebb. Evenings alone in my Greenwich Village apartment, I stared at the floor while I paced the tiny room. Sometimes on the streets of the Village or in my apartment, walking was my meditation. I posed life questions to myself as the rhythm of my stride punctuated them, over and over, again and again. Why am I here? What am I doing? What is the meaning of life? How do I find peace? How do I find out who I am? How do I find out what I am?

I didn't know what to do. I took long walks in the city, examining the meaning and purpose of my life. One day, at the corner of 23rd Street and Fifth Avenue, a word bubbled up and burst into my consciousness, and that word was *image*. That moment of awareness changed the focus of my life forever. I saw that my whole life had centered around and was being driven by an image of who I should be and what I should be doing. Instantly, I was free of fear and constriction. I was a child again, and life was an adventure. The barriers that had discouraged me from following the promptings of my heart had vanished.

Over the next few months, my lifestyle changed dramatically. I stopped much of my drinking and womanizing and found joy in simple things; a true sense of peace pervaded my being. My stamina and physical strength doubled. I understood people far better and could even see into their minds and hearts. Pictures of pastoral art brought tears to my eyes, and I spent hours in the Metropolitan Museum, drinking in the wonders of beauty, something I had never done before.

My friends questioned me about this dramatic change, but I could not explain. The experience, which lasted for months, was the catalyst for my spiritual search. I was thirsty to understand what I was experiencing and, more important, how and why it had happened.

I can tell you what it is not.

I cannot tell you what it is.

It is not seeking.

It is not lonely.

It is not inside or outside.

It is.

—LOCKE RUSH

-4-

I CANNOT TELL YOU WHAT IT IS

Letting go of Mary felt almost like letting go of life, my most precious possession, but at last I had made an honorable decision and I was living it through. I could not go back, but I didn't know where I was going. This fear of the unknown was intense and pervaded my being. After some time had passed, however, a new spark appeared within me. I was grateful to be alive, so grateful that I lost all fear, even the fear of death. I recognized the spark: it was not new; it had always been there. It was the spark of joy and self-reliance. I believe this spark was what the Buddha must have been referring to when he said, "'neath Heaven above and the earth below, I am the world's most honored one." I had surrendered to life, expecting that it would crush me, and was surprised to find that it nourished me. I had been resisting my unfoldment, and now I embraced it wholeheartedly.

I saw myself clearly. Everything I had been doing up to then was for the purpose of projecting a favorable image. Oh, how funny and smooth and witty and wonderful I was! Yet I was not really any of those things. I remembered myself as a young child, running through the meadows, feeling good inside and out, at one with nature and myself. I had no fear in me then. I could see and feel the good in each person, each thing, and each situation. Instead of focusing on myself, I focused on what was around me. I wanted to help and to comfort everyone I came in contact with. In those childhood years, innocence translated into certainty: I did not doubt myself; I did not suffer from inner confusion. The good in me instinctively cried out for expression, and I acted unerringly on it every day. As I walked the streets of New York City, pondering the meaning of my life, I saw that the real me underneath the role-playing playboy was a different me; the real me was truly expansive, free of the enormous weight of maintaining an image. Life is wonderful when we stop associating who we are with the mask we have been wearing.

This second birth by its force and energy crowded out and transformed my old existence. The positive process of transformation absorbed and thrilled me. The manure of old habits fed new and healthy habits. I understood what Christ meant about being converted and becoming again like a little child. We cannot open to the flow of life and feel the joy of living as long as we are caught up in maintaining a role or depending on others for our happiness. When we let go of the role and the dependency, rebirth takes place spontaneously.

Although my central issue was learning to live without Mary, a subtle change crept into all aspects of my life. I stopped worrying. I scaled way back on everything that was getting in the way of finding out who I was so that I could see the good parts poking through.

I stopped smoking, a habit I have never again started. Since I was consuming three packs of cigarettes a day, this was an amazing turnabout, and it was extremely difficult in the early stages. I think I was able to do it because I was determined to show the advertising companies that they didn't have power over me. I started taking Hatha Yoga lessons with a Hindu yoga instructor, and I practiced yoga for two hours a day.

I stopped eating meat, not because of spiritual principles but quite naturally, because meat no longer appealed to me. I started doing regular fasts. I lost thirty-five pounds. I found I could easily forego meals without missing them. I stopped my heavy drinking— content with a glass of wine at dinner or a beer at social gatherings. I went out less and less; although I still enjoyed meeting friends at bars occasionally, I had lost my taste for noise and nightlife.

I developed the ability to listen. I no longer got bored, and I could listen to even the longest ramblings or conversations with interest and compassion. I was asked to many dinner parties where before my modus operandi had been to avoid the plain or physically ugly people and to associate with glittering people who titillated me. My strange, emerging new being was acutely sensitive to the sadness of the homely, the outcasts, and the ignored ones who sat apart, hoping they would be included. Consciously, I often singled out the most distressed person I saw and spent the evening with her or him, asking and listening and saying nothing about myself. The part of me that increasingly yearned to be good and to be of service was insistent, so I listened and followed and acted. I don't know if I helped or made anyone less lonely. I only know that I found satisfaction and peace in this action.

My dependence on women and my need to control them nearly vanished. I found peace inside, and it gave me a wonderful sense of completeness: nothing was lacking; I had everything I needed. I spent more and more evenings at home, and when I did go to parties, I usually left alone. I was more honest with myself, and it changed the quality of my relationships. I still dated from time to time, but now I focused more on the friendship than on the sex. The spark inside had become a tiny flame of emerging light, and in it I saw clearly the waste and sorrow of using women for my own gratification.

I was reminded of this at the oddest times. Once when I had gone back to my companion's apartment for a drink, I was assailed by awareness of what I was doing. Both of us knew that 'having a drink' meant spending the night, and soon after we arrived, she changed into a silky negligee. As if by rote, we began intimacies. Suddenly, I stood up, put on my clothes, and left a very bewildered young woman sitting on the sofa.

Part of what I experienced at this time may have been a result of the dramatic decrease in my alcohol consumption. The depressant aura shrouding my consciousness had lifted. And there was something else: my faith in God had been rekindled. Something higher than myself had become real to me. I could feel a vibration of goodness in me that touched everything I did.

I was flooded with physical energy and a sense of goodness and self-sufficiency. The energy begged to be used—nothing was too much for it. *Just try me,* it said. I remember moving all my furniture by myself from my Greenwich Village flat to a fifth floor walkup in the 90s on York Avenue. By myself I carried a sofa weighing over three hundred pounds up five flights of narrow stairs.

Even my professional life had been touched by this wonderful grace. I had always had a good eye for detail and a sense of curiosity, and that made camera work a natural occupation. Framing a picture, however, which required imparting the correct sense of tension and proportion, had always been difficult for me. My friend and boss Bob Gaffney, who had an impeccable eye for framing, had always corrected my compositions before we shot. I was surprised to discover that framing had become easy; it felt natural. I didn't have to struggle to get the right perspective. The elements fell into place effortlessly, and my pictures were excellent. Bob noticed. He was quite surprised, and from then on he left me on my own in this respect.

During this time we made a documentary called *Rooftops of New York*, which was about people's lives on their rooftops in the summer when they didn't have enough money to go to the beaches. Bob McCarty and I wrote the screenplay, and Bob Gaffney did the camera work. We made it funny. By hiring a lot of starving actors and using leftover film, we were able to make the film for three thousand dollars. We also got Lionel Hampton to compose a song for us, free, because he liked us. The film was to open in New York City with *The Guns of Navarone*, guaranteeing it a huge audience. Unfortunately, the New York opening was halted: we had not shot the film union. We couldn't afford union scale. We had spliced a union seal into the leader of the film, but a meticulous projectionist discovered the splice and prevented the opening, limiting the film's exposure. Even so, *Rooftops* was nominated for an Academy Award, and we spent an exciting few months. We attended the ceremonies and heard that the film had been well received. The buzz was that our lack of exposure had cost us the Oscar.

After *Rooftops*, another college friend, Billy Mellon of the Mellon family, asked me to help with camera work and production for a film he was shooting in Peru at the headwaters of the Amazon River. The film was a documentary on the Albert Schweitzer Hospital, which was providing free medical care to the Indians. We lived in the Amazon for two or three months, working on the film.

It was a great experience. The director was Erica Anderson, who had won an Academy Award for an earlier film on Albert Schweitzer. While we were on location, I wandered around and shot film on my own, just for the experience and the fun of it. Back in New York, Dede Allen, who went on to win several awards for her film editing, cut the film, and she taught me how to edit. We discovered that we had no footage of jungle and birds and people walking around the streets. Since that's what I had shot for my own pleasure, they used my footage in the final cut. I was thrilled. I also saved the day with my childhood talent for mimicry by making all the bird sounds myself. Any ornithologist who saw that film probably went crazy.

Erica had done another film about a Schweitzer Hospital in Haiti, run by Larry Mellon, Billy Mellon's father. She had shot some dramatic before-and-after footage, showing the transformation of a snake pit mental institution into a modern hospital. Instead of writhing on a muddy floor, the patients were cleaner and calmer, thanks partly to a new drug called Thorazine.

SmithKline heard about the film and requested it. Guess who arrived with the film? Their old employee, Locke. They were all over me.

"Hi, Locke. How are you?"

"We've missed you, boy!"

All those old friends who had claimed to be disenchanted with SmithKline and on their way out the door after me were still there. I was king of the roost for a day. It was satisfying. I had taken a big risk when I left; I had followed my instincts and now I was doing a job I loved and living the way I wanted to live.

I also went to Chile to do a documentary. I was freelancing and was hired as a cameraman/producer to do a film there about the *piqueñéros*, a dying breed of gold miners like the character Humphrey Bogart portrayed in *The Treasure of Sierra Madre*. A Chilean couple, Silvia and Raphael Vega-Querat, were funding the project. The

Querats took a liking to me. "You must be our guest," they insisted.

The social life that revolved around the Querats was stimulating. In the evenings, they left their doors wide open, and many artists came by, among them the Pulitzer Prize winning poet Pablo Neruda. No one even thought of eating until nine or ten at night, and the festivities went on until at least one in the morning, when people would go home or pass out or fall asleep. This went on every night. There was great camaraderie and spirit. It seemed to me like my fantasy of Paris during the thirties.

My camera assistant and I shot some footage, and I think it would have been a great little film, but the Querats ran out of money and we couldn't finish it.

Also during this time, I was called upon to speak publicly, a situation that before had terrified me. I was not afraid. I felt no need to prepare. My words emerged effortlessly, and people said my talks were humorous and profound.

Emerging from the darkness felt strange and wonderful. As my depression lifted, the light inside was radiant. It filled me. This spiritual awakening was as close to a conversion experience as I can imagine. I remember pinching myself and whispering, *My God, is this really happening?*

I read voraciously, searching for some clue to the wonderful thing that was happening to me. I inhaled books on Eastern religion, finding it less cluttered than Western religion. I read my first book on Zen, *Zen Flesh, Zen Bones* by Paul Reps. I found that I easily understood the concept of koans and the strange paradoxical dialogues of the old Zen masters. I laughed helplessly at passages that friends found humorless.

On a Sunday afternoon at the Metropolitan Museum, I discovered the joy to be found in works of art. I had been dead to the world of art, but now it so captivated me that I could spend thirty minutes in front of one painting, absorbed in the scene and in the sense of wonder that it touched in me. As I sat in front of a Corot landscape, I wept at its beauty and serenity. My life had become like that painting. Who could I thank for the priceless gifts I was finding in my heart and in the world around me? I started going to Russian Orthodox services. Amidst the incense and chanting, I thanked God and asked what I had done to deserve this wondrous state.

I no longer needed external stimuli. My pace of living slowed. I dropped my activities, one by one, and sought solitude. I looked forward to returning home alone and eating alone. Phone calls or unexpected guests were tolerated interruptions to a strange new sense of centeredness that I knew must be nourished. My aloneness became precious. I was fully aware of myself and my surroundings for the first time since childhood. I spent evenings browsing in my room as if it belonged to a stranger, humming to myself, joyful, stopping occasionally to look at a picture or a book. I felt complete, whole. My old black-and-white world had transformed into a Technicolor marvel. Situations that had previously provoked fear or irritation felt perfectly comfortable. I was happy. Whether I was with someone or alone, I was not lonely.

It made little difference to me what I did or where I went. I acted on my whims as a child would, unafraid of the future. One day I stood in the rain for an hour to get tickets to a show that I didn't really care to see just because I felt like standing in the rain. I was conscious always of a new essence within, which eliminated worry and fear and revealed the deep significance of the most normal objects, people, and situations.

Later in my life, some of the religious literature I read made me recognize that what had happened to me during those last months in New York City was profound, but it seemed pretentious to call it spiritual. I felt utterly *natural;* what I experienced was something so ordinary and obvious that it is hard to describe in a meaningful way. I had been thirsty, and suddenly I was a fish in a vast expanse of water. Can a fish say its thirst has been quenched? A fish has no conception of thirst.

The experience of this particular state lasted for quite a long time. In fact, it has never completely gone away, but it has never again been as full as it was at that time, so full that it seemed to be emanating from the pores of my skin.

I wanted others around me to know and understand what I was feeling, but I was afraid they wouldn't and did not dare try to explain lest it go away. But my demeanor expressed everything. Friends asked me what was different. Had I taken happy pills? they wanted to know. Some attributed the change to yoga and took up the practice themselves, hoping it might be the key. Yoga was not the key. It seemed to me that a mysterious and delightful Visitor had come to stay in the house of my life, bringing grace and joy and peace I had never imagined could exist.

For I was afraid Thou wouldst hear me too soon, and heal me at once of my disease of lust, which I wished to satiate rather than to see extinguished.

—U.A. Asrami, "The Experience," The Psychic International, May 1963

-5-

FOR I WAS AFRAID THOU WOULDST HEAR ME TOO SOON

Ever since my summer in Europe during college, the memory of Paris had haunted my imagination. I remembered my first impression of that splendid city: emerging from the subway and stepping onto the street was like waking up in a movie. The cobblestones gleamed from a recent rain. Shopkeepers were unrolling their awnings. The fragrance of freshly baked baguettes drifted on the morning air. The sweetness and freshness of that morning in Paris had the flavor of early childhood magic. I felt I had come home.

Ten years had passed since then, and I longed to experience those feelings again. Therefore, when I inherited some money from my grandfather in 1963, I quickly decided I would use it to spend a year in Europe. My spiritual awakening had left me feeling as unconstrained and full of wonder as a child. I was no longer burdened by internal or external pressure to do anything, to produce anything, or to lead a conventional life. I had just turned thirty, and moving my life into a new arena seemed a symbol of my rebirth.

I don't think I would have returned to Paris at that time had it not been for the boon from my grandfather. As it turned out, his gift may have been responsible for dramatically altering the course of my life, for I did not come back to live in the States for nearly eight years. At the time, however, I did not think of the journey as part of a spiritual quest. I went to recapture the smell of freshly baked bread.

In Europe, my nine-to-five existence gave way to a leisurely world where shopkeepers closed their doors at noon for a three-hour siesta. In the pie of life, work was only one slice. The other tasty sections were reserved for family, vacations, theater, meals, and travel. Nations that had been bombed and inhabited by foreign armies, cultures that stretched back fifteen hundred years, cities that proudly displayed their landmarks of the past, all imparted a richness and a balanced perspective on daily life that was absent in the States. People lived their days fully instead of racing through them on their way to the weekend.

Like a child in a candy shop with a pocketful of money, I delighted in this relaxed and more epicurean way of life. I wanted to make use of the new currency of my awakening. I wanted to find out whether my sense of wonder was unlimited.

I made some good friends—a few expatriates and several French. Most Americans think the French are spiteful or angry or laughing at them, but the French are just very independent. They have a strong sense of property, which gives them a certain attitude that Americans misinterpret. It is true that the French consider Americans bourgeois, or square. It is also rather strange since the French are much more bourgeois than Americans. They also keep their home lives private. I dated a woman from an old family for two years before she invited me to her family home for lunch.

What is it that draws millions of tourists abroad each year, and what is it that keeps some of them there? On one level, it is simply the desire to experience new sights and sounds; deeper down, it is part of man's eternal quest, the search for a Shangri-La that will end all wanting and searching.

A few years later, when I interviewed several dozen people about their peak experiences, several spoke of foreign travel as producing rare states of mind. All of us carry in our deepest core the memory of a true state of happiness, and we seek it in one way or another. The true state of happiness is a state of freedom from ambition, escape, and compulsion. It is *pure being*. Any experience that reminds us of this center of pure being is joyful.

For many people I met, Europe was what in AA terminology is

called 'a geographical cure.' When you are busy being an explorer, you don't have time to look at yourself. It is titillating to escape the reality of a familiar, tedious, or unpleasant past. Daily life in our familiar surroundings becomes routine; the grooves carved by habit are deep and rigid. We categorize, differentiate, and judge because it makes us feel important and in control. We lose track of the cosmic flow and the unity we share underneath the differences presented by our personality masks.

A new culture is a mild shock treatment to our rigidity. A sojourn in a foreign land can clear the lens of perception for a while. New surroundings interrupt the habitual patterns and reactions that inhibit our ability to listen, to observe, and to experience life objectively. It is difficult to categorize and differentiate when everything is so new and mysterious.

As strangers, we are accepted as we are. No one expects us to play the old roles we have perfected, and so we can relate more honestly to other human beings. We can take a true interest in the desk clerk, the waiter, the stranger. Detachment becomes part of life yet allows us to enter more fully into the flow around us. We let the dance of life unfold. We become less concerned with our image, our small sense of ego, and more concerned with experiencing and seeing with the fresh vision of a child exploring a new world.

In time, however, the old habits re-emerge, and the wide-eyed traveler becomes the jaded tourist. Of course, I did not realize this for quite a while. I was certain I had found my Shangri-La.

Europe was a huge and satisfying novel, each page revealing a new adventure. The first months in Paris were exhilarating. I reveled in the life of the Left Bank. I was freer than I had ever been. I wandered the streets, inhaling the many fragrances of the city, its espresso coffee, perfumes, fresh bread, and pungent cheeses. I sat for hours in a cafe on Blvd. St. Germain des Pres and watched the passersby. The Bois de Boulogne, the Tuileries, and the Jardins du Luxembourg were feasts for my eyes and heart. I loved Paris, and I loved it that there was no one to tell me what to do. When I wanted to go exploring in the middle of the night, I jumped on my

Lambretta motor scooter and wheeled down to Les Halles to enjoy an onion soup as I watched the produce come in to market from all over France.

As spring approached, I wandered further. I vacationed on the Riviera, hitchhiked to Greece, lived on a small isle off the coast of Turkey, skied in Austria, drank wine in the Vienna Woods, and read voraciously. Almost out of money, I journeyed back to Paris in time to watch the fall colors transform the tree-lined boulevards. I needed a job. Fortunately, my old friend and colleague Bob McCarty had just arrived in Paris. Bob introduced me to a woman named Mara, who worked at a modeling agency, and Mara encouraged me to seek work as a model. First, however, I needed a portfolio of photographs. Thanks to a photographer friend of Mara's, I was able to trade an afternoon of modeling for prints of all the photos.

The photographer sold one of the photos to a leading French magazine. It appeared on the cover, launching my new career as a photographic model for a top Paris agency. What an ideal job! The modeling was lucrative and made it possible for me to stay in Europe. Americans were á la mode in Paris. My face reminded photographers of Steve McQueen and Mel Ferrer, so the jobs flowed in. I traveled around Europe to do TV commercials, small movie parts, and magazine modeling. I worked hard and the work was pleasant, but I played equally hard. It seemed like a joke to receive a hundred dollars an hour for posing with beautiful women when it was something I had done for free all my life. I spent more and more time out on the town, often with the same women with whom I worked.

My headquarters was La Louisiane, a small Left Bank hotel that was home for many expatriates, musicians, artists, writers, 'in' tourists, and, in earlier times, for the likes of Sartre and Camus. La Louisiane was a Paris microcosm. While I was there, many famous artists lived there or in the neighborhood—sax man Dexter Gordon, jazz pianist Bud Powell, Irwin Shaw, Brian Geison. William Burroughs, author of *The Naked Lunch*, lived down the street. Salvador Dali also lived nearby, and a whole gang of us gathered there on Thursday nights.

Tall shapely American models waited for dates in La Louisiane's tiny lobby, people on the make flowed through the doors, and the smell of marijuana lingered in the corridors. La Louisiane had the secret of success: it was 'in.' People went because other people went because other people went. The hotel fronted on Rue de la Seine, a market street that was a convenient source of food and drink.

This hedonistic life was interspersed with periods of reading, reflection, and spiritual searching. There was no need to spend more than six months a year working, which left me free to ski in the winter as well as to continue my spiritual explorations. Now, looking back on the years from 1963 to1966 in Europe, I see my contradictions. The budding will of my awakening was not yet strong enough to conquer my worldly will, which had grown formidable through long indulgence. And so, these two wills, the spiritual and the carnal, contended with each other and disturbed my soul.

I was engrossed in reading books on Zen and other spiritual paths. In my hotel room, Ramakrishna, Gurdjieff, Krishnamurti, and Ramana Maharshi were stacked up alongside James Bond and Mickey Spillane. Wherever I went, I took my books. I read for hours in the parks and cafes, and my whole being was reaffirmed and nourished by what I read. I'd sit down in a cafe with a bottle of wine and read Ramana Maharshi until I got bored then switch to Mickey Spillane or James Bond until I felt guilty, then turn back again to Ramana Maharshi.

Krishnamurti's words were like swords, cutting away the entangling underbrush of emotions and attachments. Yet practicing his 'choiceless awareness' was next to impossible. Books on Zen pointed the way to *satori** and spoke of the 'free man.' I was freer than I had ever been, but I strained ahead of myself, searching for enlightenment. My awakening had changed the entire focus of my life, but the experience had receded a bit. I experienced occasional moments of insecurity and depression, but never again as during my early days in New York. These moments served as quiet reminders that more work lay ahead.

I sought places where I might find others with similar interests.

I met Dr. Hubert Benoit, a highly respected psychiatrist who had written several books on Zen. One of them, *Zen and the Psychology of Transformation: The Supreme Doctrine,* was a great discovery. When I read something I really like, I go straight to the horse's mouth. I didn't know anyone who knew Benoit, but I found his phone number, called out of the blue, and requested a meeting with him. He asked if I wanted to see him professionally. I told him about my consultation with the psychiatrist Dr. Bond a few years before and explained that Dr. Bond's assessment was that I did not need psychoanalysis.

I met informally with Dr. Benoit several times. He was gracious and wise. We discussed Eastern and Western Zen. Through Benoit, I met another author on Zen, Dr. Karlfried Von Durckheim. A Jungian analyst associated with the Jung Institute in Zurich, Durckheim had spent many years in the Orient. His primary focus was the spiritual path as it relates to Zen Buddhism. I read his book, *Hara the Vital Center of Man*, and arranged to meet him.

Durckheim was a solid man with a ruddy complexion, a fringe of white hair, and twinkling blue eyes. He spoke three languages fluently in measured philosophic and somewhat enigmatic phrases. He invited me to do dream analysis work with him at his retreat center in the Black Forest, and I accepted eagerly.

The retreat center was in Todtmoos Rütte, a small valley hidden in a lovely niche of the Black Forest. An hour from Basel, it is a truly pastoral setting. A tumbling stream splashes down waterfalls at the foot of the valley. Many paths wander through the forest, and there is little to remind one of the outside world. Simple cottages rim the meadows of the valley, and the small central lodge, Herzl House, sits at the head of the valley. Herzl House, which translates as House of the Heart, accommodated visitors and some of the residents of the center. I spent six months living in one of the cottages at Todtmoos while undergoing intensive dream analysis and a form of therapy unique to Durckheim.

I learned to record my dreams. I had a special writing instrument with a pressure-sensitive light on it so that I could record a dream

My home for 6 months at Todtmoos Rütte in the Black Forest where I underwent Jungian Therapy

the moment I awakened without turning on a lamp. I recorded as many as six or seven dreams a night, some of them quite significant. Once you tune your system to the intention of remembering your dreams and set up a method of doing so, it seems natural to wake up, roll over, record a dream, and go back to sleep.

Life at Todtmoos followed a routine. I got up fairly early in the morning and fixed myself a little breakfast in my room or went to the dining room in the main building. After breakfast, I read over my dreams and wrote down my understanding of their significance. We gathered every day to do zazen and certain diaphragmatic breathing exercises, practices that complemented and enhanced the inner sense of calm I had enjoyed since my awakening. Late in the morning, I spent an hour or so with Durckheim or with his associate, Frau Dr. Hippius, analyzing my dreams.

These sessions took place five or six days a week. Both Dr. Durckheim and Frau Dr. Hippius wisely refrained from interpreting my dreams for me. That was my job. When I related my dreams and what I thought about them. Durckheim would sit back, scratch his head, and cup his chin in his hand as he mused. His method was to gently probe deeper and deeper into the meaning of a dream as he invited my reflections. The truth to be found in my dream life therefore revealed itself to me naturally, as I was able to assimilate it.

After my session with Durckheim, I enjoyed lunch at Herzl House. Afternoons were free. I took long walks, wrote in my journal, and read. After dinner, we all gathered until nine or ten o'clock for coffee and interesting discussions, storytelling, or Mozart. The author of *Mary Poppins*, Pamela Travers, was there when I was, and she often told stories. We became great friends.

Pamela Travers had been a disciple of Russian mystic G.I. Gurdjieff and had spent some time with him in person. I found the works of both Gurdjieff and his collaborator, P.D. Ouspensky, fascinating, but also very complicated. After a while, I decided that the 'answer' couldn't possibly be so convoluted and so difficult to comprehend. I was looking for a simpler way. Even so, I was interested to know about Pamela's experience.

She saw Gurdjieff as a man of prodigious intellect and great power who was very helpful to a number of people in terms of provoking their thinking about themselves and life. However, she also said that he was not her cup of tea. She and some others had left him because of his moral and other imperfections. He craved power and insisted that people do what he wanted them to do.

'The great Gurdjieff was quite a man," Pamela said, with a hint of a smile.

I asked her to explain. "His feelings toward the opposite sex were well known," she continued. "It was common knowledge that he had a kind of harem. I was not that close to him and I never fell into that category, but I saw what often happened when women met him. Mr. Gurdjieff had developed certain powers from his practice of various forms of meditation and yoga, and he could arouse a woman simply by focusing his energy on her genitals, which he did quite openly."

However, unlike many of the so-called gurus who came on the scene in the late sixties, at least Gurdjieff was not keeping his nature a secret. He lived in a world unto himself. He had experienced levels of consciousness that the people around him had not, which would have made it difficult for them to differentiate a true spiritual path from a path governed by what I would now call psychic powers. The wiser disciples, including Pamela, stuck around until they saw the fuller picture, and then they left.

If you look at pictures of Gurdjieff, you see that he had a big belly. I had read about this phenomenon in Durckheim's book. According to Eastern thought, the vital center of man is the *hara,* which is located two inches below the navel. The *hara* is where energy or prana is accumulated and doled out to the rest of the organism, like a treasure chest of money you can spend anywhere you want. Because of my later experiences with the *hara* energy during my Zen period, I can well imagine that Gurdjieff's desire to understand and utilize this energy may have led him into some fascinating realms.

Such were the engrossing discussions we enjoyed over our evening coffee at Herzl House. I stayed there for six months or so, from summer and into the winter. The weather was beautiful in the summer, hot and windy and not humid. When the snows came in the winter, the tiny town of Todtmoos became a wonderland, a living Christmas card with twinkling shops and reindeer and horse-drawn sleighs.

During my time in the Black Forest with Durckheim, I focused all my energy on self-exploration. I had little else to do. I went into myself through dreams to discover who I was and how my inner consciousness was expressing itself. I had the opportunity to work on issues of my own identity and my relationship with my parents—all the classic things that therapy addresses.

I watched unfold the various fantasies and fears that arose from my childhood attitudes toward my parents and life in general. I saw how my desire to be the best in everything resulted from the strict discipline of my childhood and a fear of being inadequate and displeasing my parents. My high grades and outstanding achievements in grade school had been as much a form of approval seeking, as they were natural, productive activities. I also saw my libidinous sexual energy with greater understanding and more compassion. My parents were not emotionally demonstrative, nor were those around us. I felt cut off, and my precocious and frequent masturbation gave vent to my repressed longing for emotional connection. Naturally I felt guilty about this because of the strong, Protestant aura that dominated our home.

Three dreams were keys to my process. One reflected an important step in my inner growth.

> I was in an office. It was my office. It was quite well furnished. My secretary said, "Someone is here to see you." "Send him in," I said. It was obvious that I was in charge of my company.
>
> The man who came in was my father. He took off his hat and held it over his stomach respectfully, as a peasant would do when visiting a landowner. He asked me for a job. I treated him kindly.

I don't remember whether I gave him a job. The important part was that he came to me on a subordinate level. The dream had shown my father as human and flawed. It represented my letting go of my idealization of him, which was unreal because, in fact, he was not there to father me after I was nine years old.

Another dream was especially vivid.

> I was in a large arena that made me think of the Roman coliseum. But it was smaller, it was indoors, it had a ceiling, and I saw some knights. I also saw a huge man called Eric the Dane, but he was Irish. He had red hair and a big, bushy, red beard. He was at least seven feet tall. He was the embodiment of animus. He was the dominant male. I worshipped him. He was my father. He took me by the hand. The experience was beautiful. He had a spiritual quality about him of immense strength and immense goodness expressed in the male form.

Durckheim was thrilled as he listened and made notes. "This is what you really need in your life. You need the father you never had, the father who left you when you were young."

In Jungian work, there are two major elements in the psyche: the anima and the animus. The anima is the feminine side of us and the animus is the masculine side. My feminine side had been very well developed. I knew how to be appealing. I knew how to flirt, how to use my eyes and my body to attract women. The masculine had been asleep.

I had always admired strength and prowess. In my early teens, I had read the muscle building magazines. I was wiry, but I wanted to look like Charles Atlas and there was no way I ever could. I was skinny and had biceps like Ping-Pong balls. Although eventually I became quite tall, I grew more slowly than my classmates and puberty came late for me, so I felt fragile and not as masculine as my taller, more muscular classmates.

The dream signified my need to strengthen the male element within me and bring it into balance with the female element. Eric the Dane represented the physical being of a man of power whom I could trust and respect.

My father, physically strong from his work on the farm and the most powerful person in my life, had left me. My confidence left with him. It must have been so. My grades plummeted. My former athletic prowess deserted me. Instead of appropriately building up my male side, I compensated by womanizing, thinking it was masculine. Alcohol helped me become the most pleasing, the most flirtatious, and the real life of the party. It was all compensation, and it served to strengthen my feminine side, the anima.

Durckheim gave me a more accurate picture of myself. He saw a young man with potential who had neglected the qualities of self-discipline, initiative, follow-through, inner strength, and perseverance.

I recognized that I must find a way to internalize the strength and the purity represented by the huge man in my dream, who was like a Christ.

In my analysis with Durckheim, I had been looking into my issues with sexuality. I had seen that, although I was not unkind or dishonest, since adolescence I had been using women for my own purposes. The following dream pointed directly to a shift in my perspective toward women and sexual conquest.

> I was fishing in the surf with a big rod. I could feel something big on the line. I had to strain, but finally I managed to reel it in. It was a huge seal, six or seven feet long and weighing perhaps a hundred pounds. I took it off the hook and carried it in my arms as I climbed a ladder onto a stilted pier. On the pier was a huge room, where I placed the seal in a bed. I wanted to take care of it. The seal was very feminine, with beautiful, sad eyes. It was a rich chocolate brown seal, and so I called it Hershey. I tenderly pulled a blanket up over it. Eventually I had to let it go back into the ocean. I felt sad, but I knew I had to give the seal its freedom. I looked at it in a fond and respectful way, and I handled it compassionately.

Durckheim was scribbling excitedly on his notepad. "This is wonderful," he said. "Now, do you know who that seal is?"

"The seal's name is Hershey."

"Oh ho." He was even more excited.

"What's so interesting about a Hershey bar," I asked.

"Her-She." Durckheim gave me a significant look.

My dream seal, Hershey, was woman incarnate. Durckheim felt that this dream signaled a turning point in how I would deal with women.

As might be expected, I did not change my ways drastically when I returned to Paris, but the dream did indeed signal a gradual shift toward a more normal interaction with women.

By the time of the Her-She dream, I had been at Herzl House for six months or so, and the dreams I have recounted here convinced Durckheim that I had finished my work. He told me I had done very well and accomplished a lot in a short time. He praised my one-pointedness and my openness and invited me to stay and help him with his clients.

I could not accept. Durckheim was a good man, a nice man. He had a great sense of humor and he was certainly intelligent, but I wanted something more. I was looking for enlightenment. I was fascinated with Zen Buddhism, and I knew that I wanted to go to Japan as soon as I could swing it. I was just waiting for the time to be right.

I returned to Paris and picked up where I had left off. Life seemed perfect. Money, wine, women, song, spiritual exploration, travel—all in unlimited quantity. Even guilt, my constant companion for years, had taken a siesta.

I all but did it, yet I did not do it. I made another effort and almost succeeded, yet I did not reach it, and did not grasp it, hesitating to die to death, and to live to life; and the evil to which I was so wonted held me more than the better life I had not tried."

—William James,
    The Varieties of Religious Experience

–6–

I ALL BUT DID IT

My life was perfectly pleasant, but I was beginning to realize the mistake in thinking that a perfectly pleasant life could provide deep satisfaction. In my experience, when you do pretty much what you want to do, you don't grow very much.

To me as a foreigner, Europe had been hypnotic, a magic ingredient in my morning espresso that perpetuated a sense of the unreal. It had been easy to believe I had left my psychological hang-ups behind. As time passed, however, the magic lost its power. By then, I became accustomed to the language, customs, food, and countryside, and I saw that under the cultural veneer, people are the same the world over. My attitude toward acquaintances visiting from the States had progressed from avoidance during my early days there *(How crass can a tourist be!)* to simple acceptance, and finally to delight in their company and appreciation of American openness.

Expatriates go through these stages, too, but the difference is that they stay on. They relate to their adopted life with a built-in detachment. To enforce this detachment, some even disdain learning the language beyond the necessary minimum. Others avoid the States and their old customs, becoming more European than the Europeans. If you scratch deep enough into the expatriate psyche, you often find unresolved issues that spring from some aspect of life back home.

My extended stay in Europe was no longer a question of escape from the past. I knew my European karma was finished, yet I was strangely inert. I was a sucker for the good life, not so much courting it but finding it hard to refuse.

Every year, I spent a couple of months in England. I had a good friend there who was my mother's godchild. She had a big apartment with an extra bedroom, so I always had a place to stay. I spent hours at the Buddhist Society in London, poring over old books and meeting others who practiced spiritual disciplines. One such man was Douglas Harding, the author of several books on religion and one in particular, *On Having No Head.* I found his book in a little bookstore, drawn to the title and the cover illustration, which showed a man looking into a mirror and seeing himself without a head.

The book talked about the layers of personality and our identifications. We keep expanding the layers of our personality to include our car, our lawn, our political party, our country, our religion—even our football team. We put on many, many heads: *I am a Republican. I am an American. I am a Christian. And don't you dare cast aspersions on me.* The scrape on your new car is a scrape off your hide, the tire marks on your lawn are scars on your sense of self, and the aspersions cast on your football team are personal insults. In Harding's view, human development is a matter of first recognizing the heads we have put on and then attaining the state of having no head, of having no false identifications.

Fascinated by what I read, I contacted Harding. He invited me to visit. I spent a number of weekends at his home in the English countryside. Harding was interesting, but he certainly had all the fallacies of a normal human being. He was interested in Ramana Maharshi and Eastern mystical thought in general, but he was not into doing zazen and studying the tenets of Buddhism. He was an intellectual and a quasi-mystic who made some very good points in his books, and he was a very good friend.

I wanted to make a documentary on Harding. I got hold of a camera and shot ten hours of film, but nothing ever came of it. I also had an affair with a pretty woman who was a student of Harding's. She and I took a trip through the northern part of England and into Scotland, where we met Kalu Rinpoche, a Tibetan wise man who was staying there and receiving visitors. I was doing several Tibetan practices at the time, prostrations and recitations of certain mantras, so I was interested to see for myself what a Tibetan master was like.

We went in and sat on the floor. It was the typical Tibetan scene. People were doing prostrations. Colorful flags abounded, and everyone was smiling and chanting and humming. We joined in and listened to Rinpoche's talk, which was translated. He was old and highly regarded, and he certainly seemed to be a saintly person.

While I was visiting London, I also met Krishnamurti, whose books had so affected me. I greeted him briefly after a talk in London. Later, I had the opportunity to get close to Krishnamurti through a friend, an Italian painter named Margarita who lived in a Paris loft. Margarita was like Mother Earth, a big woman who wore muumuus and had long black hair. She was quite charming and sexy and also very pretty. Margarita loved Krishnamurti. She had lived in his enclave and handled his public relations, and she knew him well.

As with all the great authors and thinkers I met, when I gained more intimate access to Krishnamurti I discovered that he too had warts and imperfections. Krishnamurti, Harding, Benoit, and so many others I met later in my life are just very famous people with the normal imperfections. They write and speak eloquently, they put forth certain truths, and people make them into something they are not.

Like the others, Krishnamurti had part of the pie, a couple of good-sized slices that were very well defined. I found his work on the cutting-away process wonderful. He provided a hatchet for chopping away at the underbrush, showing us that, ultimately, nothing is there. There is no cottage in the woods, no pathway to nirvana. There is nothing but the void, and you just have to let go of each thing that comes, minute by minute. I believe this is part of an important truth, but the fact is, according to Margarita, Krishnamurti did not live his own life that way.

Reading the work of these philosophers and spiritual inquirers was important to me. I extracted what I needed from them and discarded the rest. They all had bits and pieces of the truth, but they also had a lot of flotsam and jetsam. Much later, when I met a teacher of a higher order, I recognized that much of what Krishnamurti said was similar: don't trust this; don't trust that; nothing you think is real is real; everything is illusion and mind. The problem was that Krishnamurti left me dangling in the void. Even then, I could see that there must be something real. Krishnamurti either did not know that or didn't understand it or chose not to put it forth. Still, I found his cutting process valuable.

I realize I was holding these men to a very high standard. During my work with Durckheim, I had seen through my longing for my father to be something he wasn't. I was looking for a true father, a spiritual father, someone who could inspire my trust, someone who was knowledgeable and wise, someone who had transcended ego. I knew I needed a guide, but I also knew I had to be cautious about who I might put in that position.

Harding, Durckheim, and some of the others I got to know were ordinary human beings with good hearts and keen intellects. The portion of wisdom each of them possessed certainly enriched my life, but I knew they were not masters, and so I moved on.

I learned from all the people I met. One extraordinary person was Jacqueline, a prostitute I met at a Left Bank cafe. We became close friends. Jacqueline worked for the most famous whorehouse in Paris. Well protected by the police, the place catered to Saudi princes, rulers from around the world, and other famous personages.

Jacqueline liked me. Strangely, our relationship never became sexual. The first time she came to visit me at La Louisiane, I was not expecting her. I was sleeping in my room when I heard a tap on the door. Jacqueline came in. She was beautiful, a gamine. She got in bed with me. Although I think she would have acquiesced to my advances, I sensed it was important not to take the relationship in that direction. She needed something far more valuable from me. I held her in my arms. She confided in me. I felt a real tenderness for her as a human being.

We continued to see each other for perhaps six months in this fashion. She would appear at my door from time to time, and we would lie in bed and talk or perhaps just rest quietly together. My relationship with Jacqueline may have been the first manifestation of the Her-She seal dream and the beginning of a new way of relating to women. Apart from Jacqueline, though, my womanizing continued.

All went smoothly for quite a while as I continued my spiritual search and my travels around Europe to work and play. Eventually, however, some cracks began to appear in the façade of my European life, breaking through my inertia and making me seriously question the direction I was heading.

Early one morning, as I was coming home on my motor scooter after a night on the town, a large Simca ran a red light and smashed into me, broadside. My body was thrown into the air and I landed on my head on the hood of the Simca. Yoga breathing kept me from going into shock as I lay bloody on the sidewalk. My face was a mess. I could have been killed but I escaped with a concussion, a knee fracture, and facial contusions.

I refused to go to the hospital. I asked for a blanket. After the police station formalities, I hibernated in my hotel room for three days. Eventually a friend who was a brain surgeon urged me to get an x-ray, and I discovered I had cracked my skull. By then, nothing could be done about it.

Although the accident clearly was not my fault, I had been drinking, and I viewed the incident as a wake-up call. I saw how vulnerable I was. No matter how much I thought I had, I could lose it all in an instant.

Several weeks later, more or less back to normal, I discovered that I had contracted gonorrhea from a Danish countess woman. Everyone in the group I saw frequently was either infected with the disease or had been exposed to it. What got to me was not so much the discomfort, which was easily cured by penicillin, but the sense of dirtiness I felt inside, something no antibiotic or soap could cleanse. Even worse, I was having an affair at the same time with a high-society French lady to whom I had to explain the whole situation. I felt truly immoral.

Other aspects of the company I was keeping were also disillusioning me. Seen from up close, the social scene in the romantic little village of St. Anton, where I skied for several months a year, was not as idyllic as I had imagined. The fairyland was not a fairyland, after all. Behind the smooth, tanned Alpine faces that so captivate tourists lurked the same passions and pettiness that motivate and provoke people the world over. I saw intense and often cruel rivalry between ski instructors. One instructor was kept from teaching a better class because he was an *auslander,* an outsider. (He came from Salzburg, which was only a hundred miles away.) Rivalry between merchants was common and fierce. The social life of this small community, I found, bore striking similarities to the goings on of the New York Social Register. People and places were distinctly 'in' and 'out.' The sexual promiscuity I was accustomed to seeing in a larger city was more than matched by the nocturnal dramas I became privy to year after year.

And then one night I got drunk. I had been congratulating myself on how well I was behaving with regard to alcohol and decided to reward myself with more latitude in my drinking. The next morning, I was informed by somewhat shocked friends that I had openly propositioned the hostess, a Viennese Countess, insulted the guest of honor with loud Bronx cheers, and passed out at the bar in full view of all. My old habits had returned, surprising me with their tenacity. I had humiliated myself.

I returned to Zurich where my work as a model for a large department store paid for my St. Anton excesses. Modeling was profitable in Zurich because few Americans liked to work there. The city was off the beaten track and had a rigid, righteous air that did not appeal to the 'in' crowd. The first time I was there, I parked my car two inches over the line and a citizen, not a policeman but a *citizen*, reprimanded me. "That is forbidden," he said sternly. I asked why and he just kept saying the same thing over and over. When I started to walk away, he reported me to a nearby policeman, who made me re-park my car.

There was virtually no nightlife. Evenings were lonely, yet I had no desire to fill the time with drinking or boring conversation. Instead, I retired to my room or a local restaurant with my current reading matter. I had an odd feeling that something was going to happen.

While on a visit to Berne, I was walking across a bridge that stretched high over a turbulent river. It was a bright, sunny day. My spirits were bright. Halfway across I felt a strange sensation, an icy tremor that began in my solar plexus and moved up through my chakras into my head. I had never experienced anything like it. I stood immobile, terrified, transfixed. I was seized by an intense desire to vault over the waist-high guardrail just to escape the fear. Finally, I pulled my gaze away from the guardrail and forced myself to walk the rest of the way across the bridge.

I stood on the other side, shaken. I decided I would have to cross the bridge again to keep from developing a phobia. I did, but it took all my willpower. I stayed close to the traffic and away from the rail because I dared not tempt that feeling again.

In Amsterdam several months later, I was sitting in a friend's apartment reading a book on drugs. The apartment was on the sixth floor of a building overlooking the North Sea. My friend was out of town so, except for me, the apartment was deserted. The wind rattled the windows and moaned through the building. Suddenly, I felt the same icy tremor I had felt on the bridge. It began in my solar plexus. As it moved upward, I was seized again with a nameless fear. I had the sense that something was not right and that I had to do something about it. This time I panicked. Although I felt intuitively that the experience would be valuable if I could let it manifest, I dared not risk it. I ran to the phone and called the only person in the city I could think of, which effectively interrupted the panic and brought me back to normal, but I was still very upset. In the weeks that followed, I spoke of these two experiences to a psychiatrist friend and to a priest. No one could explain them.

On the bridge, and when the wind was whistling around the apartment building in Amsterdam, awareness of my vulnerability had awakened existential terror. But for the grace of God, I realized later, I might have plunged over the side or out the window to my death. In both instances, an insistent voice inside warned me to get busy and do something about the way I was living my life.

A few months later, I received another jolt, something that impressed upon me the darker side of life, the side I did not want to face.

I had just enjoyed a very sensual night in London. My partner had cried out loudly with pleasure, her voice growing to such a crescendo of ecstasy that I was sure Buckingham Palace had been alerted! To avoid the glances of curious neighbors, I left her apartment very early in the morning. It was dawn and the city was quiet except for a milk truck that sped by the door as I stepped out. As I began to walk, I was stopped cold in my tracks by a terrible wailing. I looked back. I could not help but think of the night before. The milk truck careened around the corner and out of sight. In the street lay a tiny black kitten, ripped open and bleeding away its last few seconds of life. Over it stood its mother, wailing with an almost human sound and sniffing helplessly at the final convulsions of her offspring.

There followed an eerie silence and then again came the wailing, plaintive and rising. Again I heard in my mind the wails of pleasure that had rung in my ears only a few hours before.

I was certain this was no ordinary coincidence. It was too dramatic and too specific to be a random occurrence. My own contradictions had slapped me in the face. I saw the ephemeral quality of life and what I was doing with mine. The Master Planner had given me a glimpse of reality, a stark view of life and the inevitability of death, a preview of things to come. Like the kitten, I could die at any instant, totally unaware.

I returned to Paris, hoping to shake off the experience and take up life as usual. Despite all that had occurred, I was not yet ready to move on. Then, as if to underscore the absurdity of my lifestyle, during my last few months in Paris I found myself in the middle of a real-life French farce with three women from my past, all of whom showed up at La Louisiane at the same time. For several months, all three lived with me in the hotel, one woman on each floor.

Woman Number One was Tricia. I had met Tricia before I left New York. She lived in the fast lane. She was from Texas and was

Locke Rush on photo shoot for fashion store, in Paris 1966

reputed to have been a mistress of the late Jack Kennedy. She was very tall and very beautiful, and her lifestyle suggested that she had plenty of money.

Woman Number Two was Larissa, a poet from Greece. While I was on the Greek island of Patmos during my first year abroad, a mutual friend introduced Larissa and me in the town square. She was with a young man, and I assumed she was married. Later my friend told me that the young man was her brother and that Larissa lived in Athens. When I returned to Athens, I looked her up. She was beautiful and captivating, and we had an affair. She mentioned that she was thinking of taking a trip to Paris and would get in touch with me.

Woman Number Three was Simone, an opera singer who was half French and half American. Simone was very sweet and very dedicated to her career. Simone was the first to arrive, and I was probably most attached to her. We had a good relationship, one I thought might become deeper over time. Simone wanted me to give up my modeling and live with her in Switzerland, where she had a six-month singing engagement. I wasn't quite ready to be so tied down, but I was enjoying our relationship.

Soon, Tricia arrived, hoping to surprise me and certainly succeeding, followed shortly after by Larissa. I didn't tell any of them about the others, and the lobby was a scary place for me: I raced through as if hot coals were scorching my feet. Some people would consider the situation a bachelor's delight, but for me it was a nightmare. Remember, at this time I was caught up in a struggle between the spiritual and the carnal. It seemed as if God was saying, "All right, if you want some flesh, here it is." Even one of those women would have been enough for a healthy young man, and there were three of them. I felt obligated to give my attention to them all, and it nearly killed me. It wasn't the physical strain that got to me in the end. It was the lying.

It was a difficult period. I could see only one way out of the life I was living and into a new life: Zen Buddhism. For several years I had been reading everything I could find on Zen. Sparkling, eccentric, and wonderful, the ancient texts pulled me in. Then I found Philip

Kapleau's book, *Three Pillars of Zen,* and it became my constant companion. The book revealed Zen in a new light. I had been under the impression that enlightenment experiences had happened to a few famous monks in an earlier era but were not happening in the present day. Kapleau's book told me that enlightenment was possible in the here and now and spoke of ways I could pursue it. I read the book voraciously; it was my salvation. I was sure that Zen was my answer. Most books on Zen are philosophical, dogmatic, or academic, but Kapleau spoke of action. He provided descriptions of kensho, or satori, and said that kensho is possible—now! He described temples and disciplines in Japan that awaited the true seeker. Kapleau's book put the spiritual experience in the here and now, something no other book had done for me. He had gone to Japan to study, had become a monk, and had experienced kensho, enlightenment. I saw that Zen might open and expand my spiritual experience.

Kapleau's book also described the necessity of submission to a spiritual master. The true seeker, he said, gave his whole life, twenty-four hours a day, to a Zen master who would guide him to enlightenment. I pictured enlightenment: the doors to heaven would open and all my problems would vanish.

In New York, when I had my awakening, I was not looking for a master. I had the master inside. I felt complete. I didn't need anything or anyone outside myself. However, the further I moved from that experience, the more curious I was and the more I wondered how I could get back to it. Now, Kapleau's book was speaking directly to my heart, and I thrilled to every page. I had found my direction. The heart has wisdom. It knows what it wants.

I bought an airline ticket. People asked me why on earth I wanted to leave Paris. From the outside, my life appeared ideal. I was making a lot of money as a model, I had my own little Triumph Spitfire convertible and could travel as much as I wanted, and I was living in the most fascinating hotel in Paris with three beautiful women. Every sensual pleasure that any man could ever want was mine. The problem was, I had no peace. I was confident that much more meaningful experiences awaited me in Japan. A voice whispered,

It's all here in Kapleau's book. Devote yourself to the practice of zazen and you can break through to the world of reality and true spiritual experience. Other people have done it. Kapleau did it.

Meanwhile, I also was a serious contender for the American lead in Jacques Tati's film *Mon Oncle*. Tati liked my audition. "There's only one problem," he said. "You're going bald. See this man and come back in a week," he said. He had arranged for me to get a high-quality toupee that cost a fortune. More fortunately, I didn't have to pay for it. When I went back, wearing my new hair, I asked Tati how long it would take to make the film. When he said it would take two years, I told him I couldn't do it because I was going to Japan. "What a shame," he said, and I was out of the running.

I gave away all my ski clothes, packed what I thought I would need, and stored the rest. And then I did something I never thought I would do. I burned my black book containing the names, telephone numbers, and addresses of some of the most beautiful women in Europe. A priceless treasure of sorts went up in smoke in the wastebasket in my hotel room, and I saw it as a step toward freedom. A few days later, in July of 1966, I left for Tokyo. I had no qualms as I boarded the plane. I had made no calls and written no letters. I knew I had to go, so I went.

Learning consists in adding to one's stock day by day. The practice of Tao consists in subtracting day by day: subtracting and yet again subtracting until one has reached inactivity.

—Lao Tzu

-7-

SUBTRACTING DAY BY DAY

Japan was mystical and exotic to my mind and my imagination—foggy mountain peaks with ancient temples poking above the clouds, the ring of temple bells signifying prayer times, blue-robed monks in a silent procession with their begging bowls. The newness of the customs, the demeanor of the people, the sound of chanting, the architecture, and especially the religion nourished me with their quiet power, simplicity, and timeless flavor.

I wandered the streets of Tokyo, taking in my new environment. It was intolerably humid out in the streets and intolerably cold in the air-conditioned buildings. The Japanese are fastidiously clean and fresh, their immaculate shirts and pressed trousers contrasting dramatically with the clutter in the back streets and the jumble of advertising. The faces I saw were strong, solid, and reserved, but when people recognized their friends, their smiles were brilliant.

The food intrigued me. I enjoyed my first meal, which consisted of raw beans, rice cakes, seaweed, cheese, salmon eggs, bean curd fried in sesame seed, and beer. Afterwards, I looked up Philip Kapleau's phone number. When I called, he invited me to visit him at his home in Kamakura.

I left immediately and found a hotel near Kamakura in the Enoshima resort area, which was peaceful and beautifully landscaped with rocks and trees. In the mornings, adults and children performed calisthenics on the beach, and it was a beautiful sight. The people I encountered were friendly. I noticed very little complaining. They laughed a lot and giggled politely at me, the odd American.

When I met the small, sturdy, and rather plain man whose book had so transformed me, Kapleau asked why I had come to Japan for Zen. He said he was just about to leave for Rochester, New York, to open a Zen temple there. "Well," he said finally, "I guess if you're here, you might as well make use of it." He said he would speak with his Zen Master, Nakagawa Soen Roshi, who was the Abbott of Ryutaku-ji, a small temple in Mishima City, two hours away by train.

Several days later, Kapleau informed me that the roshi, or Zen master, had given him permission to send me to the temple for one week so that he could determine whether I was serious. He also wanted to make sure I would fit in. Apparently some Westerners had not fared well at the monastery, so he would not commit himself in advance.

One week later, I walked through the historic wooden gates of the monastery and into the ancient yet intensely practical world of Zen.

Ryutaku-ji (Dragon's Tooth Pond Monastery) was a cluster of wooden buildings on the side of a hill. Nestled in a bamboo forest, the main building—the *zendo*—rose above the others, marking sharp, clean lines against the skyline. It was an ancient structure with traditional Japanese wooden rafters. Much of the original wood and ornamentation was intact, dating back three or four centuries. From the top of the hill above the monastery, I looked across a wooded valley to see Mt. Fuji rising majestically into the clouds, just ten miles away. The valley below the monastery was dotted with small farmhouses and neat fields of rice and soybeans. It was a lovely setting.

Ryutaku-ji was considered a traditional temple, although the roshi, Nakagawa Soen, was an innovative master who was often unconventional in his teaching. There were sixteen monks at Ryutaku-ji while I was there. Half of them had been there for years. Most of the rest were there for a two-year training that would qualify them to take over their family temples. In my estimation, only three or four were true seekers, fully dedicated to the inner search.

Soen Roshi was a small, slight man with a shaved head. He was dressed in a dark blue outer robe, which is the traditional daily garb of a monk. His demeanor was quiet as he greeted me with a quizzical

Locke Rush in courtyard of Ryutaku-ji Dragon's Tooth Pond
Monastery

smile and invited me into his chambers.

He gave me whipped green tea and sweets, and we chanted a sutra. He seemed very wise, not the great sage I had expected, but dedicated and enlightened. He was peaceful yet forceful, not by pushing but by his presence alone.

"What have you studied about Zen Buddhism?" he asked me.

I told him I had read D.T. Suzuki, Allan Watts, and Philip Kapleau.

He was silent for a while.

"All that you have read," he said, "will be of no use to you. You must empty your mind and begin with a clean page."

And so I did.

Next morning, a gong resounded at 4:30 A.M. and immediately the day began. There was no dallying in bed. Blankets and mattresses were quickly and neatly folded and stored. Within five minutes we all had completed our morning toilet and were seated motionless on cushions in the *zendo*, doing formal Zen sitting, or zazen. Shortly, new bells sounded and we all filed silently into the main temple, quickly lining up in two rows on opposite sides of the altar, facing each other. For several minutes all was quiet. Only the incense rising from the altar lent movement to an otherwise frozen scene. The temple was large, with rafters that soared to a high ceiling. The tatami floor was shiny and cold. The red and gold altar housed life-sized statues of the Buddha, which impassively observed the goings on.

Drums and morning chanting began: *Maka hanya haramito shingyo*. The words were meaningless to me. My lower back began to ache from the pressure of keeping straight; my knees, unaccustomed to the half-lotus position, protested only ten minutes after beginning. I tried to disregard the physical and lose myself in the sounds and rhythms. The tempo increased and so did my pain. I felt I must shift position, so I re-crossed my legs and leaned back a bit. The monk to the left noticed. His disapproval was nearly imperceptible, but I felt guilty. I watched Soen Roshi chanting and moving through his ritual. He must have done it ten thousand times, yet his concentration and way of moving told me that he was intensely engaged. How poor was my attitude in contrast. The ceremony dragged on endlessly until the final sound of the *kanzeon*, after which there was deafening silence. As the silence deepened, I could hear water dripping into the pond outside.

We got up. I was unable to stand straight because of the pain my back. We filed out and returned to the *zendo* for more sitting, this time quiet zazen. After a while, bells rang and we moved quickly to breakfast. Chanting prayers as the food was served, we sat on our heels at a low table formed by benches. By then my knees were a mass of pain that spoiled the pleasure of breakfast. The food was hot rice gruel, sesame seed, and sour pickles. The drink was hot water, which served as a cleansing agent for the shiny wooden bowls and which we swallowed after our utensils were clean.

Breakfast was followed by house cleaning chores. The work continued, quiet and unhurried, throughout the morning: sweeping, scrubbing, dusting, weeding, harvesting, clearing and trimming undergrowth, and so forth. There was no talking. It was cold, even in summer, and I learned to move quickly to stay warm.

Lunch was the main meal of the day. Vegetables, herbs, rice, and green tea were the standard fare. Afterwards, there was an hour of rest followed by additional work until dusk. Although strict Buddhists do not eat after lunch, at Ryutaku-ji we were served an evening meal of leftovers from lunch, and there was always enough rice to fill my belly. The evening hours were for bathing and zazen.

The bath was a round metal tub some six feet in diameter, which was heated from beneath by a wood fire. Two monks bathed at a time. There was no talking. Evening zazen lasted for one or two hours and was punctuated by the whack of the *kyosaku*, a stick used by the head monk to rouse drowsy sitters and rekindle enthusiasm for sitting. The lights were extinguished after prayers, and by ten o'clock everyone was asleep.

It was difficult being cut off not only by culture but also by language in a place where I was not even sure what I was doing. During my first weeks at Ryutaku-ji I was frustrated and confused, but also determined. When I had dropped everything to come halfway across the world to meditate, I hadn't envisioned too many difficulties. I was there to 'get' kensho, and I hadn't expected anything to stand in my way. I was to learn slowly and painfully that the Zen life is not one of glories and witty intellectualization but one of hard work, pain, and humility.

Sitting continued to be extremely painful. In the beginning, my back, knees, ankles, and hip joints were incredibly sore. I was discouraged to discover that I couldn't sit in good half-lotus position for five minutes without twitching. My hip sockets were not accustomed to it, and my sciatic nerve was badly pinched from the effort of keeping my back straight. Japanese sit this way from birth and can do it easily, but I realized it would take a lot of hard work to get my Western bones and ligaments sorted out.

I was angry at my futile efforts and determined to conquer the problem. Once, during my free time, I sat for one hour, punishing my legs. Afterwards I realized I couldn't push myself so hard. My right knee was painfully swollen; I bent over, got up, and sat down like a man of seventy. I was so frustrated that I visited a surgeon in Tokyo and asked him to cut some of the ligaments in my legs. Fortunately, my request horrified him and he refused.

Although my years in the Marine Corps had been a good introduction to this hard and disciplined life, in the Corps I had been able to share my feelings with others. Now, I was cut off from most communication. To make matters worse, my work boss was one of several high school boys with whom I shared quarters. They had been sent to Ryutaku-ji by parents who hoped some of the discipline would rub off on them. The young men I took orders from were delighted to be in command; not only was a foreigner an oddity, but to be able to reprimand and order him about was a rare privilege. This situation made my first weeks even more difficult. The hawk eye of my 'superior' was always watching me, and I found it difficult to concentrate.

I learned that work is considered 'moving zazen' and is highly praised. Any task is to be done wholeheartedly, with full concentration and devoid of any attachment to the outcome. This concept is alien to most Western thought, and it is crucial to understanding the Japanese mind and zazen. Work practice relaxes the mind. Thoughts such as *I must get it done on time* or *I'll be punished if it's not good* or *I must do better work than my neighbor to prove my worth* give way to acceptance. When performed without striving and resentment, sweeping the walk can be as happy a task as watching a favorite movie.

I confess that during my first weeks at Ryutaku-ji I could not appreciate this, and, because most of the day is spent in physical work, I became upset. I approached Soen Roshi one day. "Roshi San, I must have more time for zazen. I know how to work. I have done physical work all my life, but I do not know zazen and I want to learn. I didn't come ten thousand miles to sweep. I came to meditate."

Roshi looked at me quietly as he mixed green tea. After pouring our tea and looking at the garden for several minutes, he said, "No, I cannot let you do this. Work is your zazen. You will understand later. Your work is most important."

Practice of zazen is the basis for any action in a monastery, whether this action is eating, defecating, working, walking, or sitting in meditation. The true monk is at all times to be aware. His zazen practice will, over the years, give him the spiritual energy to be centered and aware in all activities.

In Rinzai Zen, one is given a koan, a puzzle to solve not with the mind but with the whole being. The koan often given to Westerners is *Mu*, which is translated as *no thing* or emptiness. The entire koan I was given was this: A monk asked his teacher, "Has a dog Buddha nature?" The teacher answered, "*Mu!*" and this was the puzzle. My challenge was to discover what *Mu*, or *no thing*, was. I was instructed to focus on *Mu* every minute of the day. Every breath I took and every action I performed was to center on *Mu* until I 'became' *Mu*.

Every month for one week a *sesshin* was held at Ryutaku-ji, a one-week uninterrupted period of zazen, with most of the work time shifted to sitting time. *Sesshin* differs from ordinary monastic life in its intensity. The tension builds. Laymen from as far away as Tokyo mix with monks and often evidence more enthusiasm and effort to solve their koans. They regard the seven days as a rare privilege and an opportunity to get enlightenment.

No cost was too high. The idea was that the more you sat, the more you did *Mu,* and the more you struggled, the quicker you would storm the gates of enlightenment and experience kensho, the breakthrough into Buddha nature.

During the final days of a *sesshin,* sitting deepens. You can feel it. Concentration is excellent, fidgeting decreases, and you are so intent on your koan that you lose track of time. Once in a while we would hear that a monk or visitor had experienced kensho. We were awestruck, respectful, and somewhat jealous.

During *sesshins, dokusan* (a private meeting with the roshi) takes place two or three times daily. *Dokusan* with the roshi can be a delight or a terror. Going to see Roshi, I prostrated myself three times to Buddha. Soen Roshi asked me, "Where is your *Mu?* " I fumbled for an answer, and he dismissed me with a whack of a small stick. Sometimes I slid open the door to Roshi's room and he waved me off sternly, knowing by the way I arrived that I was not 'ripe.'

When one's sitting has matured, kensho can happen at any moment. *Dokusan* at such times is a no-holds-barred meeting. Screams, shouts, and uproarious laughter echo from the roshi's inner sanctum. Anything goes. As understanding of his true nature grows, the student loses his fear of the master. In psychological terms, the healthy child eventually incorporates the father and mother into his own being, finding within the natural balance and harmony of the actualized man. So in Zen does the roshi become the new father, the Godfather, the representative link, presiding and sculpting the rebirth that is emerging.

The structure and discipline of meditation threw me back into a neurotic childhood pattern. An element of early psychological growth involves coming to understand, accept, and value proper discipline. When mature and conscious parents do not guide this development, as is generally the case, anger, resentment, and inadequacy arise. Being forced to live up to a standard that is imposed without love and understanding can set a deeply neurotic life pattern. My parents, like most parents, had been dealing with their own unresolved neurotic patterns when they were raising me, and so it was inevitable that I had developed a neurotic pattern in regard to discipline. I resented any imposition, but I also sought approval because of a feeling of inadequacy. In this situation, Soen Roshi became the father I wanted so much to please.

I was determined to be a good boy, keep quiet, sit hard, and earnestly gain his love, admiration, and respect. I became so humble that it was hard to fault me. All my actions were measured not simply by my desire for realization, which was genuine, but also and more predominantly by a feeling that I must live up to the standards of the perfect Zen student. I was deeply frustrated because my body and mind would not respond the way I wanted them to. As time went on, I began to see this frustration as a barrier to my unfoldment.

My attempts at zazen were frustrated not only by physical pain but also by pleasurable fantasies of Europe and my old life of the flesh, which came up in meditation as thought waves. Fortunately, my direction was strong and was aided by my heartfelt knowledge that the worldly life I had led could never be truly satisfying.

Acute awareness of my inability to function at a high level increased my sense of inadequacy. The result was that I strove harder and harder to still my mind and force my body into submission, which is exactly the opposite of what is required for any real development in zazen.

One day Roshi and I were walking down the long path to the gate. A warm wind blew across the fields and moaned through the deep pines. "How is your Zen, Rocku?" he asked.

"Very bad. Very slow," I said with a sigh.

"Ho," he guffawed, thumping me on the back, "Rocku Zen best Zen, slow Zen, natural Zen."

It was early March. A premature warm spell had settled over the countryside. Six weeks early, spring had appeared. Green shoots had appeared on trees. Flowers had blossomed. I was joyful at the respite from winter, but Roshi was merely reflective.

"Too soon," he said. "Everything come in right time." A few

days later winter set in again and all of that giddy, premature spring withered. Roshi's words stuck in my mind. He knew I was seeking an early spring, but I was not ready, not yet ripe.

Another American arrived at the monastery, relieving my sense of cultural isolation. Ed Dullahan was a redheaded schoolteacher from Long Island. He reminded me of an Irish imp with a red beard. He played the flute and was a very funny guy as well as a serious student of Zen. Ed was confident that anyone could be enlightened if only they would stop pushing the process. "Don't be in such a rush," he advised.

Ed told me of an experience in which the flowers he had been looking at seemed much brighter. Suddenly, everything stood out like a brilliant picture or photograph. The roshi he was working with at the time told him that he had experienced a taste of kensho. I was excited: brightness and clarity of vision were part of what I had experienced in New York City, and I was still trying to place what had occurred in some context.

I sought a definite answer, a formula, something I could apply to brighten my life at will. The memory of the secret elixir that had sweetened and filled those months in New York City haunted me, and I began to find within me some similarities of mood and insight. What bothered me was that during such moments, there was no zazen. I was not striving. I was not even consciously letting go of thoughts or trying to just 'be.' When I was relaxed and my mind was still, everything I sought was present within me. Peace and a vibrant glow in my heart showed me that all is good and in its fullness just as it is. It was so simple: no zazen, no *Mu*, no striving. Why, then, was I living in a monastery?

The quality I sought and that which became manifest at certain times was not at all limited to Japan, to meditation, or to travel. It was a joyful, complete sense of oneness which, when present, required no reflection and which, when gone, prompted endless introspection and frustrated attempts to recapture.

What makes zazen so difficult for beginners is that the practice bypasses or thwarts the rational mind each time the mind attempts to intervene. In psychotherapy one is usually working *with* the mind to explore, evaluate, judge, compare, suggest. Psychotherapy values these functions. A therapist's reputation and professional practice may even depend on his perspicacity and mental agility. In zazen, the rational mind is useless. There is no therapist; meditation is the therapy. This presupposes that the person sitting has an intense desire to get at the root of his problems, which requires strength, courage, and patience.

Although the purpose of zazen is not essentially therapeutic in psychological terms, long and persistent sitting does foster relaxation, calm, and inner poise. In *Zen in Psychotherapy—The Virtue of Sitting*, psychologist Akahisa Kondo wrote that many of his patients reported a decrease in irritability and considerable reduction of tension as a result of sitting in zazen. He wrote that only sitting in zazen could prevent us from trying to solve our problems in the false and ineffective way that has become habitual. The solutions the rational mind is capable of producing are, in reality, pseudo-solutions, escape mechanisms that scatter our energy and divert us from facing our patterns. Sitting leaves us no alternative but to turn inward and look at ourselves. Looking inward, of course, confronts us with another problem: mental distraction in the form of fantasies or ideas.

The struggle with these mental distractions is a common problem. One day as I sat in zazen, I became sexually aroused. This was the result of a sexual fantasy that had started because my mind was restless. I saw that all thoughts of pleasure come from a restless mind. Bringing my mind back to *Mu* was difficult. *Why should I?* I asked myself. Moreover, I found that it was as hard to let go of unpleasant thoughts as it was to let go of pleasant ones. I clung just as obstinately to guilt, anger, and fear as I did to pleasure and joy. Habit and obligation led me to dissect and linger over my unpleasant thoughts with the delight of a gourmet savoring a selection of tasty morsels. Over and over, I caught myself thinking that my pleasurable thoughts were harmless and that I could resolve my unpleasant states of mind by thinking about them.

One early morning as I walked in the temple compound, a fresh insight came to me. Worry and fear and anger are only thoughts, and thoughts can be changed. Therefore, worry and fear and anger can be eliminated, along with the compensatory actions that only reinforce our negative state. Buddhism stresses right action because a 'guiltless' life enables us to meditate much better and, in turn, the meditation enables us to more easily lead a guiltless life, which further enhances the benefits of meditation, and so on. Unproductive, neurotic action fans the fires of neurotic thought and works against the absolving qualities of sitting.

Most religions talk of surrender, of letting go. What does this mean? What is it that hangs on? The mind is what hangs on. The mind is both the original sin that separates us from God and is also a sixth sense. The mind is a valuable tool when it us operating as a sixth sense. Like sight, intuition is a sense, but it has reason as a faculty. The problem is that reason doesn't serve only its proper function, which is self-preservation, but ventures into other domains.

For many people, for example, the scent of burning leaves is sweet and lovely, reminding us, perhaps, of the childhood joys of autumn. For someone whose house has burned to the ground, however, the scent of burning leaves evokes another association entirely. The scent of burning leaves is just an odor; the mind supplies a positive or negative association. This is how our mental habit patterns distort our perceptions of the world.

Watching the petty functions of my mind required constant effort. I practiced zazen as diligently as I could, believing that awareness of the activity of my mind would reduce its hold over my consciousness, but it was a slow process. I persisted and, finally, I tasted occasional sips of an unruffled state.

Zazen was teaching me to surrender. Surrender in the deepest sense means letting go of our thoughts. Children can teach us about letting go. Fascinated and absorbed in observing an insect or a tree, they are unconsciously practicing perfect zazen: their minds do not get in the way of their intuitive appreciation and union with the object. I tried to do the same. Whenever I became aware of clinging to a thought, I practiced letting go. My koan was my weapon. *Mu* gave me something to hang on to as I strove to let go of my attachment to mental concepts about objects, people, and situations.

Mu is simple but arduous. After a few months of sitting and working with my koan, the pain in my legs had decreased considerably, but I felt I was making little headway with *Mu.* Concentrating on a meaningless *Mu* that I knew was meaningless, to the exclusion of 'meaningful' thoughts, was hard. I told myself to have faith in *Mu,* the sword. *Straight ahead,* I told myself. I needed faith and determination. Every time I went to Roshi with an answer to *Mu,* he dismissed my latest profound revelation as *makkyo,* illusion. Once when he asked me how my Zen was progressing, I said my legs were hurting badly. "Good," he replied. "Continue."

In the cold months, the bath was the only place to get warm. The walls of the monastery were made of rice paper, and the temperature was almost the same inside as outside, just above freezing when we were lucky. One of my jobs was to build the fire under the bathing tub. When the water was steaming hot, one by one we monks would slip into the water—a torturous yet delicious experience and a fitting end to a hard day. For 'the man who wears six sweaters' as the monks laughingly called me, the bath was a salvation. It was the only time during the day that I was warm. Because I could never get warm except during the bath, I learned to stop thinking about shivering all the time and turn my mind elsewhere. Since that time, I never have had a serious problem with the cold.

Life at Ryutaku-ji was conducive to peace of mind. The days proceeded in a regular and healthy routine of retiring early and rising early. Physical exercise toned my body and zazen toned my mind. Refraining from idle conversation taught me the therapeutic value of stillness. The diet was light and totally pure. Towering pine trees, swaying bamboo, and flowers of all varieties enriched my contact with nature. Life was simplicity. My physical senses became acute.

I had entered into a period of celibacy. In the beginning, I had experienced nocturnal emissions and was subject to frequent sexual fantasies. A few months after my entrance to the monastery, however, these distractions ceased. I can honestly say that much of my sexual desire had vanished during that time, replaced by zazen and the desire for enlightenment. I journeyed to Tokyo occasionally, but I felt no drive to partake of the many sexual pleasures so abundant in that city.

I remembered a line I had read somewhere: "All sexual desire is but thought." If someone had told me this only a few months before, not only would I have laughed, I also would have considered that individual seriously neurotic. At Ryutaku-ji, I finally saw the truth in those words. Since then, I have occasionally offered this insight to others, but invariably it is met with ridicule and sometimes even hostility. Even so, I know it is true. Hundreds of hours of zazen showed me how my mind works. I watched thoughts arise and I watched them die. I discovered for myself that the only reality is awareness and that all the things I thought were real were merely reflections of a restless mind.

Fear, ambition, lust, and anger are only as real as thoughts are real. If we dwell on them, they will push us around almost as if they were tangible. However, the moment we turn toward the deeper truth of our inherited completeness, fear, ambition, lust, and anger dissolve. The dissolution of bothersome thoughts is not immediate; it is the result of a process. Repeatedly returning to the thought of *Mu* eventually causes them to shrink in importance.

The Japanese have a word for this process: *joriki. Joriki* can be interpreted loosely as psychic energy or life energy, but I experienced it as a spiritual energy born of dedication, strength, and will. *Joriki* arises directly from concentration, but concentration is due to strength of will and strength of will is a result of faith and faith is grace. *Joriki* is grace with muscles, a calm, subtle, yet powerful force felt throughout the body. It is neither physical nor mental yet it is both. In the beginning, *joriki* may be felt as a subtle vibration; over time it may become a euphoric strength. It is largely due to *joriki* that the sexual appetite diminishes. Why seek something you already have? It is the height of redundancy. The subtle inner emanations, relaxation, and peace are akin to the feeling that arises after the sexual act.

I suppose I thought I had solved my obsession with sex forever, but Soen Roshi knew better. One day as he and I walked in the courtyard, he pointed to a monk and said, "You see that monk? He is married, you know." He paused for a moment. "He is a good monk now, much better than when he was single." I did not understand why he pointed this out to me until many years later.

Occasionally there was a break in our routine. The monastery owned land that the local tenant farmers lived on. Whenever someone in the tenant farm community got married, all the monks were invited to the wedding, including me. At one of these celebrations, we monks sat around a low table on the floor, drinking hot saki. The monks toasted me. *"Kampai!"* each of the sixteen monks said in turn, downing his saki in one gulp. I responded in kind. In less than five minutes, sixteen ounces of hot, sweet saki had flooded my system. I was flying.

"I'll show these hillbillies a thing or two about drinking," I thought, flushed with the memory of my superior track record of evenings spent with Jack Daniels. I stumbled off into the bamboo forest to relieve myself and when I returned, I drank more. Soon I leaped onto the small stage and began to dance. I don't know if tradition permitted it, but there I was anyway, doing my Zorba version of kabuki. Suddenly I fell, hitting my eye on the corner of the stage. Blood spurted out as I struggled to get to my feet. Thankfully, the party ended just as I noticed how pretty the young bride was. God knows what I might have done had the celebration continued for another five minutes. The monks had to carry me up the hill, stopping every few feet so that I could vomit. Invincible Westerner! Man of iron! When we finally made it back to the monastery, the monks bathed me and tucked me into bed quite gently.

Next day, hung over and with a black eye and a large gash above my eyebrow, I realized how lucky I had been not to puncture my eye in the fall. Soen Roshi called for me. He poured me a cup of tea and gazed at my eye. "Hmmm," he mused. After a long pause, he said, "Did you learn anything from last evening?"

"Yes."

"Good. That is what is important."

Although I continued to drink socially, that was the last time I ever got drunk.

The episode was put into fuller context by an event that occurred the following week. In early morning prayer, the final chanting of *kanzeon* before the silence, which was customarily repeated seven times, went on endlessly then came to an abrupt end, punctuated by Roshi with *"Kwatz!"* a violent exclamation with more power in it than any sound I have ever heard. Following this outburst, the silence and the sound of dripping water from the pond outside were broken by the sobs of several monks. It was an eerie sound; monks rarely cry and never in public. Later I learned that a monk in a nearby monastery had hung himself that morning because he had behaved unceremoniously the night before.

To the Japanese, disgracing yourself by saying something wrong or doing something inappropriate is the worst thing you can do. They call it 'losing face,' and losing face is considered a grievous offense. Word had it that the monk who hanged himself had struggled with a drinking problem, and my guess is that he must have done something so awful while he was drunk that he felt he could not face anyone.

Public expression of grief in a society in which people never show emotion is especially moving because of its spontaneity. Likewise, the spontaneity of my drunkenness at the wedding, although my behavior certainly had been unwise and disgraceful, had moved the other monks. It cut across the social barriers that had kept our relationship formal and distant. In my early months at Ryutaku-ji, I had kept a wall between them and me. I wanted to make sure they saw me as a sincere student of Zen, so instead of actually being sincerely myself, I projected a sincere image and protected it fiercely. They felt my stiffness and responded accordingly. On the night of the wedding celebration, I got too drunk to keep up my pose. Surprisingly, I was greeted with nothing but smiles and claps on the back the next day. This puzzled me at first, especially when the monk who had disgraced himself took his own life. As a *gaijin*, a heathen from the arrogant West, obviously I was not held to such a high standard. Instead, by disgracing myself I had become more approachable. From then on, my relationship with the other monks was more natural and real.

Soen Roshi had once mentioned an old Zen saying, "Never put another head on your own." Personality and everything we have learned to think of as who we are—these are not who we really are. They are the heads we put on top of our true identity, which is the same identity that exists in all of us. I had behaved badly at the wedding, it is true, but at least I had stopped putting another head on my own in my relationships at the monastery.

I was fascinated by a phrase I found in a book by Seng So S'ang, a Tang Dynasty Chinese poet. It read,

"All in one, one in all, if only this is realized then no worry about our not being perfect."

Meditation can lead to this realization, but another and perhaps more accessible route is through human interaction. Since we human beings have the potential to recognize our own spirit or Buddha nature, we must have the capacity to see and feel Buddha nature in other human beings. Touching another's center is equivalent to touching our own center. It opens us to the eternal being within us, our own cosmos, our own flow. And to know the eternal cosmic flow in yourself is to know it in another. It is a most positive action. Arrogance, posing, and passing judgments on others about right and wrong are some of the ways we put another head on our own. Projecting and defending an image prevents us from communicating center-to-center.

Not judging others is Christ-like. Accepting others as they are honors the eternal cosmic flow. Accepting others as they are weakens our strutting little ego by robbing it of an opportunity to proclaim our superiority and our uniqueness by putting others down. Meditation that does not lead to self-acceptance and acceptance of others is not true meditation. Like many Westerners, I had approached my spiritual growth as a competition. I had been striving to become more Eastern, more serious, and more ascetic than the Easterners around me. I had been striving to be the best meditator and trained myself in the most difficult postures. In short, I had put another head on my own, a Japanese head. Instead of being myself, I had been imitating who I thought I ought to be.

Soen Roshi was a walking example of spontaneous being. He made a place in his life for the formality of his culture, but his life energy was apparent even in his formality. Soen Roshi's childlike simplicity and lack of pretense were his true teaching, and he sought always to evoke these qualities in others.

One day, for example, Ed Dullahan and I were sitting with Soen Roshi in his chambers, discussing the flavor of coffee. Roshi produced an old jar of coffee beans. He took out three beans, popped one in his mouth, and gave one to Ed and one to me. "The true flavor of coffee is in the bean," he said, chewing away with apparent savor.

Ed spat his out right away. "This tastes like sawdust," he said.

Playing the stoic philosopher, I chewed on the dry, tasteless bean for twenty minutes. Only days later did I realize what Roshi had been teaching. My response was false, an attempt to emulate Roshi by imitating his action. Ed's act was spontaneous; it was a Zen act, natural and uninhibited.

I became increasingly appreciative of monastic life and the Zen way. I had never before seen men who combined strength and gentleness so beautifully. The strength of purpose and the character of Zen monks are the result of thousands of hours of sitting quietly, immersed in the stillness at the center of their being. A Zen monk rarely asks for anything. He never takes the last sweet on a tea tray, and he is always the last person to enter a room, insisting on your precedence. In a Zen monastery, life is basic and the essentials are minimal. Economy of action and economy of speech are cultivated. What need is there for more when real fulfillment can be found within yourself? As practice of zazen deepens, acceptance is the dominant theme. Reactivity to events and people diminishes. Why try to change other people or the order of things if the order of things inside you is right?

As we sat in the *zendo* one evening shortly after dusk, I witnessed a remarkable example of Zen conduct that demonstrated both acceptance and right action. The air was heavy and incense hovered in the room. The occasional bark of a dog in the distance and the faint rustle of bamboo were the only sounds. Each monk was deeply engrossed in his koan or practice. In Zen, the object is not to become lost to the outside world in trance but to be aware of your internal being as part of the entire being of the cosmos and the physical world.

On this evening, the stillness was interrupted by the sounds of someone coming up the path to the monastery. By his uneven gate and the noises he made, we all knew that the visitor was an eccentric, slightly demented peasant who occasionally did odd jobs at Ryutaku-ji. This man was given to drinking spells, and on that night, he was very drunk. When he reached the door to the *zendo,* he stopped.

Not a figure moved. The blue-robed monks were as motionless as Buddhas, each man a barely distinguishable form in the dim light. Muttering to himself, the man lurched down the aisle, heading toward the priceless statue of Boddhidharma at the far end of the *zendo.* Becoming aware of his surroundings, the man gave vent to anger, derision, and laughter as he approached the statue. On reaching it, he ceremoniously bowed and then began rocking the table on which the statue was placed.

Several yards away on the *tan* (a raised portion of the *zendo* used for sleeping and sitting), was the head monk. He sat immobile, his features inscrutable, indrawn. As the rocking progressed, it became obvious even from where I sat some ten yards away that one more movement would topple the centuries' old statue and shatter it to pieces.

Suddenly, the head monk exploded into action. In one cat-like movement, he flew off the *tan,* reached out to steady the statue on the table, folded his palms together in reverence to Buddha, and returned to his seat. His action was spontaneous. He recognized what was needed and acted instinctively. An instant too early and his act would have been awkward and formal; an instant too late and the statue would have fallen. There was no premeditation, no measuring, no lingering, no lecturing, and no posturing.

The effect on the intruder was staggering. He fell to his knees and began to pray, awed by the purity and compassion of the head monk's act. Even in his stupor, the man's contrition and humility were real. For some minutes his sobbing echoed through the dark hall. The incident was never mentioned. It had been a small part of the day's activities, no less and no more than washing dishes or weeding the garden.

One year after I entered the monastery, I had to leave Japan for a while in order to maintain my tourist/study status. I chose to go to Thailand because of its beauty and Buddhist culture. I also wanted to observe the practice of Hinayana, the Southern school of Buddhism.

On my way to Thailand, I stopped over in Tokyo to visit my older brother, who was staying at the Hilton Hotel while doing business in Japan.

It was a shock to be thrust into the world of businessmen and their endless drinking. I adjusted as best I could, feeling like a third foot and not caring to enter the conversation. After the silence of the monastery, all talk seemed absurd, emotional, and trivial.

In the evening, Tock coaxed me to a nightclub, the Copacabana, which is known to have the most beautiful hostesses in Tokyo. I was given a delightful woman who spoke English, was an artist, and had lived in Europe. She made excellent money as a hostess and seemed to enjoy her work. At evening's end, she pleaded with me to take her back to my hotel room. After much discussion, I reluctantly said yes; her insistence was flattering, especially since she had offered to waive the hundred-dollar fee. I had no desire for her, but it would have felt awkward to turn her down and, also, I was curious.

When we arrived at my room, she disappeared for a long while to bathe and to change. She returned in a silk gown. She was a ravishing sight. She was expert in her trade, and gentle and humorous as well, yet I found it difficult to become aroused. Eventually, all normal sexual functions took place, but even orgasm felt strangely incomplete. The emotions that normally charge the sex act with meaning had left me. Habit and instinct remained, but I felt separate from the act. Any Oedipal, dependent, or clinging aspect had vanished.

It seemed I had changed profoundly and that zazen or spiritual absorption had become distinctly more rewarding and more sensual than intercourse. It came to me then for the first time that true renunciation does not involve renouncing anything. It is, in fact, misnamed. Renunciation takes place naturally; it is the falling away or shriveling up of a habit as it is replaced by something vastly more fulfilling.

The next morning, my brother grinned as he asked about my evening. "Oh, I didn't want to hurt her feelings," I said. "After all, she even waived her fee for me."

Tock roared with laughter. "The hell she did," he said. "I paid her a hundred dollars at the beginning of the evening."

Despite my insights about renunciation, it appeared that I had not yet reached that point in my development. Habits may indeed shrivel and lose their appeal under the right circumstances, but given a little encouragement, they can also spring back to life. In the monastery I was rarely exposed to temptation, and when I was, the daily routine of work and zazen made indulgence difficult or undesirable. In the weeks I spent in Thailand, however, I found myself sliding back into my old grooves. Although I continued daily meditation, distractions became more the rule than the exception.

In Bangkok, for example, I met Fred, an American who had lived in Thailand for several years. He invited me to stay at his home. Shortly after my arrival, Fred took me to a very elegant nightclub. Like most nightclubs in Bangkok, it had a large room in the back where girls waited to be chosen. Through a one-way mirror we could see Thai women of all sizes and shapes smoking, drinking, doing their nails, and chatting with one another. I was intrigued by their beauty and delicate qualities. Although the women knew they were being watched, they were not self-conscious as they moved about. Each girl had a number pinned to her scanty dress. The procedure was to choose a girl by number and place your order. Prices were very low. A few minutes later, your selection arrived at your table, almost as if she were a sirloin steak. And so I was introduced to the pleasures of Bangkok and was back to where I started before all my rigorous Zen training.

When I returned to Ryutaku-ji, I told Soen Roshi that I was leaving the monastery. I was not a monk. Very few people can truly be monks, celibate, focused, eyes on God full time. It had taken only a brief sojourn outside the monastery to reawaken my old habits. All the Zen in the world hadn't helped. The same is probably true for many would-be monks. As healthy as monastic life is, its promise is still deceiving. I concluded that it would be better to make slow, solid progress amidst the hustle and bustle of worldly life than to artificially leap ahead in a monastic setting, only to have my progress undermined upon re-entering society.

I moved out of the monastery and into a small annex apartment in Kamakura where I stayed for the next two years. My landlords were Mr. and Mrs. Oshima. My new home was only a few hours from Ryutaku-ji, so I would be able to visit Soen Roshi with ease. Also, I had heard about a small and earnest group of Westerners who were practicing zazen in Kamakura. They did *dokusan* with Yamada Sensei and Yasutani Roshi, both good friends of Soen Roshi.

No pious practice is so perfect that it may not be an obstacle to spirituality.

—*Meister Eckhart*

-8-

No Pious Practice Is Perfect

Kamakura, once the capitol city of Japan, is a small city on the west coast about thirty miles south of Tokyo. It is known for its temples and particularly for the Daibutsu, a large metal Buddha some thirteen meters high. The population of Kamakura swells in the summer months as thousands of visitors flock to the beaches. The rest of the year it is a small, quiet town and ideal for contemplation with its many peaceful temples and wooded paths.

I soon made friends with the Westerners who practiced zazen there: Philip Kapleau's wife, deLancey; Jane, a Canadian *sansei;**and Birgitta, a German woman and translator of Kapleau's book, *Three Pillars of Zen*. We went as a group to Sunday all-day *zazenkai* meditation meetings led by Yamada Sensei* and attended *sesshins* in the area.

My home in Kamakura was in a separate wing of the Oshima family home. I had a large living room enclosed in glass with sliding doors that looked out on a beautiful garden. A guest room, kitchen, meditation room, and bathroom completed my living quarters. The house was situated on the outskirts of town and so there was little noise save for the nearby river and the locusts and birds so abundant in Japan.

For the next two years, I lived a simple life. I had no stereo, radio, or television. I did my own cooking. Furniture consisted of cushions

---

* Traditionally, a *sansei* is a third generation, pure blood Japanese born outside Japan, while the word *sensei* means 'wise person.'

on the tatami floor, a low table, and a roll-up mattress that served as my bed. Otherwise the room was bare except for an occasional flower arrangement. I followed the lovely Japanese custom of placing carefully chosen objects against a plain background. Paucity of decoration seems to assist in clearing the mind. After a while, I became accustomed to this simplicity and also to silence in the course of a regular life. Even when I dined with the Oshima family, it was not uncommon for us to enjoy silence for five minutes at a time while we ate our meals.

I kept a daily routine similar to that at Ryutaku-ji. I arose before dawn, meditated for an hour, then walked slowly, hands clasped behind me, along back paths and through nearby temples, continuing my meditation as I walked. By this time the day had begun. Temple bells rang out, and I often heard drums and chanting from neighboring Zen temples.

After my morning walk, I did another thirty-minute sitting followed by forty-five minutes of yoga. I showered, dressed, and ate a simple breakfast of fresh-juiced apple, a slice of homemade whole wheat bread with organic honey, and a cup of mint tea. Next, I allowed myself the luxury of walking uptown to buy the morning paper and enjoy a morning coffee at the Happi Shop, where I lingered over the day's news.

The old lady who ran the Happi Shop was herself a study in Zen. No matter how crowded the shop was, she never hurried. Slowly and with infinite care, she prepared each morsel and served it with enchanting delicacy. Each customer received the same attention. Whenever we talked, she laughed often and seemed absorbed in my every word and gesture. Through her and others I met in Japan, I learned that it was not necessary to enter a monastery to find genuine Zen characters. Making coffee and serving it with grace was this woman's daily prayer.

After coffee I returned to study Japanese, to write, or to read. Before lunch, I taught English to a student who came to my home. I enjoyed a vegetarian meal at noon and then walked again, this time perhaps three or four miles, continuing my practice of awareness.

I walked extremely slowly, repeating *Mu* with every breath and relaxing into my lower belly. When my concentration was good, I was aware of a solid, vibrant feeling in my belly that spread throughout my body, creating a sense of incredible well-being that bordered on the edge of compassion. It seemed to embrace all living creatures, pardoning all for what they could not help, loving all, and eliminating any feeling of fear or depression. I kept my gaze on the ground in front of me, changing my focus from time to time to concentrate totally on a lovely scene or interesting object, mindful of maintaining awareness and not letting the mind slip away. The result of doing this for hour after hour was profound and totally relaxing and refreshing. In fact, it enhanced my sitting at home, just as my sitting enhanced my walking.

In mid-afternoon I returned home to work on my journal, after which I took green tea and meditated for an hour. Dinner was usually brown rice and a vegetable soup, which I made from fresh garden vegetables. My second student arrived after dinner and stayed for an hour. I meditated again and went to bed, usually before ten o'clock.

At first, until my practice had deepened to the point where I could sit alone, I often walked to a small building on the grounds of Engaku-ji, an ancient temple in Kamakura, where the monks in charge held daily sitting for lay students who included Westerners, college students, and Tokyo businessmen. The head monk, Zengyo San, was a strong and compassionate man who had once sat for six months to experience kensho, never lying down to sleep. He knew me from Ryutaku-ji and accepted me into his daily routine, providing an extremely important bridge between Ryutaku-ji and ordinary life. I had entered a new phase in my spiritual training.

Not being in the monastery enabled me to relax more and taught me to function more naturally in a physical and social environment. The absence of formality in all aspects of daily living was a relief in many ways. The disciplines imposed on monks reminded me of my childhood. Like a child, I had rebelled at first and later conformed in order to gain acceptance and recognition.

I attended twelve *sesshins* during my first year, and these were very different from those I attended while I was at Ryutaku-ji. The difference can be explained by an old controversy in Zen meditation circles between gradual enlightenment and instantaneous enlightenment. Life in the monastery had favored gradual enlightenment. Soen Roshi had *not* stressed kensho, and *sesshins* there were no more than concentrated extensions of our daily lives. Any striving was individual and internal. You set your own standards and proceeded at your own pace toward enlightenment.

The *sesshins* I attended with Yamada Sensei's group were oriented toward instantaneous enlightenment and emphasized extreme effort. Perhaps because the group was mainly lay, *sesshins* were viewed as special opportunities to 'grab the prize.'

The operative motto was 'kensho or bust.' We were told that we must exert every fiber of our body, will, and mind to become one with *Mu*. We stormed the fortress of kensho, shouting *Mu* to achieve one-pointed focus and pierce through to an understanding of *Mu*. Anyone who did not give one hundred percent effort was considered unworthy of the task, and one hundred percent included a form of hyperventilation. Along with everyone else, I strained to increase the force of my breathing and the volume of my voice until the rafters rang with *Mu*.

During my first *sesshin* with Yamada Sensei's group, after hours of hyperventilation, I felt light-headed and my entire body was twitching. I went into spasms and toppled over to flop around on the floor. Desperate, I succumbed to my helplessness and began to sob.

The head monk quickly moved to my side. The Japanese are uncomfortable with tears, particularly if it is a man who is crying, and a Western man at that. He took hold of my arm and shook it. "You must not do this. Please. It's not right. It's not good," he said nervously.

I could sense his confusion. He knew his advice was incomplete, insensitive, and repressive, yet how else was he to deal with the situation? Later on, we discussed the incident and decided it would be best if I did not force meditation, and from then on I was careful to hold myself back from that level of extremity.

Nakagawa Soen Roshi (center) and students, author (far right)

The *sesshins* led by Yasutani Roshi were not quite so extreme. A wise old man in his eighties, he was also a champion of the instantaneous enlightenment school, but he embraced the quiet side of zazen as well. Even so, his *sesshins* were definitely success-oriented. One or two kenshos usually occurred during every *sesshin*, but sometimes none. Everyone who had not gained kensho during a *sesshin* felt disappointed.

I noticed that the people who experienced kensho were not screamers, just industrious and trusting people who, without drama, quietly did their work as best they could. Also, sixty to seventy percent were women, a high percentage given that women accounted for only about fifteen percent of attendance at *sesshins*. Something in the feminine nature seems to suit itself well to Zen and *sesshins*. The accepting, passive, yielding, embracing aspect of the feminine is a distinct aid to realization. Also, most women who had kensho did not question or doubt their koans. They worked much more on intuition and surrender, the true means to kensho.

Much of the difficulty in Koan Zen seems to be the leap of faith involved in total acceptance of the koan, which requires letting go of old patterns and concepts. In my observation, males are not so easily able to turn off the monkey mind and give in to the koan. The male mind seems more dualistic and men are prone to use the koan as a tool, always aware that 'I' am the one doing it.

Even when I had ceased shouting and had begun to see that quiet, stoic surrender was more effective for me, I continued to struggle fiercely with my mind. I used every means available to quiet my mind and put *Mu* in my belly. Focusing on the *hara*, a spot one and one-half inches below the navel, was said to stabilize the posture and still the mind. But my mind would not descend easily to the belly, so I took measures to bring it down. I scratched myself raw on that spot and rubbed hot wintergreen lotion into the skin, which helped. I did a visualization in which I drew my breath in through my toes as if it were ink moving upward through the hollow tubes of my legs until it filled my belly, reversing the process on my out breath. I tried any method I could find to aid my quest for one-pointed focus.

Eventually I discovered what it meant to 'feel the belly.' When the *hara* is activated, the belly swells and you can feel the *hara* vibrate. It is absolutely palpable. It is physiological.

For a year, I followed Yasutani Roshi throughout Japan to attend *sesshins*. Gradually, my zeal for quick enlightenment was replaced by a more realistic understanding of what was entailed. I learned to pace myself. Patience and pain became my bywords. I never attended a *sesshin* in which I did not have to deal with pain. It was interesting to discover that, in spite of pain, I could still maintain concentration and find some peace. All religions agree on the goal of getting rid of the ego, and zazen provides an excellent opportunity to do so: every time the ego urges us to change position, scratch an itch, or get up, it must return instead to one-pointed focus. Slowly, out of this self-denial and suffering, I developed a sense of inner strength and also a genuine compassion for others' suffering. Enlightenment is the knowledge that you are *not* the mind or the body, and this subtle truth begins to dawn during the long hours of sitting cross-legged and motionless.

After some months of strenuous sitting, I was getting results. My concentration was improving. Due to the effort of the past *sesshins* and the increased daily meditation, I more frequently experienced small periods of calm. To call them calm is not really doing these states justice. I had a feeling of inner vibrancy, of not needing anything to be even a hair more perfect. One day, for example, I was sitting in a local bank, waiting my turn to be served. As I sat musing and looking at my knees, I had a flash of insight. I saw that everything is *complete:* it was a staggering recognition. All my anxieties, fears, hopes, desires, opinions, comparisons, and strivings were nothing but thoughts that faded into a plain background and vanished.

On another day not long after, I was at home when again this simple but profound inner vision descended upon me. Like a child, I stood in my bedroom, giggling to myself because it was all so simple. Kensho, what is it? Whatever I was experiencing, it was effortless. It made no difference whether I was tired or energetic; the openness, perception, and fullness of vision were the same. There was no space for other thoughts. There was no mind training, no *Mu*. Everything was as it was. There was no hurry or worry. I gazed at an empty box for twenty minutes, delighted by its commonplace essence. To me, the box was as beautiful as the Taj Mahal.

In other moments, I was still confused. There was a distinct difference between the peaceful feelings I was experiencing in my daily meditations at home and what I was experiencing during the frenetic, supercharged, and strenuous *sesshins.* Struggle and more struggle just at a point when I was learning to relax and surrender presented a paradox. Struggle more and relax more. I could not doubt in my heart the efficacy of zazen effort, yet I did indeed doubt the necessity to struggle and strain toward enlightenment. I felt suspended between the path of surrendered awareness and the path of struggle and attainment.

I talked with Jane, deLancey, and Birgitta, who had struggled with similar problems. Birgitta had come to realize that the intense striving urged by the roshis was not so concerned with actual sitting as with determination and will, and she had modified her sitting. She had stopped straining and had begun to sit on her koan like a mother chicken sitting on eggs. Her attitude was that her koan would hatch when the time came, and not a minute before. She had found this attitude very beneficial. She said that the trick was to just keep sitting, to keep the constant warmth and attention there, and eventually enlightenment was bound to happen.

I felt strengthened and confirmed by her explanation. I saw that I had arrived in Japan very much a Westerner, convinced that if I strove hard at my zazen course of study, I would be awarded the kensho diploma. When I thought my process wasn't moving swiftly enough in the atmosphere of the monastery, I had left with the idea of finding a faster route to the rewards I desired. Wasn't this how everything worked? Greater effort equals quicker results? This viewpoint was strengthened by Yamada Sensei's exhortation that we must be willing to kill ourselves attaining kensho. He seemed to offer a crash course, and there I was, part of the grunting and straining group that left each *sesshin* downcast because they still didn't have kensho.

I finally accepted that in matters of the spirit one does not 'storm the gates.' God grants His boons when He is ready. I understood that I must continue to make an effort but continue with a prayer, "Not my will, but Thine, O Lord."

Soon after, I attended a *sesshin* in Osaka that Yasutani Roshi was conducting. In this *sesshin,* I moved quite smoothly into a phase in my practice that was just as intense as before only quieter and deeper. If you question from your depths, "What is *Mu?* What is this thing?" there is no room for anything else.

Now I understood what Soen Roshi had meant one day when I asked him how to still the mind. We were standing by a lotus pond. The air was all but still; just a whisper of wind moved the ferns at the water's edge.

He looked at the pond for a while before he answered, then extended both arms as if holding a tub of water, "When you have a tub of water, how to make still? By shaking tub?" A smile spread over his face. "Only let water become quiet; try not to disturb. Must happen itself."

All I had to do was to sit and hold gently but firmly to *Mu.* Unconsciously, I had been straining to force my mind into submission and criticizing myself for failing. From then on in my practice, whenever I saw that my mind had strayed, I simply brought it back to the one point, again and again and again. I didn't let anger, frustration, or impatience get in the way.

I remembered what I had discovered about playing tennis. When a 'let' serve comes at you, one that tips the top of the net and clearly does not count, and you decide to hit it just for the fun of it, you can drive that ball down to your opponent's far corner and deliver a perfect shot, a Zen shot made with complete ease because there is no thought of scoring a point.

As I relaxed and my practice deepened, I had to deal with new problems. I understood now that I must continually return to *Mu,* no matter what, but I began to experience feelings of pure joy, peace, compassion, and an incredible sense of expansiveness.

When I brought my focus back to repeating *Mu,* the subtle feelings vanished. What was I to do? It seemed the height of redundancy to throw out the food as soon as I was served. Why do *Mu* and blot out that strong joy inside? It seemed most natural to cradle gently the peaceful mood in my soul, resting in the awareness of the stillness it brought. My way out of this, eventually, was not to discard the peaceful state but to keep it in the background and continue to do *Mu.* It didn't have to be either/or; it could be both/and. I discovered that staying with *Mu* in this way helped keep me connected to the peaceful state.

My sense of well-being begged to be used. The lotus heart deep within whispered to me, and feelings of love arose. I wanted to sing to the world. I spoke more often with strangers, listened with the third ear, and accepted and forgave with ease. I had read, however, that there should be no attachments and no reliance on others. A phrase from *The Zen Teaching of Huang Po* by J. Blofeld caught my attention. It spoke of "just allowing all things to take their course the whole day long as though you were too ill to bother...innocent of any urge to be known or unknown to others...*your minds like blocks of stone that mend no holes.*" (Emphasis mine.)

Your minds like blocks of stone that mend no holes: I saw the wisdom in this phrase, but it was difficult to practice. I wondered how to reconcile the flow I felt between people and nature and me with Huang Po's exhortation. Uncertain, I tried to compromise and find a middle way that neither rejected the world nor clung woodenly to the repetition of *Mu.* I was strongly drawn to the practice of *shikan-taza,* where one merely sits, not counting breaths, but simply being aware of the incoming and outgoing breath.

Because of the confusion in my practice, I slowly drew away from my teachers, preferring to experiment in my own way. Zen Japanese masters (for all their good) are only Japanese and Zen and masters of their own way. Again I resonated to Soen Roshi's advice to stop putting another head on my own. It seemed silly, stupid, and Japanese to worry, worry, worry about kensho. Being pushed down into a system that made me feel *obliged* to attain enlightenment was only an extension of childhood admonishments to be good and do what I was told. I felt it was time for me to be an adult, to go at my own pace, to destroy my own demons, sliding back and pushing on and learning rather than trying to conform to someone else's concept of what I should be.

Even so, the writings of Hindu sages had begun to influence me strongly. Perhaps I had finally had my fill of the strict life, both in my childhood and during my stay in Japan. I was drawn to the more natural and loving approaches described by Vivekananda, Ramakrishna, and Ramana Maharshi. In one of his books, Vivekananda describes the mind as a bull. It is difficult and sometimes impossible to force a bull into a corral, but you can lure it inside with sweet grass. I found that my mind concentrated better and was more absorbed by what fascinated or pleased it.

I continued my practice of *Mu,* but at a much lower key. I began to concentrate on breathing or on the subtle vibrations that emanated from the heart. As my practice deepened, interesting things began to happen. Walking home one day, I was trying to control my mind and concentrate on Being without much success, it seemed. Suddenly, I looked up and realized I didn't know where I was, what street or even what country. Everything was new and unfamiliar. I was seeing the world as a newborn child must see it, fresh and free of conceptions. The feeling was extremely strange, and I was afraid. I felt out of my body and totally disoriented. After a few seconds I blinked, and my thoughts and mental processes flooded back in.

I experienced something similar on another day when I was riding the train to Tokyo. Everything seemed strange, and I didn't know where I was for a few moments. Although the intensity passed quickly, the whole day felt rather unreal. I wondered if this was the detachment that sages speak of. It was not unpleasant, but it felt stunningly new.

In meditation one evening, I watched my breathing become irregular and fast. I could not adjust it, so I let go. The breaths became shorter and faster and a black void enveloped me. I tried to plunge into it, but it was somewhat static and I couldn't penetrate it.

My eyes went out of focus. I opened them and stared at a picture of Ramana Maharshi. He became large, then tiny. I lost track of time. I seemed to be floating sideways in the room. Gradually my normal perception returned. *What is all this?* I wondered.

At *zazenkai* one day, a bell rang, and it rang in my stomach. My whole being vibrated. The next two periods went by very fast. I could not recall segments of my sitting. *Mu* was Nothing. When I told the *sensei,* he seemed excited and encouraged me to continue.

These natural changes in my practice propelled me to return to Ryutaku-ji for *dokusan* with Soen Roshi. He met me in his chambers and, after tea, he said, "This evening we take bath together after monks finished."

We went to the bathhouse, prostrated three times to Buddha, and entered the bath. Roshi squeezed the juice of two lemons into the water and let the rinds float on the surface. The moon shone low on the horizon. Submerged in the hot water, we gazed at one another for a long time. Finally he spoke "Some people have *Mu* like cancer here," he said, pointing at his body, "when all the time it is not necessary. *Mu* is just this...me...always—not difficult, but many people make it difficult. Bath is *Mu. Mu* is a tool. *Mu* is to help you. It is strong medicine in the beginning, becoming thinner and thinner and disappearing. It should disappear. Now you understand. The one thing is Budd-ha." He said the name in two syllables and laughed, his eyes crinkling.

My interview was over. Roshi smiled. I felt a weight had been lifted. He and I understood one another. I didn't realize it then, but I had passed through *Mu.* During zazen and in my daily life from then on, my meditation practice shifted to watching my breath flow in and out and centered more on stillness and quality of being.

What is known as the teaching of the Buddha is not the teaching of the Buddha.

—*Diamond Sutra*

-9-

Not the Teaching of the Buddha

My life in Kamakura continued, following a comfortable routine of meditation, contemplation, tutoring, and *sesshins*. I had already received what I wanted when I came to Japan, but I kept putting off my departure, uncertain of my direction. It took a catalyst to mobilize me.

The catalyst came in the form of a hippie couple from California, Frank and Gisele. Frank was in his late fifties, bearded, tall, and thin, with the lingering smile of someone who thinks he knows. His aristocratic and nubile wife, Gisele, was a few years younger. One evening, I had dinner with Frank and Gisele and a few friends, including Ruth, the youngest of the group. Frank had brought with him a large lump of strong black hashish. Would we like some? he asked.

"Of course!" we said, eager as serious seekers to try any new experience of consciousness. Except for Frank and Gisele, none of us had ever tried hashish or even marijuana. Espresso coffee was the strongest thing that had entered our bodies for several years. So we were clean physically as well as mentally, fresh and receptive to an intriguing experiment. "You'll like this," Frank promised. "It'll really expand your consciousness."

Because none of us were smokers, we decided to eat the hashish. Except for Ruth, we each took an amount the size of a pea and swallowed it with green tea. Ruth had no reservations: she cut a hunk of hashish the size of a walnut. Because we were ingesting the hashish instead of smoking it, Frank told us it would take forty-five minutes or so before we felt the effects of the drug.

We waited patiently, drinking tea and talking about India and gurus. Frank told us about a swami in India who could do for us in a few weeks what all our Zen practice had so far failed to do. It was rumored that this man could confer instant enlightenment on anyone simply by his touch or the power of his gaze. The process was called *shaktipat diksha*, and the man was Swami Muktananda, a master of Siddha Yoga, the yoga of unusual powers.

Wow! A quick fix for Locke. That appealed to me. I was fascinated but also skeptical. I wanted to meet Swami Muktananda. Frank gave me the name of a disciple in Delhi to contact whenever I decided to make the trip.

By now an hour had passed and we felt a little strange and unfocused, as if we had drunk a glass of wine. We were fairly certain that the effects would not get stronger. I was disappointed to note that my consciousness had not expanded as promised.

Ruth was having a different trip. She sat in a corner crying and mumbling incoherently. She got up and stood on her head for a few minutes, then sat down and sobbed uncontrollably. After a while, I went home. Ruth spent the night.

The next morning a breathless Ruth arrived at my house. She was beaming. "I've solved my koan," she gushed. "I know *Mu.*" As we talked I realized that she was fully confident about her drug-induced enlightenment. To make it official, she planned to have it sanctioned by a true Zen master. A few days later, Yasutani Roshi delivered the sanction.

In the ordered and intense world of Zen discipline, solving a koan is no easy task. Some people work on it for years, and here was a twenty-five-year-old who had taken hashish and solved her koan immediately.

Somewhat anxious, Ruth asked, "Do you think I should go back and tell the roshi I took hashish?" A wise inner voice warned me that the truth in this instance could cause a catastrophe. "No," I said. "Don't do that. Leave well enough alone. There's no need for him to know."

Ruth went on to solve successive koans, each of which was

sanctioned by a highly respected Zen master.

I was happy for Ruth, but uneasy. Her experience prompted many doubts and questions. I was curious about what had happened to her. What did it mean that a drug-induced experience had produced a breakthrough sanctioned by not just one but several masters of the highest rank in one of the most traditional Eastern disciplines? I wondered about the connection between a drug experience and a true spiritual breakthrough.

I had learned that primal energy, also referred to in different disciplines as shakti or prana, can be collected, stored, intensified, and directed. It can be liberated in a variety of ways, and I suspect this is what happened to Ruth when she ingested the hashish.

I found it incomprehensible and upsetting that Ruth's experiences were able to withstand scrutiny and be formally sanctioned by several great masters whose guidance and wisdom I had relied upon. Couldn't they tell the difference between a drug-induced experience and a true experience? Ruth's state had not changed. She did not appear to be coping any better with her life, nor was she endowed with special powers or with the lofty spiritual states I had envisioned. She was a young girl who had taken a lot of hashish and solved several koans. *If that's how it works,* I thought, *why are we wasting our time sitting in these agonizing positions for hour after hour and year after year? Let's just take hashish instead.*

All the spiritual texts on Zen, from Dogen Zenji and Rinzai to D.T. Suzuki and Paul Reps, clearly say that when you experience kensho your life is transformed. According to Zen literature, when you demonstrate a koan to a master, your understanding of the koan is not intellectual. The truth is in the taste: you *know* the truth and you *know* that you know; through the experience you assimilate the truth. If what I had read was correct, there should have been some visible change in my friend.

I could have understood it if the roshis who sanctioned my friend's kensho had been lesser masters, but they were among the most respected in Japan. Their lineage could be traced back to the great Rinzai and Soto masters, even to the Buddha. They were the real

thing, masters of an ancient tradition who provided guidance from
the most lofty old temples and rigorous monastic orders in Japan.
My confidence in the promises of Zen Buddhist practice had been
rudely shaken. Kensho* was highly revered and sought after. For those
who practice zazen, kensho is the pinnacle of spiritual achievement;
throughout the centuries, people have died trying to gain it.

I still find it astonishing that ingesting a heavy dose of hashish
enabled a young woman to break through the veil-less veil and 'see
reality.' I loved the years I spent in Japan and found them quite
valuable in my development. I also respect and admire the Zen
tradition, but this incident can never be explained to my satisfaction.
It simply was what it was, an enlightenment experience that occurred
during a drug experience. This was a new koan for me: take drug…
have experience…experience is kensho. How could this be?

I have never wanted to risk unduly influencing another person's
spiritual practice, which is why until now I have told this story to
very few people. I have no desire to destroy anyone else's faith. Over
the years, people have asked my opinion about Zen practice and
about spiritual disciplines in general. I have been careful to consider
my responses carefully. I don't have the answers for anyone else's life.
Usually I proceed slowly and offer my opinion and my experience
only to the degree it is sought. I don't push. On the other hand, if
someone really presses me for my opinion, I have to be honest.

I decided to tell the story here because I want to be honest about
my journey, and this incident left me at a crossroads so far as Zen
and Zen masters were concerned.

Was my time studying Zen a waste? No. Although Zen didn't take
me where I wanted to go, I learned some things of value. I certainly
grew in patience from learning to sit still for hours at a time. Zen
practice strengthened my discipline. It calmed my nervous system
and gave me a pronounced sense of physical well-being. I benefited
from the sense of unity that came from sharing Buddha nature. I

---

* *Satori* and *kensho* are used to refer to enlightenment. *Satori* is the more classical
term; *kensho* is the word used commonly in Japan.

benefited from learning the breathing techniques, the principle of right action, and the practice of work without attachment to the outcome. In the end, though, my eagerness to storm the gates of enlightenment resulted in seizures. What made it more ridiculous was that the koan was *Mu*. We were *Mu*-ing like a bunch of cows.

Meanwhile, I was having some unexpected experiences of a clairvoyant nature that seemed to be associated with the development of my meditation practice. One day during meditation, a scene flashed into my awareness quite clearly. I saw a new yellow car pull up in front of my house. Out jumped four men, one of whom I knew. The other three were strangers. They walked to my kitchen door and rang the buzzer. I went to meet them and the scene vanished. I had no idea why this had occurred or what it meant, if anything.

The next day, a Saturday, I was in my kitchen when I heard a car outside. I peered through the window. It was a yellow car. One of my former English students and three other men I did not know got out of the car. The men walked to the kitchen door and rang the buzzer. The scene I had witnessed in my meditation experience of twenty-four hours earlier unfolded in front of my eyes. My student, eager to show me his new car, had brought along some friends he wanted me to meet.

Many smaller versions of this phenomenon occurred, convincing me that clairvoyance could be deepened and strengthened with only a little effort. It appeared that I had discovered the psychic world, but I was not very interested. I was fairly certain that extra-sensory perception, or whatever it was, would not give me the peace and understanding I strongly wanted, so I concluded it would be a waste of time to focus on it.

At around this time, in 1968, one day I had a persistent sense of foreboding. When I came back to my house in the late afternoon, I found a telegram on the porch. Before I opened it, somehow I knew what it said. My younger brother, John, had died. Only thirty-one years old, he had died of complications of alcoholism. I learned later that one week prior to his death, he had visited a physician friend who expressed deep concern about his physical appearance and condition. The doctor had advised John to stop drinking or he would probably be dead in a week. My brother's answer was to leave the doctor's office and buy a fifth of whiskey.

Six days later John lay in an intensive care unit. His last act was to tear out all the IV drips and tubes that were his life support systems. With a final burst of energy, he dressed himself and was halfway out the front door, heading for a bar, when the attendants brought him back. A few hours later he died. His need for a drink had killed him. Left unchecked, our dependencies will indeed kill us.

I left for the States immediately. The funeral brought my father and mother together for the first time in years. I watched them in the library of my mother's house after the funeral. I thought that John might not have been dead had they stuck it out. I felt removed from them.

Our parents affect us in two ways, first in our unconscious and second in our normal interactions with them. The unconscious is much deeper, for it is the repository of all our conditioning, dependency, fear, love, resentment, and admiration. To my eyes when I was a young child, my parents belonged together. I assumed there always had been and always would be mutual love, caring, and respect between them. I believed this even though I had never seen them show real love and respect to each other or to me. They were always arguing, working, or going somewhere.

It had taken the death of a son to free them from the social and emotional trappings of their lives and give them a palpable compassion and understanding of each other's pain. My father, who was leaning against the mantelpiece, looked at my mother, who was sitting a few feet away, and she returned his look and held his gaze. My inner camera snapped this picture. In that instant, my parents became human for the first time in my eyes, vulnerable and fallible. The umbilical cord had been cut yet again, and this time I knew it was truly severed. My dependency on them was over.

I stayed in the Philadelphia area for a few days to meet with old friends, moving among them as if I were in a dream. All the old reactions, interplay, joking, and frivolous talk were gone—not because of the funeral, but because I had changed. I was working on inner things. The situation was not unpleasant; in some ways it was deeply satisfying.

When I returned to Japan after John's funeral, I knew the time had come to move on. I had lived in Japan for two and a half years, and life was smooth, fulfilling, and quiet. I had assimilated what the spiritual practices of Zen had to offer, and I knew I would never lose what I had gained. I felt good about leaving, for although I wanted very much to visit India, I knew I was not leaving Japan prematurely. The fruit I found there had ripened and dropped. An inner voice had spoken to me, perhaps my intuition, and it was quietly insistent. I have learned over the years to listen to that voice and respect its urgings, so I packed my bags and left for India.

Whosoever studies to reach contemplation…should begin by searchingly enquiring of himself how much he loves.

—St. Gregory the Great

–10–

HOW DO I LOVE?

India, land of swamis, beggars, incredible wealth, and grinding poverty. The sounds, sights, and smells are overwhelming. It is a land of thousands of gurus, each offering a different path and different answers to a seeker's deepest questions.

For me, India was a magic carpet, a mysterious and sublime continent, a place I knew already in my heart. Often when I approached an ancient city for the first time, I experienced a strong and poetic feeling of déjà vu. However, I had never before responded to a foreign country with such a feeling of nostalgia.

During my first week there, an incident occurred that showed me what I could expect in the months to follow. While walking near the Tibetan Bazaar in Delhi, I was approached by a small, dark man with flashing eyes. Already accustomed to the many fortunetellers in India, I was amused at his pitch, which started out in the usual way.

"Sir, I will tell your fortune and the many things to come in your life." I smiled pleasantly and continued on my way. He followed me through the crowded bazaar, periodically tugging on my shirt.

Finally he stopped me, "Sir, I am very good, not like all the rest. I see and know your spiritual yearning. So that I may show you my power, in all good faith, give me two rupees, and I shall tell you your mother's first name. If I am correct, you pay me the full sum and I will tell your fortune, yes?"

I stopped and considered his offer. If this man could tell me my mother's name, he might prove to be an excellent fortuneteller. It certainly would be worth two rupees to check him out. I handed him the money.

He pocketed the two rupees and continued. "Your mother's Christian name is Deborah. Now please give me another five rupees and we shall begin."

I was stupefied. I was not carrying a passport, and I was not conscious of thinking of my mother's name. Either the man was a genius or he was far luckier than chance would dictate.

He told me many things about myself, and he was so accurate that I was afraid to ask him about my death. When he had finished, I asked him to take a cup of tea with me, which he quickly accepted.

When I asked him how he had become such a marvelous fortuneteller, he told me that he had practiced Hatha Yoga for many years and had become expert at certain meditative disciplines taught in Raja Yoga. He had belonged to a sect that performed these kinds of 'miracles,' which were not nearly as difficult as I might think. In the West, he went on, people consider only five senses, while Eastern philosophy recognizes a sixth sense seated in the mind. A person who has developed certain powers and abilities through yoga practice can enter another person's mind and read it. He said it was similar to reading Braille. If you know the code, you can read it easily. If not, you may touch a message repeatedly, totally unaware of its meaning, or even that there *is* a meaning contained in the raised dots. Being able to read another person's mind or perform other such magical feats, he said, had nothing whatsoever to do with a spiritual state or with being a good person. It was simply a developed clairvoyance that could be turned into a business. He offered to teach me—for a price.

I thought of my meditative experiences in Japan. After a few years of *shikan-taza* (watching the breath), I had become much more aware of the powers of the mind. It was fascinating, for example, to see experiences before they happened, and I knew that with some effort this and other powers could be developed. However, I also knew that such abilities were not sufficient to change my character. By then, I was fairly certain that the peace I sought had more to do with goodness than with psychic powers. I needed answers about my life and its purpose. I needed to move toward full understanding. I needed a man of wisdom to guide me on the path to enlightenment. I did not need to learn how to read minds.

I had come directly to Delhi because I had been told that Swami Muktananda would be there at the time, conducting an intensive, a period during which followers chanted and prayed and might receive *shaktipat*, or activation of divine inner light. I was eager to see him. I hoped he was the man of wisdom I was seeking.

Shakti is a Hindu term for the energy that exists in all things. An abundance of shakti is said to reside in the base of the spine, waiting to be activated and guided upward from the lower chakras, or energy centers, to the head. As shakti rises through the channel in the spine and touches successively the chakras in the genitals, belly, solar plexus, heart, throat, forehead, and crown of the head, it is supposed to confer wisdom and the higher states of consciousness. This phenomenon is also referred to as awakening the *kundalini* energy. I had heard that Muktananda could activate this process with a word, a glance, or a gesture, producing in the recipient an 'Aha!' experience of the highest order. I wanted to receive *shaktipat*.

I went to the intensive, which was taking place at the home of a disciple in the suburbs of Delhi. When I had the opportunity for *darshan*,* Swami Muktananda looked at me for a few seconds with a piercing gaze and said, "You have done a lot of hard work. You will stay with me a long time." He invited me to return with him to his ashram.

And so I followed Muktananda to his home in Ganeshpuri, some sixty miles north of Bombay near the coast, to join the congregation of the faithful and near faithful. I took happily to the sounds, fragrances, and sensual side of the ashram. Almost everything about ashram life in India was 180 degrees opposite to my experience of Japan. The seekers were extroverted and the climate was warm. I lived on the roof of the ashram and slept out under the stars, occasionally sharing my space with a Westerner who was passing through. Most of the time I was pleasantly alone up there.

I arose each morning at three o'clock, showered, and joined

the other disciples to recite mantras on the porch outside of Swami Muktananda's bedroom. It was pre-monsoon season when I arrived, and the heat was oppressive. We sweltered in the pre-dawn stillness, chanting the *Soham japa* (I am That), hoping to awaken the *kundalini* energy. We could hear the blast of the air conditioner as the Swami rested in his cool inner chambers.

One fellow, I believe he was a businessman from Bombay, turned into a human lion on more than one occasion, taken over by what we assumed was shakti. He roared as the shakti moved through his chakras, and he literally tried to climb up the walls. We all sat there, trying to keep the *japa* going and watching wide-eyed as this man roamed the meditation room, snarling and growling. We were so brainwashed that we exclaimed over his accomplishment because we had heard Muktananda praise the man. "You see how he is progressing, how well he is doing?" he had told the rest of us.

It didn't make any sense to me that acting like an animal was a good thing, but I tried to quell my doubts. Like most people there, I had come to the guru with fully functional common sense and had willingly thrown it away. The mind must go. Questioning must go. I accepted the necessity of surrendering my old state to make room for something new, but the doubts crept in anyway. "Why?" I often asked about this or that. "It doesn't make any sense," I muttered, mostly to myself.

Also, I had not had the *shaktipat* experience that so many people raved about. Muktananda had touched me a few times, but nothing had happened. This, too, increased my doubts.

Those in the guru's inner circle reassured me. "Don't question the guru," they counseled. "He is supreme in wisdom." Perhaps so, I pondered. Perhaps when you are with the right guru or teacher you truly *are* in the presence of such high wisdom, but I was beginning to question the scope of Muktananda's wisdom. What I know now is that out of a thousand gurus, you will be fortunate to find even one who has a sincere and true connection to God.

At the ashram I was one of only two or three Westerners. This was before Swami Muktananda attracted some celebrities, socialites, and diplomats and hit the big time. When I was there in 1969, most of his followers came from in and around Bombay, arriving in a regular flow to pay their respects and 'get' the shakti that so far had eluded me.

It was customary for visitors to bring a gift; if you had not thought to bring something, you could buy a rose at the door for two dollars. When you presented the rose to Swami Muktananda, he acknowledged it and set it aside. Soon, a disciple quietly whisked it away. I discovered later that one rose did very good service to the guru. After it was bought, presented to the guru, and whisked away, it soon reappeared at the ashram door, where it was sold again. This is not a rumor; it is something I saw with my own eyes. A good rose might bring in fifty or sixty dollars in its working day, more than an average Indian laborer could earn in two months.

Even before I learned of such practices, it was difficult not to be judgmental. I was seeking a true sage, one whose every action, word, and gesture demonstrated real wisdom and true compassion. I was disappointed in Swami Muktananda. Too often I saw him display arrogance, impatience, irritability, and anger. I thought of the dictum, "What you are speaks louder than what you say." I could not find fault with many of the ideas he put forth, such as his anti-drug messages and his advocacy of prayer, service, and gratitude to God. However, I noticed that the people in the ashram focused most of their attention on seeking experiences rather than on developing good character.

I went along this way for several months at the ashram, chanting the chants and being a good student while silencing or rejecting my doubts. Perhaps the peacocks and the dog that roamed freely on the ashram grounds suspected my infidelity, for the dog bit me once when I returned to the ashram late after a visit to town, and the peacocks chased me and pecked at me. On the morning after I was bitten, Swami Muktananda publicly chastised the dog and told him to bite me no more. The dog continued to growl every time I passed from then on, but he never bit me again. I considered this a miracle of sorts, though not the kind of miracle

I had expected from Muktananda.

While I was staying at the ashram, I made forays into the nearby town to drink tea and talk with other spiritual seekers. I also visited Bombay, where I met a very interesting woman, a psychic and a Bahai named Caramanli Dawn. She was big and strong, perhaps five foot ten, with broad shoulders, a shock of red hair, and very blue eyes. She was knowledgeable about homeopathy and natural healing. Everywhere she went, she used her remedies to cure children. She also gave freely to the poor. She was a dear person, and we became good friends.

Dawn told me she had the gift of talking to the elves. If anyone else had told me this, I would have dismissed the person as a crackpot. But Dawn was as solid in her character as she was in her physique.

"When I was a child, I would go into the woods near our home, where the elves would come out and talk to me. I told my parents; they thought I was making it up and were angry. The elves didn't want me to get in trouble, so they stopped coming."

At the time we met, Dawn was just finishing a book on palm reading. She read palms with great accuracy. She had told fortunes at the Russian Tea Room in New York City for a couple of years, and she was so good that her palm reading had been used in clinical work at the University of California.

She read my palm. "You will follow a Middle Eastern path," she said. I just looked at her. Briefly, I wondered if she were crazy. "You will leave all this and go in another direction."

"What do you think of Muktananda?" I asked her.

"No. Not for you. I get nothing special from him. He's a magician."

I left the ashram after six months to continue my search. I wanted so much to believe in a wise and compassionate father who would guide me to God and the enlightenment I sought, and I had not felt this connection with Muktananda. Nor did I feel the kind of emotional and spiritual bond I had enjoyed with Soen Roshi. Even so, I met with Muktananda to inform him that I was leaving.

"It's time for me to go," I said. He did not try to convince me to stay or tell me I was doing the wrong thing. He gave me a blessing, and I went on my way.

I went to Bombay and stayed there for perhaps a month, helping Dawn edit her book and exploring the bookstores, libraries, and cafes. Before I left, Dawn said something that penetrated my heart. "Locke, after you have seen it all, remember, your character is your religion."

Thinking of Dawn's parting words reminds me of a true story I heard about a wealthy follower of Muktananda who invited my friend Rudy to his house for tea. The host was a refined gentleman, swathed in white silk. As they enjoyed their tea, the man spoke of compassion and devotion and the unity of mankind. While he was holding forth, a nervous servant spilled some food on his white robe. The man slapped the servant across the face with the careless ease of someone swatting a fly, never pausing in his lofty discourse.

Dawn was right. A person's character is his religion. It is too easy to use outer trappings and wise words as a substitute for the very dirty daily work of coming to grips with your inner conflicts and bad conduct.

I had several destinations in mind as 'must-sees' when I left Bombay, most in South India. I wanted to visit the ashrams of Sri Aurobindo and Ramana Maharshi, and I also wanted to have *darshan* with Sai Baba and Sri Anandamayi Ma. It was fortunate that I had a plan, because that's what kept me from being waylaid nearly every day I was traveling. Indians love to talk. Whenever I climbed on a bus or a train, I soon found myself deep in conversation with the nearest passenger who eagerly pressed me to stop and see 'his' guru, who was superior to all the rest.

My first stop was Sri Aurobindo's ashram in Pondicherry, where lived The Mother. She had been a close companion of Sri Aurobindo, who had died a few years before. People said The Mother was immortal but she looked frail and, in fact, she died a few years after I saw her. She appeared on her balcony and inched along, blessing people with a feeble wave. I got into her room with a few other people for *darshan*. She blessed us.

Back on the bus and headed for Tiruvannamalai and the ashram of the late Ramana Maharshi, a 125-mile trip, I was almost persuaded to dismount halfway there by an eager devotee who insisted I just had to see the 'best guru in India.' It made no impression on him that I had just left Sri Aurobindo's ashram and was on my way to the ashram of Sri Ramana Maharshi.

Every day I became more aware of the rivalry among gurus and ashrams, most of it perpetuated by ardent devotees. I saw so much of it during my time in India that I soon learned to disregard it. However, I encountered many Westerners who were so naively open to 'sagedom' that their heads were being twisted in a thousand different directions as they strove to assess, weed out, and collate the mass of often-contradictory advice that bombarded them from every direction.

I arrived at the dwelling place of the late Bhagawan Ramana Maharshi, a great Gnana Yogi. The ashram was a bit different from many in India. First, it was not showy and, second, it had the distinction of harboring devotees who had migrated there because of the master's *spiritual* presence rather than his *physical* presence. Other ashrams criticized this, holding that it was better to work with a spiritual presence that resided in a physical body. My own observation was that in many of those other ashrams the devotees usually mistook the body of the guru for the spirit, constantly worshipping it instead of heeding the guru's message that the true guru is inside.

At Ramanasram, the presence of Ramana Maharshi was palpable; those who lived anywhere near his ashram at the foot of Arunachala, the sacred mountain, bore witness to his presence. Unlike other ashrams where the guru was the center of attraction and people organized their lives around the holy one's comings and goings, at this ashram people went serenely about their routine of meditation, prayer, and daily duties, breathing in the presence of Bhagawan.

Sir Arthur Osborne lived close by the ashram, and I had the opportunity to meet him. He was the chronicler of Sri Ramana Maharshi's life and work and the pillar of the ashram. His books had drawn me there, so as soon as I got settled into my little hut on the grounds, I walked over to his place and introduced myself. He was an old gentleman, tall and stooped, with thin white hair and a prominent nose. He invited me to dinner.

I spent a few weeks at the ashram and had a few more dinners with Sir Arthur. He was gentle yet vibrant, and he was generous with his thorough knowledge of Ramana Maharshi and his teachings.

While I was traveling in India, I had some odd and rather disturbing dreams.

Sometimes while in *sesshin* in Japan, and also when coming out of deep sleep, I had noticed an involuntary trembling and convulsion of the body, almost as if someone were shaking me. Always the sensation was associated with the feeling of crying or deep laughter and heaving of the chest. Once during *sesshin* I had experienced a violent explosion deep in my unconscious. I had the sense that if I could be fully present to it, I might be purged and also understand the terror and force behind it. I could find no explanation for these incidents, but I knew they were meaningful; they welled up from a deep source close to my psyche, and they were associated with fear and anger.

One night, while I was staying in Bangalore, the shaking and convulsions occurred in a dream.

> A woman was meditating, and I opened her door while she was in a trance. Her third eye opened and stared at me in a horrible, accusing, punishing way, as if to say, "Damn you! Look what you've done. It's all your fault. The power of God will descend. You are vulnerable. I'll fix you now."
>
> My whole body began to shake violently. I was terrified. Even the bed and the room were shaking uncontrollably. I beseeched almighty God to stop, but He continued even as I cried out to Him from my heart that I was sorry for my sin. I had the distinct feeling that I had disturbed someone and was being punished for something I had done in innocence. I knew that the shaking and convulsions were about to break through to a basic answer, and I was desperate to find the answer and find my freedom.

I searched my childhood memories for a psychological explanation. If I had surprised my mother and father during sex, I might have interpreted the sex act as violence toward my mother. Might my father have reacted violently, even physically shaking me? I visualized a scene in which he shook me furiously and chastised me. On the other hand, perhaps I was simply reliving one of the many times my father shook me for being disobedient. Whatever the incident this dream had recalled, incredible fear and guilt were associated with it.

At around the same time, I had several other dreams with a similar theme. In each was a woman who, for some reason, I was unable to love or who was taken away by another person. Always these dreams ended with me alone, sobbing, my body convulsing and straining toward deep, emotional release that was constantly thwarted. The dreams were cinema-like and the action unreal; I sobbed but without tears. I felt cheated and inadequate, unable to express love or other deep emotions, unable to dissolve my hard ego in tears of surrender.

Finally I thought I understood the shaking and the spasms at *sesshin*. Meditation seeks the depth of the mind and can loosen it, releasing the 'frozen tears' of an innocent child who was bewildered by his parents' rejection. My inner energy and faith in constructive action had been bottled up and redirected into self-preoccupation, pleasure seeking, and later a revenge against women and a fear of commitment lest I be betrayed again.

So it was that in the strange and esoteric land that has fostered so many loving saints, I truly became aware of my own lack of love. How was I to love? How does anyone learn to love? The austere years in Japan had been valuable in quieting the mind, but I knew that the true answer to life lay beyond the bounds of meditation and in the experiences of daily life. Watch a mother with her child, asking nothing, giving all, totally absorbed. She is doing perfect zazen. On rare occasions I had felt the incredible sweetness of life. Everything glowed. Enemies became friends. My desire to recapture this state, I realized, was the root of my alcoholism. Drinking had been an attempt to suppress the categorizing, judging mind and to evoke instead this wonderful sense of unity that didn't choose or prefer.

I confided my fears and my desire to love and be loved unconditionally to Hugo, a German homeopathic doctor who had lived at Ramana Maharshi's ashram for at least a decade. He was a healer and a quiet and gentle man, strong in his faith and simplicity. Many Indians in the area thought of him as a saint, and certainly he was deeply dedicated to relieving suffering, both physically and spiritually.

Hugo's tiny hut was simple and threadbare, holding only a few religious items and a writing desk. When I first saw him, he was wearing nothing but a *lungi*,* and he walked with a measured and aware pace, intent on his actions.

We talked in his hut for several hours. I poured out my analysis of my neurotic state and asked him what action he might recommend. Hugo, whom I discovered was extremely versed in Freudian and Western psychology, took a long time in answering. When he did, the words came gently, quietly, and without urgency. "There is only one neurosis in man," he said, "and that is not knowing *what* we are." As we talked I felt my tension and confusion dissolve. I felt the truth of his words. The great fallacy in our lives is that we do not know our true nature, the essence of our being, the true Self. That is, indeed, our biggest neurosis.

We also talked about Ramana Maharshi's path of commitment and giving and about the challenge of living a celibate life. When the creative force is not satisfied constructively, it comes out in the form of the sex drive. Hugo said that following the Maharshi's way satisfies the need for fulfillment and love at a very wholesome level. I found Hugo a beautiful and wise man and, above all, very loving. He was also a gifted healer.

A few days later on my way back north, I stopped at the Adyar outside of Madras. A lovely piece of land with banyan trees and gardens bathed by the waters of the Indian Ocean, the Adyar is the

---

* Sarong-like garment that wraps around the waist.

home of the Theosophical Society. During the days I perused the books in its exceptional library. Evenings and afternoons I talked with Michelle, the manager of the center.

Michelle was French and had always been a seeker. She saw my confusion and responded wisely and warmly to my hesitancies and fears. She emphasized the danger of blindly following and being emotionally swayed by others' ideas without thorough testing and checking. "The first rule is to go slowly and go your own way," she said. I felt free again. I felt free to go my own way in my own time, slowly, surely.

It is paradoxical that in a land abounding in mysterious Indian sages, the two people who did most to clear my confusion and encourage me were Westerners, totally accessible, friendly, and decidedly not mysterious. In Japan as well, the people who had most touched my heart were the people at the Christian Zen Center in Tokyo, many of whom were Westerners. Their friendliness and openness made a welcome contrast to the formal and somewhat impersonal atmosphere of the Japanese Zen communities I visited.

I made one last stop in South India to visit Sattya Sai Baba, who many considered to be the reincarnation of the great sage Sai Baba of Shirdi. Sai Baba, a small man, was dressed in a short-sleeved saffron muumuu. Someone explained that his sleeves were short so that people could see that Baba had no tricks up them as he performed his miracles. And miracles he did perform. I heard about many but saw only one: sacred ash seemed to flow out of his hands and fingers as he rubbed them.

I tried to get an audience with Sai Baba. Although he seemed to have favorites and was available to them, access was limited. From time to time he emerged, performed, and then retreated back into his inner sanctum. I was curious but not overwhelmed. The feat I had seen him perform seemed no more miraculous than a really good magic trick. Since then, I have heard that he funneled money into charities, and he probably had some wisdom to have attracted such a big following, but I never heard him speak about God or the spiritual path. Even so, I took every chance to observe him carefully while I was there, and I felt no resonance in my heart.

The ache in my heart persisted. I desperately wanted to be able to manifest real love. I prized it higher than any gift. I knew that something locked up inside was capable of love, but I didn't have the key to this chamber. It had been hidden from me by suspicion and doubt. All around me people spoke of love, but all I saw was its antithesis. As I searched for the key or for some clue to its whereabouts, I found myself sitting at the feet of one of India's greatest saints.

Before coming to India I had read books by a number of Indian saints. One had stood out from the others by the clarity of her message and the light in her eyes as seen in the photograph on the front page of her book. Her name was Sri Anandamayi Ma, and she was reputed to be a Bengali saint of the highest order.

She was accepting visitors at a temple a few miles outside of Delhi. The temple was large and stood in the middle of a plain. Hundreds of devotees waited for the opportunity to speak personally with Sri Anandamayi Ma. I took my place in line for the rest of the day, slept on the floor that night, and waited all next day for an interview. When I was next in line, a large commotion arose. A caravan of shiny black cars appeared in a flurry of dust and pulled up outside the temple. I heard later that the visitor was either the prime minister or another very high government official.

He was ushered in ahead of me for a long interview, after which we were told that Mayi Ma needed a rest. I was discouraged and was on the point of giving up my quest when one of the attendants noticed me and beckoned me into the inner sanctum. I could not believe that finally I was being admitted into Sri Anandamayi Ma's room.

She sat, dressed in white, on a raised dais. She was over seventy but looked much younger. She had virtually no lines in her face. She had a beautiful smile, and her eyes were very dark, deep, and wise. She spoke no English. I sat down below her and looked up into her eyes.

"What is your question?" asked the interpreter.

"How do I love?" I asked in a tremulous voice.

There was silence for several moments before she asked, "Do

you have a religion?"

"I have been following the Buddhist path."

"Do you have a guru?"

I said I did not. We talked a little about meditation, and she gave me some valuable advice. Again I asked, "How do I love?"

She looked knowingly down at me and with a slight yet firm voice answered gently, "Love is service to others—you may serve others."

I was perplexed. I thought she hadn't understood my question. "But how do I serve others?"

"With your body. Do you have any other questions?"

When I said no, I was gently ushered out of her room. I walked out into the sunshine of the Delhi plain. I was disappointed. Her answer to my burning question seemed commonplace and lacking in mystique. Serve others with my body? Big deal. That's not what I wanted. I wanted the esoteric path. Little did I know until years later how accurate her words would prove. She gave me exactly what I needed, but I was the one who had not understood. I still believe that Sri Anandamayi Ma was a true child of God. Her eyes seemed to look right through me, and she spoke wisdom.

Still, I had not discovered the source of my spiritual dryness. I knew that service was necessary and that probably I would enter a serving profession, but to do so without love would be pointless. I looked back over my life and saw the familiar pattern caused by my inability to love.

I had filled the gap caused by my early childhood fears and the divorce of my parents with a long string of affairs, none of which could evolve into marriage because the seeds of destruction were deep inside me from the beginning. I had derived some satisfaction from the love I received, but when I was asked to return that love, I drew back, protecting myself from old hurts. When as a child I had tried to love or to expand my heart, I had been cut off in various ways, so I quickly learned to stop opening. No matter how much love was poured into me, none ever flowed out. I had gathered about me those things that pleased me and enhanced my ego. I avoided pain and sought pleasure. Any flow or constructive growth always came to a halt when I saw it involved pain or giving up what I felt was mine.

Slowly and almost imperceptibly over the years, I had come to lean on the negative side. Always a perfectionist, I enlarged the imperfections of others instead of focusing on their assets and accepting and forgiving their imperfections. I could not accept and appreciate the good in others because I could not accept my own imperfections and my own pain. I could not forgive my parents or myself, and deep inside I had a diamond-hard core of resentment, anger, fear, and guilt that prevented me from truly forgiving and loving others.

How can we love if we constantly find fault with others? Christ's injunction to love thy neighbor as thyself came to mind. I had always focused on the love of neighbor part. Now I saw that I could not love or even accept my neighbor as myself because I did not totally accept and love myself. This emotion-charged area deep inside me was like a dynamite cap. I wanted to detonate it but was afraid of the consequences.

Restless and not yet ready to return to the West, I decided to check out Maharishi Mahesh Yogi, who was giving talks in Delhi at the time. This was before the Beatles had made him so famous, but even then, he drew a pretty good crowd. To gain entry, you had to bring a flower or pay something at the door. Seeing that someone had left a flower on a table outside, I picked it up and used it to get in.

The hotel conference room was fairly large and perhaps half full. It was similar to the Muktananda scene. Maharishi was a small man. People waved fans as he spoke. He seemed benign, even kindly. I felt nothing new from him and certainly not the spark of the divine that some others had reported. I stayed afterward to talk with a couple of his disciples then took my leave.

I also visited the site along the Ganges where the Kumbamela, a big guru fest, is held every twelve years. It was an off year, but I saw some old yogis sitting in the sun who had been in full lotus position and motionless for two weeks and other such wonders. Maharishi's ashram was near there, so I stopped by for a brief visit.

He was not in residence, which didn't surprise me since it had not been long since I had seen him in Delhi. The ashram was a pleasant place. They gave me literature. A few other Americans were hanging around. It was no big deal. I was pretty well guru-ed out by then.

The most interesting part of my visit to India was not Muktananda or Sai Baba or even Sri Anandamayi Ma, it was a vivid, superconscious dream I had early one morning.

In this dream, I was standing on a hill looking down at a small village. A road wound up through the village and coming up the road was a small, dark-skinned man dressed very simply in white. A turban was wrapped loosely around his head. He seemed to glow. He walked effortlessly, as if he were floating, his demeanor childlike. A small group of adults and children walked with him. They were laughing and peaceful. I felt a *Yes!* resound through my being. I sensed unity and sweetness and goodness in this man and in those who walked with him. I was entranced. I thought, *What a lovely scene. Perhaps this is my teacher.*

I woke up and lay in bed, enjoying the lingering presence of the dream. *If this is my teacher,* I thought, *who is he and where is he?* Finally, I stored the dream away. *Those people were all laughing,* I told myself. *That can't be right.*

It was time to leave India.

I decided to journey back to the West and see how the cosmic plan would unfold. I didn't know in which direction I might go, but I was sure my place was back in the Western world. I was determined to find a way to deal with the emotional and psychological issues that my dreams had uncovered. Hidden deep inside me, bound up with fear, guilt, and anger, lay what I sought most in life, an opportunity to forgive and to love.

On my way home, I visited Europe again. I wanted to see my old friends, and I also was curious as to how Paris and London would affect me after all I had been through. How would I react? Would I be able to stay centered?

Paris was lovely. It was autumn and the trees lining the boulevards were golden. The bustle and noise in the market streets warmed me. I returned to La Louisiane Hotel in the heart of my old stomping ground. Many old friends had moved on. Most of the others I contacted were glad to see me, but I found our conversations oddly limited. For the most part they did not show enough interest to make me feel comfortable about sharing details of my experiences in the East. More than that, I knew I could not communicate the gradual internal changes that had come about as a result of hundreds of hours of quiet sitting. In turn, I found that conversation about movies, personalities, politics, automobiles, and fashions no longer held my attention for long. I had lost my enthusiasm for it. "So what?" I often wanted to say, but I didn't. "That's fine but let's get down to brass tacks, to what *really* matters."

I had a few sexual encounters while I was there. Getting to know another person was still titillating, but the relationships had no meat on them. Playing sexual and personality games was just an old habit, and I needed more than games to satisfy me.

One old friend who had stayed on in Paris was Jean Claude, who had been one of the most way-out artists on the Left Bank. A true ex-patriot, he had discarded his American name, grown a beard, and learned French. In those days he had looked very French and sometimes even spoke English with a French accent.

We met in a small cafe. Jean Claude had changed. He was Jack once again, he was wearing a suit and tie, and the beard was gone. He greeted me warmly without a trace of French accent. "How ya doin', man?"

When I asked about his plans, he surprised me. "I'm going back to Chicago to teach art," he said. "It's a good-paying job. I'm through with Paris. *Les Parisiens sont carrés,*" he explained, his hands forming a square to reinforce his point. "*Sont des petits bourgeois,*" he went on. "Anyway, I've had it with this trip. I'm going back to the good old U S of A and some real work."

We parted with an affectionate hug. Something inside was pushing me to get home. It was time for me to do some real work, too. I had decided to teach or to counsel or to work with people in some other capacity. During the eight years I had been abroad, I had learned things I might be able to share with others. I might even get paid for it.

The day before I left Paris, I borrowed a friend's convertible and took a drive in the countryside. It was a lovely day, the top was down, and I was with a woman I had known from my old days in Paris. As I rounded a corner I happened to glance up to my right. There on a huge billboard was a giant man dressed in a yellow slicker and smoking a pipe as he gazed down at the passing cars with a slight smile. I nearly drove off the road. The man on the billboard was me. It was an ad I had posed for years before, a canned fish ad with the caption *"Filets de maquereaux."* The word *maquereaux* means mackerel, but it is also a slang term used to describe a man's character, and it is *not* a compliment. The universe had given me a reminder of my past that was too big to overlook.

As my plane took off for London, I was perplexed to find myself gripping the seat. Takeoffs and landings have always been excellent gauges to my internal calm or spiritual centeredness, to my trust that everything happens as it is meant to happen in the cosmic flow, even accidents. Yet there I was, back in the Western world with all my 'new' knowledge and spiritual insight, and I was still seized by the ancient and deep fear of death that I had felt on the bridge in Berne and in the windy apartment in Amsterdam. Apparently all my hours of meditation had not been enough to resolve my deepest fears.

Our own life is the instrument with which we experiment with truth.

—*Thich Nhat Hanh*

–11–

EXPERIMENTING WITH TRUTH

Being back in the United States felt peculiar. We were like old friends who reconnect to discover each other uncomfortably different. I was considerably more peaceful. In my meetings with old friends and acquaintances, I could see I had moved forward and had a somewhat broader and deeper view of life than they. I resisted the pull to resume my former lifestyle.

I recall in particular my reunion with a former college roommate. We met in a bar. He sat down and ordered a double scotch while I excused myself to go the restroom. When I returned a few minutes later, he had already finished it. He ordered another and was halfway through it before he was able to relax.

For a while I tried to keep up with my old friends until I recognized the truth in something Philip Kapleau had told me. "Locke," he had said, "you probably will not have much in common with old friends; you'll have to make new ones." Too many of these reunion conversations reminded me of the snarl of worldly thoughts I had learned to let go of in meditation. It was a difficult time, for I loved my friends and tried to go out with them, to listen, empathize, and encourage, but my heart was not in it. Offering advice on meditation or how to get off the frenetic treadmill was pointless and unwelcome. They thought I was weird or had 'gone 'round the bend.' There was little common ground on which to base a relationship. Gradually, I let go of my friends and left them to their pursuits. They were probably as relieved as I was.

A few months after my return, I was persuaded to shoot a film on Zen in Japan. I was in New York City and met a young sound technician, Phil Pearl. When he heard about my time in Japan, he said, "This is great stuff, man! You should go back there and do a film. We'll talk to my father—I bet he'll help you out."

His father and another man gave me two thousand dollars to get the equipment I needed. They said they'd get me over to Japan and then send more money when I needed it. It was a shoestring operation, and ill fated from the beginning. When I got to Japan, I told the Customs officials that I would be there for three months and discovered that, through some error, my visa was good for only two weeks. They put me under house arrest. I didn't know what to do.

I called on one of my father's old friends from his Princeton days, an influential Japanese man who eventually straightened out my problem but not until his own affairs had been scrutinized. It was an unpleasant situation, and I still regret the inconvenience it caused him.

Soen Roshi had agreed to let me film at the monastery, but just as I began the shoot, my camera started malfunctioning. It wouldn't focus properly. I tried everything. Finally, I traveled back to Tokyo and took it to a dealer. They thought I was crazy but replaced the lens, anyway. While I was in Tokyo, I took the opportunity to wire my backers for more money. The reply came the next day: they couldn't send me more. I had no choice but to abandon the project and return home.

Back in New York City in the fall of 1970, I took stock of my situation. I was nearly thirty-nine years old, and the cold fact of employment loomed in front of me. What exactly did I want to do? What did I know how to do best? I looked back on my life and saw that in everything I had done, what interested me most were people. I wanted to use the knowledge I had gathered to help others in their search for inner peace. I knew I could teach people breathing and meditation techniques, ways of centering, and ways of blocking out the world that I had found effective.

American life in the late sixties and early seventies was like a circus with many acts going on simultaneously. Woodstock, the Beatles, Ram Dass, the influx of swamis, yogis, and gurus from the East—all were embraced by the younger generation and also by many members of my generation. Music, drugs, and various touchy-feely therapies tugged people into the sphere of exploring their emotions and seeking transcendent experiences. The widespread quest for peace and self-understanding through these channels excited me, if only because it was a refreshing change from my conservative upbringing.

I understood that I would need a post-graduate degree to pursue the kind of work I wanted to do with people, and so I decided upon the Union Institute Program, an outgrowth of the Antioch System. My doctoral program was a forerunner of the University Without Walls. Graduate students entering the doctoral program were required to spend six weeks in residence at a colloquium, during which they defined their area of focus and chose a doctoral committee to review and guide their work. My area of focus was counseling psychology viewed through the perspective of Eastern meditative experience. I believed that the basis for true happiness lay in the discovery of self and in exploring and opening the inner heart.

As I worked to define my area of focus, I considered the diverse paths I had explored: yoga, Jungian analysis and dream work, Zen Buddhism, and Hinduism. My challenge was to blend all these experiences into a cohesive and intelligent statement. Each contained a measure of truth, and I needed to melt away the superfluous and extract the substance in each to create a workable therapeutic approach. This synthesis proved more difficult than I had imagined. I sensed that all paths and all religions are but expressions of one truth, but what was that truth?

Once I had organized and refined my program, I was required to do work in my chosen area (referred to as a PDE, a project demonstrating excellence) as I developed my doctoral dissertation. I pondered whom I might ask to be on my doctoral committee and where I might work on my project, I decided it would be a good idea to attend the Annual American Psychological Association Conference in Miami, which was being held just before my six-week colloquium at the Union Institute. There I met Dr. Stanislav Grof, a Czechoslovakian psychiatrist from Prague. Grof, considered the foremost expert on psychedelia, gave a fascinating talk on LSD.

LSD was first discovered by a Swiss scientist, Dr. Hoffman, who one day accidentally ingested a tiny portion of something he had created in his laboratory at Sandoz: LSD-25. His experience led him to realize that he had created a drug of rare potency, one that induced astounding transcendental states in ordinary people who took it. Best of all, the drug seemed to have no serious or lasting side effects. In Prague, Grof had supervised over two thousand training sessions to study the effects of LSD on subjects who wished to understand themselves better. These sessions almost invariably elicited profound and meaningful experiences. By maintaining the correct dosage and the purity of the chemical LSD, Grof felt he could achieve in several LSD sessions the same effects as a successful Freudian analysis might take years to achieve. His description of breakthrough experiences was reminiscent of what I had heard about kensho experiences in Japan.

I was fascinated and more enthusiastic than I could remember. A few times in my life, while reading a book or watching a film or listening to someone speak, I have felt an instant connection to some truth that was being expressed. This was one of those times.

Dr. Hoffman's discovery seemed to indicate a genuine shortcut to enlightenment. In all spiritual traditions, great achievements have been gained only after years and years of the utmost effort. Yogis and Zen adepts have dedicated their lives to meditating on an inner point in the quest for transcendental states. When LSD came along, spiritual pioneers in America were ready to bottle it! People including Timothy Leary and Richard Alpert (Ram Dass) became vocal proponents of the new wonder drug, and other people both known and unknown swore by the powerful visions and states of wonderment it produced. Some were convinced that LSD could indeed produce instant enlightenment, and anyone who has taken LSD would have to agree that it provides at the very least an earth-shaking experience.

I had declined to take LSD several times because I did not trust the guides or the purity of the chemical. The reports of LSD-induced insanity naturally made me leery. This was a different situation. Grof was a physician who had taken the drug and taken it often, and I detected no hint of mental derangement. On the contrary, Grof's manner and what he said were quite impressive. His words came from a calm center. I sensed no attempt to manipulate or coerce his audience. His facts were scientific, and his illustrations were simple and dramatic. He *knew* something, and I very much wanted to know what he knew.

During his lecture on the day we met, Stan Grof spoke of birth and death and the phenomenon of regressing back to the womb. He said that we carry within us the fear of death, which is usually due to the fear of death we suffer during the birth process. His experience had convinced him that reliving as adults the birth experience and the persistent fears associated with it can free us from those fears. I thought about my death fear while crossing the bridge in Berne, my vertigo in the apartment in Amsterdam, the deep and subtle fears that arose during many *sesshins* in Japan, my frozen tears in India, my fear of takeoffs and landings and heights: Grof had provided my first real clue to the source of these intense fears and perhaps even a way to resolve them. Through this man and his technique I finally might be able to understand myself and find internal freedom.

I sought out Grof after the talk to ask about the possible correlation between his work and what I had experienced. Grof was a large man, well over six feet, and probably 235 pounds. His broad, somewhat stoic face had a quiet intensity. I was somewhat unprepared for his mannerisms, for he seemed to weigh the universe before responding to a question or comment. Nevertheless, our rapport was instantaneous, and we talked well into the night. Grof had a habit of looking fixedly and with great intensity at whoever was talking to him. It was somewhat unnerving. To this day I'm not sure if it stemmed from his great curiosity and analytical mind or if it was a carryover from his psychoanalytic training. Underneath this impassive exterior was a kind-hearted man of immense good nature and generosity.

Grof was working at the Maryland Psychiatric Research Center, located on the grounds of Spring Grove State Hospital in Catonsville, Maryland, not far from Baltimore. The Center had received state and federal funding to research the effects of LSD, and Grof was administering pure LSD to terminal cancer patients, alcoholics, and professionals from many fields, including psychiatrists and psychologists. Grof suggested that I come to the Center to undergo a training session with LSD, which he would guide.

I was thrilled. I was not about to turn down a chance for instant enlightenment! I hoped that, unlike hashish (or zazen or *shaktipat*, for that matter), LSD could create in me the deep and lasting transformation I had been seeking.

I told Grof I would like to arrange the session before my six-week colloquium.

...Normal waking consciousness...is but one special type of consciousness, whilst all about it...lie potential forms of consciousness entirely different.

—William James,
The Varieties of Religious Experience

–12–

POTENTIAL FORMS OF CONSCIOUSNESS

For logistical reasons, I could not arrange an LSD session at the Research Center for a few weeks, so Grof suggested I do the session at his home.

The day arrived. Stan and I spent the morning talking. I poured out my fears, hates, ambitions, and secret desires. I wanted him to know me thoroughly before I took the drug so he could better steer me into emotion-charged areas during the session.

After receiving guidance on the coming LSD experience, I swallowed the odorless and tasteless drug, a rare substance received direct from Sandoz Laboratories in Switzerland. This was not the kind of acid available on the street. It was far more powerful and pure. I lay down on the couch.

For a while, I just lay there, waiting for the drug to take effect. I had not eaten breakfast, so I expected an early onslaught. After thirty minutes I felt nothing, and my boastful (but unspoken) attitude was, *So this is LSD. Come on. Show me something good.*

As I continued to lie there, listening to music and still skeptical, I felt something strange. It felt as if the cells in my body were stirring, each one waking up from a deep slumber. I got up to use the bathroom, and that's when I knew something was going on. My walk was unsteady, and there was something strange in my vision, a distinct perceptual shift in my depth perception. When I returned to the living room, Stan suggested I lie down again. He instructed me to put on eyeshades to block out visual distractions and stereo headphones, through which I heard music that Helen Bonny had carefully selected to guide and intensify the experience. Soon the trip began. As the immensity of other realities swept over me, enfolding me, I felt the power of LSD and knew why I had resisted taking it for so long. "My God!" I exclaimed. "It's true. It really *is* a trip!"

It was a trip into territory I had never seen before, a trip into a reality that has existed since primordial times. I became aware of the power that is in me, and it was staggering. I felt wonder and foreboding and terror, and I didn't know whether I was in the experience or the experience was in me. I spent the next six or seven hours under the influence of the drug. During the session I lost seven pounds! I cried for hours, tears of every kind, and I sweated profusely, tossing and turning on the couch.

Here is some of what I wrote down directly after the session.

> *I went immediately into the birth experience—shaking, trembling, body spasms. I became my mother giving birth. The terror and gasping for breath stretched into the mystical sphere. I saw the inevitable cycle of birth, death, and rebirth. I saw the necessity of death for life to go on. I became the pulsating eye-center, nucleus-cell out of which all life comes and to which it returns. The eye became a vortex, swirling, sucking all life (myself) into it and spewing it out again—the cosmic recycling. I saw the enormity and relentless quality of the flow and how one cannot stop it; that it sweeps all before it like a tide. I saw Christ on the cross and then became him on Calvary Hill, across which tramped hundreds of people. I felt the lacerations of body and soul and understood what suffering is and why it is necessary, a part of the whole.*

Re-entry from LSD feels similar to re-entry from a Zen *sesshin*, although the latter feels clearer, more vibrant, and cleaner. The LSD aftermath, in contrast, feels somewhat like leaving a sickbed after a long illness. I was weak but happy to be moving about once again and inhaling life, happy to allow all things to take their course.

I walked with Grof in the garden after the major effects had abated, but I was still high and overflowing with the residual horrors and wonders of what I had seen. As we moved slowly along the path, Stan said "Well, Locke, welcome to the club." He paused. "Well? What do you think?" He was eager to see how my entry into the farthest reaches of psychedelia compared with my Zen experiences.

I said, "Stan, this will never bring you to God."

He responded with a smile, "I know, but isn't the scenery wonderful! Isn't the journey a wonder?"

Following my LSD session, the Research Center hired me to work as a therapist and guide for others undergoing LSD therapy, which nicely resolved the question of how I would be able to complete my PDE work project and support myself at the same time. I also asked Grof if he would serve on my doctoral committee, and he agreed.

My committee of five was complete. It included, among others, Stan Grof; Frank Haronian PhD, a leading psychologist on the East Coast who was working with a technique of therapy and self-discovery called psychosynthesis; and Helen Bonny, the leading music therapist in the US. Helen's work focused on the effects of music on the mind and emotions, and she was an integral part of the LSD research project.

And so, at the age of thirty-nine, I embarked on my new career as a student. After my colloquium, I joined the team at the Research Center and worked there for nearly three years. I also underwent several more LSD sessions. Although my intuition told me that LSD would not take me or anyone to God, it was still fascinating to explore a realm that seemed boundless and full of many mysteries. What's more, Grof was persistent in his assertion that it was vital to undergo at least six sessions to fully reap the psychological benefits.

Previously, my only significant experience with any drug was with alcohol, and alcohol never plunged me so deeply into myself or lifted me to such extreme heights. Like my friend in Japan who took hashish and was said to have attained enlightenment, I was seeing visions and realizing metaphysical truths, yet even as I was unwinding after my first session, I knew that LSD would neither give me the permanent spiritual transformation I longed for nor establish in me an open heart of love for others.

Even so, I continued to take it. I did so partly because I was hoping Grof's theory was correct: that several carefully controlled sessions would equal a successful Freudian analysis. This was the carrot I kept trying to grab. I was poised, waiting to consciously make my way through the perinatal matrices and achieve the final result.

There were three tracks to the LSD research project being conducted at the Maryland Psychiatric Research Center. The first track was for alcoholics who resided nearby on the hospital grounds. The theory was that LSD would open the alcoholics to hidden memories and thereby free them from the unconscious compulsion to drink.

The second track was for terminal cancer patients, people who had only a few months or less to live. The theory was that experiencing the cosmic inner worlds by means of LSD would reassure the dying and enable them to approach death in a more relaxed, open, and accepting way, which might even alleviate some of their pain.

The third track was for selected professionals from a variety of fields. Here the theory was that one or more carefully administered LSD sessions would deepen and enrich their professional and personal lives. The sessions were usually conducted on the second floor of the Research Center in rooms specifically designed for psychedelic experiences. A video camera unobtrusively recorded portions of sessions.

At the Center, we approached LSD therapy in a serious and respectful way. We did not take the LSD to 'trip.' The way we administered the LSD set up certain psychological obstacles that could not be avoided. The only way out was to go through them. You had to face them squarely. When your eyes were covered and the music was playing, you were facing total darkness and a sense of death and the only thing you could do was surrender. As soon as you surrendered, the darkness became light.

The backbone of Stan's theory was that progressing through several carefully designed LSD sessions would bring to the fore and resolve experiences and traumas that occurred during the four stages of development from conception to birth. These four stages of development are called the perinatal matrices. What occurs during each perinatal matrix imprints our being. The effects may be even more intense than the effects of early childhood experiences. The pain, pleasure, and joy that we feel in the womb and in the birth passage affect the quality of our lives and may resurface years later to cause seemingly inexplicable problems, fears, and desires. Grof believed that we could become consciously aware of this imprint by reliving these experiences, thereby gaining the opportunity to resolve the negative imprint of trauma.

The first perinatal matrix or stage is the time of quiet stillness when the fetus is at rest in the womb. The second perinatal matrix is the time when the fetus has begun to move; it is characterized by vague foreboding of what is to come. The third perinatal matrix is the passage down the birth canal, which is usually torturous and frightening to the unborn child. The fourth stage is birth, the breakthrough into the outer world and the drawing in of the first breath

In my sessions with LSD, I re-experienced all of these stages, and I had some valuable insights.

Our longing for love and undisturbed peace has its roots in the prenatal experience. It arises out of an unconscious desire to join again with the lost ecstasy of the unitive state or spiritual union as we experienced it in the womb prior to the trauma of birth, and this effort is doomed. We fall in love and our beloved is flawed. We are flawed. Whatever we gain in one moment can be lost in the next. Events and people disturb our equilibrium. There is no permanent, ecstatic union to be found in the world. No matter how permanent it appears to be, everything we find in the world is temporary—that's what it means to live in a world of illusion.

The only 'salvation' is to become aware of what is here and now, inside and outside, and this is the real value of meditation. Through true meditation and prayer we may be able to still the mind enough to touch and feel the continual internal joy of true presence, but this state needs to be made permanent.

Also through my exploration of the perinatal matrices, I understood that the impetus for neurotic action arises out of the unconscious trauma associated with our desire to escape the seemingly indefinite and nearly intolerable aloneness of the pre-birth experience with its premonitions of the birth struggle that is to come. The fetus senses itself to be in a no-exit situation, hemmed in and desperate to break free: *I'm in this situation and I have to do something about it.* During the process of birth, we struggle to escape the panic, fear, disgust, and pain of being interminably closed in and dying, as well as to escape the painful struggle for life.

Later in life this indelibly etched memory affects our lives profoundly. The underlying, unresolved trauma impels us to struggle against any situation that restricts us or causes us pain. We react intensely to the events of our lives, blaming others and ourselves and believing that we are in an intolerable situation that has no end. No wonder we panic. We are thrown back to the original, desperate struggle to save ourselves. These reactions to whatever stirs up the buried memory of birth pain account for the restlessness of the monkey mind and our endless racing to and fro. This frenetic effort translates into patterns of ambition for fame, fortune, and total satisfaction. The result is that we race past and fail to appreciate the very goal we are seeking, which is the exceeding beauty in every moment and the Source of this beauty—God.

Once we recognize this self-defeating pattern, we have the opportunity to take wise action instead of merely reacting blindly to situations. This action is of a special nature, more akin to non-action or acceptance than to the habitual reaction against maintaining a status quo that we have been taught to see as inactivity, laziness, and wastefulness. If only we had the knowledge, faith, and trust to endure, we would understand that there is no way out of the fear except through it. Just as when we were fighting for our lives in the birth canal, there is nothing we can do to stop the flow of life as it pushes us through the passages of our lives. The trials we experience are natural and necessary for our growth, and we can aid the process best by letting go and surrendering to what each passage of growth brings us.

Actually, conscious inactivity invokes effort of a special kind and leads in the direction of effacement of ego. The life of a saint is like a spinning top, moving so fast that it appears motionless. Acceptance of our helplessness and fate involves also an acceptance of a sense of 'all is well,' a center of calm that survives, no matter what. This center of calm is the result of building good qualities, one level at a time: outer patience, inner patience, contentment, trust in God, and gratitude to God for everything that comes in life. Creating and maintaining this center of awareness and calm is our only answer to suffering and also our primary purpose as human beings.

The sessions were times of great activity, trauma, bliss, and understanding. I kept hoping for a significant change in my character, but life outside of the sessions went on much the same as it always had.

I watched with great interest the LSD reactions of people who came through the program for professionals. Some fought the experience by trying to assert control over the drug. One Icelandic psychologist struggled for half an hour after the drug took effect, trying to meditate or concentrate his way around the effects of the LSD. Soon enough, he was consumed by its power and ended up writhing on the floor and sobbing.

A professor from the Midwest who had been dealing with marriage problems left his session deeply moved, effusively thanking everyone on the staff. He hurried back to Wisconsin with his new 'enlightenment' tools for mending his marriage. Six months later he returned, his marriage broken apart for good.

A West Coast rabbi cried like a baby as the LSD forced from his unconscious stored memories of childhood abandonment. "Mommy, Mommy, Mommy...why did you leave me?" The rabbi took his own life a year or so after he had taken LSD. He was a sweet man who desperately wanted peace and used the wrong medicine.

LSD therapy with alcoholics was not successful. It scared them, and although the protocol allowed for two sessions with an option for a third, none of the alcoholics wanted a second session. This makes more sense to me now that I have worked in the addiction field. We know that psychotherapy does not work with alcoholics, so it follows that psychotherapeutic use of LSD would not work either. Alcoholics have to want to stop drinking, and LSD was unable to jolt them into a desire for sobriety.

I was assigned as a therapist to the third track, the project of working with the terminally ill.

Doctors in the oncology unit at nearby Sinai Hospital referred terminally ill cancer patients to the Research Center. The patients were told only that a treatment was available that might be able to provide some psychological and physical relief. When patients arrived at the Research Center, I or another therapist met with them to discuss their illness and to describe the course of treatment.

It was not unusual in those days for medical professionals to tiptoe around the word cancer, so sometimes the job of informing patients of the nature of their illness fell to the therapists at the Center. This happened to me on one occasion with a patient who was under the impression that she had arthritis; until I talked to her, the word cancer had not been mentioned. I've always been good with words, so I was able to handle the situation, but I was shocked, sad, and angry at the insensitivity of the hospital medical staff.

Preparing someone for a high-dose LSD session was tricky. Explaining the eyeshades and the stereo headphones was the easy part. In fact, it was impossible to really prepare them for the powerful onslaught of the drug. Analogies can go only so far. I tried to paint a picture of the session without scaring patients unduly. The reality was that the treatment was intended to induce an experience of death and rebirth as preparation for the immanent death of the physical body. We were operating under the premise that re-experiencing the deep suffering and consequent release of emerging from the womb into the world would help the patient see and feel his true, immortal nature. Standard procedure called for one LSD session, but some patients requested an additional session.

Although I now disavow the use of LSD as a means to this end, patients who got in touch with their immortality in the non-physical sense and came to accept the inevitability of physical death became more communicative. I observed that in some cases their physical pain was markedly diminished, probably as a result of a significant decrease in psychological and physical tension.

My work in this area taught me a lot about the death process and about how a therapist, or anyone else for that matter, can best assist a person who is dying. Trust is the most important element. Trust can occur only when the patient has confidence in the therapist, and the therapist's confidence develops as a result of the experience of being with the dying. To be convincing, whatever reassurance or advice is forthcoming must have the ring of authenticity and knowledge. It was important that any books I quoted from or advice I gave resonated in my own heart and communicated to the patient that all was well and would continue to be so after death.

I learned to listen with dispassion to the negative, grasping, or hysterical outpourings of those faced with dying and to communicate, verbally and nonverbally, what the dying most need and search for in others: love, understanding, and quiet assurance. Surrender is key to a peaceful passage. To enable the dying person to let go of his tension and fear and surrender to what is inevitable, we stressed that the 'gateless gate' is not the end but the beginning, that one joins loved ones and sheds earthly cares and sorrows and pain.

Probably the hardest task of being with the terminally ill was dealing with their inescapable physical pain—spasmodic, wrenching, searing pain that ate away at their vital organs. What could anyone possibly say that would be sufficient? It was here that my own faith and deep acceptance of suffering as a necessary part of life gave me solid support. My experience had convinced me that suffering does indeed have meaning. Suffering is the purging fire. Suffering drives us to surrender to something greater than ourselves; it drives us to God. The understanding that suffering *has meaning* can transform the whole being of a terminally ill patient.

I seemed to know instinctively that the only way to help the dying is to be kind and gentle and compassionate with them. I surely did not know what they were experiencing or what was in store for them. I tried to be a support. I listened when they wanted to talk. I tried not to go off on philosophical tangents about life after death, because I didn't really know anything about it.

A number of the people I worked with had faith in some kind of existence in the hereafter, particularly an extraordinary woman named Joan. After two sessions at the Research Center, Joan went to California to be with her father and stepmother during her last days on earth. She wrote me a letter, and we began to correspond. Included in her first letter was the following:

> *My doctor here says I am facing death with great equanimity. That is partially true. I also have my moments of fear and anxiety about it. This happens when I get out of the Here and Now, however, and start anticipating. The one-day-at-a-time philosophy is important for us all, I believe, but especially important for me at this stage. I remember the sudden awareness, late in the LSD session, that I had found a way to legitimize my sadness, and that was to become terminally ill. The irony was that I then found happiness and a feeling of relief in this discovery.*
>
> *The great difference I felt in me and the world after that first LSD trip is due to my being in touch with my divinity... and with that same spark in others. "All that ugliness is only beauty," I remember saying (or feeling) early into the trip. And how could I experience the beauty of love if it weren't inside of me?*

Sometimes we talked on the phone. Joan was courageous. In her last months, she worked through many difficult areas, such as final goodbyes to loved ones who lived far away. In September of 1972, I went to California and spent three days with her. These were beautiful days—incense, many quiet moments, good classical music, and talk that was precious and pregnant with meaning. Joan had accepted her death. She was calm. She was the one who comforted the household, not vice-versa.

A tragic incident involving Joan sharply illustrates how little we know about what is in store for us. When she was very close to death, Joan's niece and her new husband came to say goodbye. They were about to travel to the East Coast to start new jobs, and they knew it would be the last time they saw Joan. They almost changed their minds and decided to stay till the end, but Joan said, "No, that's all right. You go ahead. We'll say goodbye now." Their parting was tender and poignant.

A little over twenty-four hours later, Joan's niece was killed in an automobile accident, and Joan was still alive. Can you imagine two healthy young people looking forward to a long life together and the next day one of them is dead? It certainly told me something. Despite all evidence to the contrary, it is the nature of the ego to assume that we will be here tomorrow and tomorrow and tomorrow.

I thought of a pre-dawn morning when I stood on the porch of the Zen monastery with Nakagawa Soen Roshi. "Are you watching the sun rise?" I asked.

"Watching to see *if* sun rise," he replied.

We cannot count on tomorrow. We might not be here. So many signs are there to tell us that death can come at any moment. I think of the vertigo and terror I experienced on the bridge in Berne, my motor scooter accident in Paris, the kitten bleeding its life away on a street in London.

I have come to believe that LSD is dangerous and can never in itself bring the real human development that so many of us are seeking. I don't think it made people die peacefully, which is what the study was trying to prove. Or if it did, it might have been because the LSD so terrified people that dying didn't seem so hard in comparison.

Perhaps I was led to work with terminal cancer patients so that I would meet people who faced death with equanimity. I saw people go to meet their Maker with no fear, like Joan. Joan came into her LSD sessions with a deep spirituality, and her experiences reflected her beliefs in a way that had great meaning for her. She was able to surrender, and she felt peace. In the end, I am convinced that it wasn't the LSD that gave her a peaceful death; it was her gentleness, faith, surrender, kindness, and lack of fear. These qualities were infectious and very beautiful.

I met several other remarkable souls. As part of my job, I went out to canvass for people who might be interested in trying LSD therapy to make their process of dying easier. Working from a list of terminally ill patients, we sent out letters informing them that someone would come by to talk with them.

One day I went to a row house in Baltimore to talk to an elderly black woman. A nurse who was obviously very close to the old woman, almost like a daughter, met me at the door. She marched me off to the kitchen. When she was sure we would not be overheard, she grabbed me by the lapels and said, "Don't you dare give that stuff to this old lady! How dare you even think about such a thing?"

"Please ma'am, I'm just here to talk with her and determine if it would be appropriate."

"She is very peaceful," the woman said in a fierce voice. "She is with God. She does not need any drug to feel better about that."

I spent some time with the dying woman. The nurse was right. The woman was in a beautiful, beautiful space.

As people move further and further away from life, it is not possible to know for certain what they are experiencing and what they are aware of. The prevailing attitude in the medical community is that a person in a coma is not aware of what is going on around him, but I always assume it is best to relate to all patients as if they were conscious. The soul cannot speak, but it may be very much present. I believe now that the soul can hear and perhaps even see everything. Therefore, it is vital to speak carefully in the presence of even the comatose, who may be deeply affected by what is said and how they are being handled.

A perfect example of this occurred years later when I went to visit Dr. Markar, a long-time disciple of Bawa Muhaiyaddeen and one of his translators. A nurse told me, "He's in a coma. He can't hear you."

"That's okay," I said. "I still want to spend some time with him."
I sat down on a chair next to Dr. Markar's bed. I took his hand. He
was completely unresponsive. "Dr. Markar? This is Locke. I'm here
to see you, to say hello." I spoke with him gently for a few moments.
Then I began to pray out loud, but very quietly. After a minute or
so, he squeezed my hand.

Because of my experience in the field, people have asked me what
they can do for someone who is dying. If you don't have an agenda,
if you can bring some peace into the room with you, if you can just
be open, that's more than enough. The learning to be derived from
the experience is as much for the living as for the dying. We may
think we are bringing them something, but often it is they who
bring us something.

One person stands out in my mind. A friend from my spiritual
community lay dying of lung cancer. Larry and I had spent some
time together over the years. He was an interesting person, but he
had a sharp tongue. Prior to my visit, mutual friends told me that
Larry had experienced quite a turnaround in his temperament. I
visited with him two days or so before he died. I was trying too hard
to be helpful, going on a bit about what our teacher had said about
death. Larry finally interrupted me, "Locke, you don't have to do
all this. I am in a very good place. The angels feed me. Don't worry
about me." There I was, trying to make Larry feel better. It was like
trying to clean a gem with mud. As he assured me, he was in a very
good place.

Beware of false prophets, who come to you in sheep's clothing…You will know them by their fruits. Are grapes gathered from thorns, or figs from thistles?

—7 Matthew 15

-13-

YOU WILL KNOW THEM
BY THEIR FRUITS

It is amusing now to see that my guru hopping had not ended in India. It was the seventies, and the guru scene was hot.

Stan Grof was interested in mystical things, and he was keen to meet Chogyam Trungpa, a Tibetan Master of high lineage. We heard Trungpa was in Washington, DC, and we traveled there to see him. He was a small, stout man, quite engaging and jovial. During our conversation, I asked him, "Should I be taking LSD? It scares the hell out of me and I don't know why I'm taking it except I want to learn all the things Stan says you can learn from it."

In a high little voice, he answered, "Oh, yes! You must continue. Yes. That is good. You must continue with it."

All right, I said to myself. *The lama says it is good, so it must be.* At that time I looked for guidance from people I deemed enlightened. Now I would say that it is important to be careful how much power over our destiny we confer on people we consider 'spiritual.' I was very much influenced then by lofty sounding titles and by so-called masters who had a throng of followers. We spiritual seekers are longing so for guidance that faulty reasoning may very well lead us to hand over control too easily, and sometimes to our detriment.

I met my share of Western gurus, too, like Grof.

Many people considered Grof the Freud of the latter half of the twentieth century. They flocked to him because he was the guy on the scene with all the latest stuff. He had approval to administer the wonder drug that promised a shortcut to self-understanding, and everyone on the cutting edge wanted to meet him. Through this avenue, I met many pioneers of transcendental psychology and what would later be known as the New Age. One was John Lilly, who also was associated with the Maryland Psychiatric Research Center. Lilly had pioneered the use of the immersion tank for sensory deprivation, and his prototype was at the Center.

The first time I used the tank was five or six hours after ingesting 400 mg. of LSD. I was *compes mentes,* so to speak, but still experiencing psychedelic effects. The tank was round, perhaps seven or eight feet in diameter, and totally enclosed in a space that was completely devoid of light and sound. The water kept the body at normal body temperature and was saline to provide buoyancy. A float device attached to and supported the feet, and a floating collar kept the face comfortably above the water. The immersion tank was designed to provide total comfort as you floated gently in a dark, womblike space.

"I'll see you in an hour," the attendant told me as he closed the door on the chamber. I drifted into a blissful, sleep-like state. Soon I heard a knocking sound. "Time's up." It didn't seem possible that a whole hour had gone by. I could have sworn I had been in the tank for no more than ten minutes. Nothing profound came from the experience, but I felt I had slept the sleep of angels.

Lilly wore glasses and was perhaps a little shorter than average. Intense, a bit abrasive, independent, and slightly cantankerous, he was a 'mad scientist' who was constantly experimenting on himself.

Grof and I spent some fascinating evenings in New York City at Lennie Schwartz's brownstone in the Village, just off Fifth Avenue. Lennie was married to Bob Schwartz, an entrepreneur and lover of the arts, and they were great friends of Milt Glaser, the famous designer.

Some of the other people who dropped in were Oscar Ichazo, the founder of Arica Institute and father of the modern Enneagram; John and Toni Lilly; the American mythologist Joseph Campbell and his wife; and Chilean psychiatrist Claudio Naranjo. One night Grof, Lilly, Ichazo, Campbell, and Naranjo were all there at the same time. What an evening! The conversation flew way off the charts. I felt like a pretty good checker player in a roomful of chess champions, one of them executing the intricate Ivanov Move #4 and me thinking, *Who is Ivanov?*

I was fairly conversant with the spiritual literature, but these people were exploring realms of the geophysical, levels of being, levels of consciousness, states of mind and being, reincarnation, past and future lives, cosmology, Indian cults, and much more. If someone had hidden a tape recorder, the tape would have been priceless. After dinner, we lingered in the dining room, which was on the ground floor and opened out onto a back garden. The conversation went on for four or five hours. We were all looking for answers, and we were all on different wavelengths. Lilly was exploring psychopharmacology, biochemistry, and how the brain was affected through the use of sensory deprivation and different chemicals. He was looking for empirical understanding of altered states and concrete answers.

Stan was more esoteric. He had less need to pin things down and organize them. He was fascinated by the mysterious realms and intrigued by the transpersonal aspects of character. He allowed for reactions in people to come from areas that he didn't know about. Stan's background was extremely broad: science, linguistics, Sanskrit, spiritual literature, and, of course, LSD research and therapy.

Campbell was much more eclectic. He was a chronicler and a teller of tales. He had a prodigious mind and knowledge of different cultures and their ways of searching for heightened experience and truth and oneness.

Oddly enough, although I found the conversation stimulating, I wasn't overawed by it. After my first LSD session, nothing much awed me. Beyond that, I was a purist. Some strange, inner, God-given wisdom told me that, as interesting and fun as it was and as much as I patted myself on the back for being included in such a gathering, none of this stuff was going to get me to God. The best way I can describe it is to say it would be like being included in a gathering with Tom Cruise and Julia Roberts: exciting while it lasted but probably not something you would go out of your way to do again. It is pretty clear that association with movie stars won't get you to heaven, but neither will association with intellectuals.

Another pioneer on the transcendental scene was Elmer Green, the originator of biofeedback and a scientist at the prestigious Menninger Clinic. Alyce and Elmer Green founded the Annual Council Grove Conference on Transpersonal Psychology. I saw them at Council conferences, where all the leaders of psychospiritual work gathered. I met the astronaut Edgar Mitchell there, as well as Pir Vilayat Khan.

Elmer was fascinated with yoga and its scientific effects on the body. He had met an Indian yogi known as Swami Rama and was so intrigued that he had brought him to the United States. Swami Rama was a tall, strikingly handsome, leonine man with long black hair. He was mysterious looking, like an Italian movie star or a youthful Omar Sharif.

Elmer convened a group of top medical people from all over the US, people from Harvard and the like. Swami Rama stretched out on a table and demonstrated remarkable control over his body, which the experts measured and verified. For example, he could make one finger ten degrees colder than another or make his heart stop beating. It blew their minds. He also diagnosed numerous cases the doctors brought to him by asking the patients to breathe on a mirror. His diagnoses were nearly always correct! He was a very advanced Hatha Yogi.

The swami developed a strong coterie. In addition to his good looks, he was funny and he was bilingual. I went to one or two of his talks. At one, I met a young and pretty woman who was quite well known in a certain therapeutic field. We became intimate and saw each other frequently in New York. One day she said, "I have to go and see Swami Rama. He has a couple of my things."

When I arrived with my friend to see the swami, he shot me a murderous look. It turned out that she had been having an affair with him. Because I knew her so well, she told me a lot about Swami Rama, what he was like, his demands, and so forth. She said the swami had an affair going in every US city he visited. Single women, married women—he cut a real swath.

Swami Rama certainly deepened my distrust of guru types. Lots of people were having affairs, including me, but Swami Rama was presenting himself as a holy man, and that made him a hypocrite in my book. The very neat wedge that separates the seemingly miraculous from true spiritual greatness became very clear during my experiences with Swami Rama. He could perform feats that even physicians with the highest credentials were unable to explain. They marveled at his powers, and many imbued him with even higher attributes that he did not possess. Eventually, however, word of his character spread, causing real problems for some of the people who had been his benefactors.

The last time I took a mind-altering drug was in 1974, just a few months before I left the Research Center. Stan had heard of an anesthetic called Ketalar, which was reputed to bring about a hallucinogenic experience similar to LSD but even stronger. Ever the guinea pig, I volunteered to try it.

Before taking any drug, it was my habit to fast and read spiritual literature. If there was to be any spiritual significance to a drug experience, I hoped to enhance it and deepen it by purifying myself inside and out. As I prepared for the Ketalar session, I was reading the Bible when I came upon Corinthians I-XIII, one of my favorite passages:

> *If I speak in human and angelic tongues, but do not have love, I am a resounding gong or a clashing cymbal.*
>
> *And if I have the gift of prophecy and comprehend all mysteries and all knowledge; if I have all faith so as to move mountains, but do not have love, I am nothing.*

As always, I was moved by these words. *With acid,* I thought, *it seems I do understand all mysteries and prophecies, but do I have love? Have any of my new insights brought me real love, true love?* I had to admit that the LSD-promised enlightenment had not been the real thing, any more than the enlightenment promised by the rigors of Zen meditation. I didn't know what to expect with the Ketalar experience, but I suspected it, too, would fail to provide a lasting connection to real love. Still, I was curious.

My Ketalar trip was powerful. I was given an intramuscular injection measured at two-thirds milligram per kilo of body weight. The effects were immediate. I felt the lower parts of my body turn cold and numb, and this sensation continued to rise up my body to my thorax. I thought of Socrates after he had drunk hemlock. I truly felt I was going to die. I stopped breathing for about a minute. Karen, a friend and registered nurse who was a member of the team at the Research Center, told me later, "We were really worried about you, Locke. We thought we might have to do something to get you breathing again."

Suddenly, I took a huge gulp of air and the session continued. A blissful and intuitive state followed, deeper in its effects than LSD. Also, unlike with LSD, the session was over in an hour, and I was perfectly able to drive myself home. Ketalar produced a euphoria that was physical, cellular. My body and mind tingled and exulted; it was a psycho-orgasmic experience. The next few days were quite peaceful. I felt a bit like a person who has been hit by a truck and wakes up in a hospital, slightly medicated, calm, relaxed, and grateful to be alive.

While I was experimenting with psychedelics, I had many experiences that other 'voyagers' considered to be of the highest order, the real spiritual thing, complete with bright lights, unity, and cosmic oneness. It will be obvious to most serious seekers that such experiences belong to the realm of illusion, but most people who have tasted these wonders would also admit that they are unforgettable. Yet my initial conclusion proved correct: these experiences did not change my basic character, and that is exactly what must change if we are to find the true self, the inner light, and thus God.

There are many theories on how LSD affects the brain. I lean toward the one that attributes the effects of LSD to anoxia. I found the effects of both LSD and *shikan-taza* similar enough that the theory of oxygen deprivation makes sense to me. In *shikan-taza,* one is barely breathing, which reduces the oxygen in the blood.

LSD converts believe that the drug opens a direct connection to God, but this simply is not so. LSD does indeed open a door, but it is a door to the mind, not a door to the soul. The mind reveals itself, while the soul remains as it was and will be, and the gulf between mind and soul remains impassable. The mind cannot transcend the mind.

I was seeing a familiar pattern: a powerful experience of cosmic consciousness or enlightenment was supposed to revolutionize your life and free you from the struggle. I never saw this happen, not with kensho or *shaktipat* or LSD. During two years of working with LSD, I never saw anyone undergo a lasting character transformation. I saw minor changes in the hours and days after a session, but nothing lasting. Only one person stands out in my mind as exceptional in this regard—Joan—and she was a highly evolved individual before ingesting the LSD. She was also dealing with an impending death, which invites transformation in those who are so inclined.

My hunch is that LSD temporarily liberates the shakti and awakens the *kundalini*, but what is the point when it leaves you right back where you were in less than twenty-four hours? Also, a very real danger exists of being so seduced by the illusions that you don't want to move on to a higher level. What would be the use of becoming like one New Age guru I met who injected himself with Ketalar every few hours to maintain an altered state?

According to Bawa, during an LSD experience the mind dumps its contents into the consciousness. I believe this is what I experienced. I have to admit I found LSD overwhelming and awe-inspiring. I was tempted to imbue my experiences with cosmic and spiritual proportions, but I am now convinced that what I found was pyrite, fool's gold, not real gold. The real gold is the wisdom I gain through understanding my daily struggles with the world and people, and it takes a lot longer to mine.

In 1975, after I had spent two years at the Research Center, the LSD project ended. I accepted invitations to lecture at various colleges—Wellesley, Amherst, MIT, and others—on the LSD work I had done with Grof. I was convinced that the LSD research project had some merit, and I got caught up with my mission. The lectures were dramatic, mostly because I showed excerpts from LSD sessions I had taped and edited. Audiences were spellbound, and I got a little taste of 'gurudom.' It is a heady experience to bring an audience under your sway, I discovered. It gave me a sense of knowing something that other people didn't know. Well, of course I did! Only six people in the world had done this research, and I was one of them. If I had traveled down the Ganges on a barge, I would also have known something that most other people didn't know, but so what? I was flattered and also appalled when a few people asked me to be their guru. I could see how easy it is to fall into that trap. Thank God I knew my limitations. I was looking for a real guru, not trying to be one.

I also accepted a job as an associate professor at the University of Massachusetts in Amherst where I conducted seminars and took charge of a high-rise student dormitory.

While I was working at Amherst, I had another meeting with Chogyam Trungpa Rinpoche. I was still somewhat awed by spiritual titles and celebrity, so when I heard that Trungpa had a spiritual center in Vermont, I drove there one weekend, hoping to have *darshan** with him.

His spiritual center was in a farmhouse, and the people who ran it were very pleasant. They told me that Trungpa was busy doing personal interviews. People were lined up on the stairs, waiting their turns. His devotees asked my name and what had prompted me to come and meet the master. I told them I had met him once before in Washington with Stan Grof.

"Oh! Stan Grof!" The word got passed on, and soon I was whisked past the people on the stairs and into the presence of the master.

Trungpa was sitting on the floor in a large, pleasant room with lots of big, brightly colored Indian cushions scattered about. He was chatting with a group of cronies, and the atmosphere was convivial.

---

* Spiritual dialogue and blessing from a master.

"Well, how are you?" he greeted me. "Good to see you. Please sit down, sit." He gestured to a spot near him.

I sat down. We all smiled. "Do you drink?" he asked.

"Yes."

"Good," he said, leaning over and picking up a half gallon bottle of saki that I had not noticed earlier. The bottle was half full. Trungpa poured me a huge cup of saki. He poured some for himself, and we toasted.

As we drank, we talked about sports and other such topics. Very little was said of a spiritual nature. We just hung out and chatted and drank. Trungpa is a likable man. Even though he was inebriated, I hung on his every word. Finally, he said, "Well, have a safe trip." He blessed me, and I left.

Later on, people who had stayed at Trungpa's ashram in Colorado told me that drinking and sexual promiscuity were common in the ashram, though Trungpa's personal overindulgences may have been limited to food and drink.

I mention it now because I saw and heard the same things so many times in reference to a number of revered spiritual teachers. It is not difficult to call yourself a guru or master and to give mantras and perform feats of magic. It takes some time and energy, but it is not that difficult. On the other hand, it is very difficult to be a fully realized human being. Thousands of people migrated to this friendly and warm guy and sought his advice. I don't know his heart, but what I saw and heard about does not fit in with my idea of a true spiritual path. It just doesn't.

Chogyam Trungpa and Swami Rama inadvertently helped me learn to differentiate what was important from what was not important. All the trappings of a yogi-guru-lama type are worthless unless the person has high moral qualities, and I had not yet met anyone of that spiritual caliber.

The walk of an enlightened man is as different from an unenlightened man as that of a giraffe from an elephant.

—Author Unknown

-14-

THE WALK OF AN ENLIGHTENED MAN

I had been teaching at the University of Massachusetts in Amherst for only a few months when I heard that Swami Muktananda was visiting the United States. Although I had not seen or communicated with him for over three years, I resigned my job at the university to travel with him.

I often question why I left a good job to do this when I had decided in India that Muktananda was not for me. My only answer is that the time with Muktananda, although obviously flawed, was at least connected to what seemed to be the search for enlightenment. As I saw it then, the job I left was purely material and had nothing to do with my search for God. I was jaded by the overload of gurus, teachers, meditation techniques, and explorations I had crowded into my consciousness. I was also confused and spiritually adrift. I did not know how to pursue enlightenment on my own, and Muktananda was my only existing connection to a spiritual path.

So, in 1975, I went off to follow Muktananda with the idea of making a documentary film about his work. I was forty-two years old. Sometimes I judged myself for still floating through life at my age. I could not help but compare myself unfavorably to my older brother. He was an established businessman in San Francisco, and I was a dissatisfied seeker without a road map. Only later did I understand that the Muktananda episode was a necessary part of closing one chapter in the search for enlightenment and opening another to a new way of life.

I traveled to Miami where Swami Muktananda was in residence. Intensive sessions were held every day, attracting people from far and wide. One of these travelers was Carole. A frail, pretty woman in her early thirties, Carole was English but had been living in the States for several years. She had cancer, fairly advanced, and had sought out Muktananda because someone had told her that Muktananda could heal her. Carole was penniless, so several of us pooled our money to get her a hotel room and did our best to feed her and care for her.

When she arrived at Muktananda's for a healing, she was told at the door that she would have to pay a fee to participate in the session. Tears came to her eyes. I spoke with friends who were Muktananda's cabinet members, so to speak, imploring them to make an exception. I told them that, sick as she was, Carole had hitchhiked all the way across the United States out of pure faith that Swami could heal her. No matter what I said, the answer was firm: she would have to pay; there were no freebies.

A group of us made the payment for Carole, but I was outraged that a so-called holy man would charge for this kind of work. I was appalled. It was as if Christ had charged a fee for performing a miracle: "Just donate twenty-five dollars to my cause and I'll cure your blindness." This episode marked the end of any relationship with Swami Muktananda. It was not the spiritual yarn out of which I wanted to weave my enlightenment. It also left me with a deep distrust of gurus or teachers of any type who encouraged blind obeisance.

I went back to my mother's home in Paoli. Several weeks later Carole called me from a hospital in North Carolina. She had left Florida and was traveling slowly north to Philadelphia to visit her 'father,' as she put it. I recalled that she had once shown me a loving, healing letter written by a holy man in Ceylon who had told her that he was her *real* father and guru.

I flew down to North Carolina and literally carried Carole out of the hospital. She could not have weighed more than eighty pounds. The doctors there wanted to perform a procedure and Carole had refused. When they became insistent, she called me. I had to sign numerous documents absolving them of responsibility if she died and taking responsibility on myself.

In Philadelphia, I took her to a place she called The Fellowship, where her 'father' from Ceylon was living. I did not care to meet him, so once I saw to it that she was settled and well taken care of, I went on my way. We talked frequently in the weeks that followed, and eventually I moved her to my mother's house so that she could live more quietly in the country. I was impressed to see that she looked much better.

Over and over, she begged me to come and meet her teacher. "Locke," she said, "this is the real thing, believe me."

I was immovable. "I've had it with gurus." I told her. "I don't believe in them, and I will not go through another boondoggle."

Carole was insistent. One day she looked much paler and sicker than usual. She said to me, "Locke, will you do me a favor?"

"I'll try."

"I want you to meet my teacher just once. It's important for you." When I started to object, she quieted me. "Locke, I'll be dead in six months. Just do this for me—as one last favor."

When she put it that way, I could not refuse to honor her request. I agreed to visit her teacher the next evening.

I already knew a little about Bawa Muhaiyaddeen. I had heard that he was a mystic who had been discovered some time in the first half of the 1900s in the island country of Sri Lanka, then known as Ceylon. The letter he had written to Carole had impressed me. I had seen his picture, and I recalled hearing glowing reports from a few other people.

One was Mary McClelland. Mary and David McClelland lived in Cambridge. David had been the head of one of the psychology departments at Harvard and was famous for his work in the field of motivational psychology. Their home was the gathering place for all kinds of gurus, great and near great. It was quite the place to hang out. I had my own little room up on the third floor where I spent my weekends. You never knew who was going to be there.

David was the one who had fired Timothy Leary and Richard Alpert for their use of LSD while they were on the faculty at Harvard. By the time I met the McClellands, Alpert had become Ram Dass and was a frequent visitor to the McClelland home. Huston Smith came through occasionally, and Chogyam Trungpa and other lamas visited.

Mary told me about Bawa Muhaiyaddeen. He had lived in Jaffna and Colombo, Sri Lanka, for many years before coming to America in 1971, and since then he had divided his time between Sri Lanka and the United States. "He is a wonderful man. You should see him, Locke." She showed me a picture of a small, dark-skinned man. The picture brought to mind other intriguing rumors about a small dark man I had assumed was African.

Therefore, when I met Carole and she told me about Bawa, it rang some bells. By then, however, I had become thoroughly disillusioned with the guru scene, and what I knew about Bawa had been stored as a question mark in my mind, along with a long list of other question marks. All the gurus and teachers I had met had proved to be much less impressive in person than they were reputed to be. Why should he be any different?

Although I had become jaded, the advantage was that often I could discern in an instant whether a teacher had anything of value to give me. The part of me that was seeking the highest truth would shake its head and say, *No, not this. Better move on.* I was not prepared for what I encountered the next evening.

The Bawa Muhaiyaddeen Fellowship in the Overbrook section of Philadelphia had once been an old synagogue. The three-story house was huge. Approximately fifty people shared rooms there. The kitchen and meeting room were on the first floor. Bawa's room was on the second floor, along with a few bedrooms and another small kitchen. On the third floor were an office where people transcribed Bawa's discourses and a number of bedrooms occupied by some of Bawa's disciples. As Bawa's health declined, he often cooked on huge hotplates in his room and served food from his bed, and three meals a day were provided in the downstairs kitchen, served without charge to anyone who visited.

When I entered the meeting room that first night, I had few positive expectations. I was there only to please Carole. I saw a number of people sitting in chairs or on the floor, listening to Bawa talk. He was seated on a slightly raised platform. He acknowledged me with a nod as I entered, and I took a seat a few yards away and to his left. It was a scene I had encountered many times before: a guru speaking to rapt followers. This time I sensed something unusual, though, a quality in Bawa that I had not encountered before, a deep stillness. His face was extraordinary, beautiful. Although he had a white beard and I had heard that he was very old, perhaps well over a hundred, I could detect no wrinkles or other signs of age on his face. But his eyes! His eyes were amazing. I felt those eyes look through me and deeply into me. I had the distinct impression that I was seeing what appeared to be eternity in his eyes. I could feel his knowledge of God. Bawa was only five feet tall, if that, and very thin. His size only enhanced his impact on me, for the power and strength that flowed from him were astounding. His face was shining. A smile played constantly around his mouth, and his movements and demeanor conveyed serenity and understanding.

After a while, Bawa turned to where I was sitting and looked directly at me as he continued his discourse. He spoke in Tamil, translated by a gentleman on his right.

"It is like this, little brother. If you take an apple and cut it cleanly in half, it will fall open into two pieces. On the left side, you have alcohol, sex, Zen, intellectual pursuits, meditation, mantras, tantras, yoga, travel, shakti, and LSD. On the right side, you have God. This is the way it is."

I sat there, amazed. It was all so simple. No one had ever told me this before. I had never cut the apple in half. I had accepted these different aspects of the spiritual life as vehicles to take me to God, but I had become so entranced and absorbed in the vehicles that I had forgotten God. It was as if I had desperately needed to get somewhere but had no car and every time someone gave me one, I lost myself in admiring it and forgot about my destination. I had not had the wisdom to clearly see what I was doing. Bawa

Muhaiyaddeen had just shown me my major error.

That was when I knew I had found my teacher. I had just met him and had never talked with him, but he had presented a chronological list of how I had spent my life. He had put all the pieces together, answered everything, and given me a solid sense of direction. What Bawa had referred to as the left side was over for me even as I sat listening to his words that first night, because I finally had seen that it had nothing whatever to do with God. I knew I needed to start eating and digesting the other half of the apple and taking nourishment from it.

Oh, of course. Of course! I thought. Bawa had seen something in my situation that no one else had seen, and when he pointed it out, I too was able to see it. Revealed in this way to me, what had seemed a mystery became stunningly apparent. At our first encounter, and without my saying a word, he had summed up my situation poetically, majestically, and absolutely to the mark. I understood what was missing in my life and what I had been searching for. It was the *Aha!* experience I had been waiting for.

As I examined each of the things Bawa enumerated, I realized that in each I had been seeking a state of being. When I saw alcohol as a way to generate a certain feeling, alcohol became my guru. When I saw sexual relationships as a way of feeling loved and experiencing pleasure, sex became my guru. The same thing happened with intellectualism, Zen Buddhism, and LSD. Of course, part of me always sensed that these experiences were not the real thing, but I had been subservient to them nonetheless. In one sentence, Bawa had shown me the connection between all of those things and neatly separated them all from God. Although I had been raised in a Christian home and had learned the Ten Commandments and the Golden Rule, I had pushed them aside, looking for something more spectacular. In the course of my quest, I had forgotten about God.

I thought back to Krishnamurti's teaching that nothing is real, which I could not accept. Even then I sensed that *something* must be real; Bawa's words made it clear to me that there is, indeed, one thing that is real, and that is God.

These realizations happened instantaneously and without much fanfare. As in conception, the one sperm hit the one egg and zzzzph!—it was done and a new life was conceived. All the other eggs and the millions of sperm were superfluous. Bawa's one little fleck of absolute truth instantly penetrated my heart. I knew I wasn't going anywhere else.

I believe now that there is a sense beyond even the sixth sense. I would call it God perception. It may be dormant, but we all have it. Mine was not very developed when I met Bawa, but it was there. It was developed enough to recognize, *Yes. This is it.* I knew I had come home. I thank God for the gift of recognizing the truth when I encountered it. Maybe it happened because, finally, I was ready.

Bawa's revelation did not bring about a dramatic, fall-down-screaming type of realization. Instead, it was a gentle, clear indication of where to go and what to do. I came to learn that this was how Bawa worked: natural, clear, and gentle. The effect was something like bathing in a clear pool after having been in a few sewers, some polluted lakes, and a swimming pool that everyone was peeing in. Finally I had found water I could drink, and it quenched my thirst. Like the stream that ran through our property when I was a boy, in Bawa's presence there were pools deep enough to swim in, and the water was so pure that I could drink it as I swam.

For the first time in years I felt some understanding and clarity and peace. I did not yet know what this path was or what it entailed, but I was certain it led to where I wanted to go.

The path, Bawa said, is like a map. A map does not describe the struggles and difficulties you might encounter on your journey. It's just a simple outline to show you how to reach your destination.

The path is like this, Bawa said:

> *You cannot see God; no one can. Even Moses saw only a burning bush and heard a voice.*
> *But you can know the qualities of God. The qualities of God are, in essence, God. If you practice them, you gradually become these qualities. As you become them,*

you come very close to God. As you come close to God,
you see and understand the meaning and the purpose of
your life on earth. And as you do this, you find peace.

At the end of Bawa's discourse that evening, everyone embraced him. We all got hugs. How simple, how nourishing, how unitive. The Zen masters and gurus I knew never hugged. What their students were missing! The physical contact was reassuring and symbolic. It immediately closed the distance between us.

Bawa called himself an 'ant man.'

"Ants are tiny creatures that do their work quietly and without complaining," he said. "It's only when we get big that we have problems."

The bigger, more obvious, and more noticeable we get, the bigger our problems grow. I could see this simple truth in my own life. When I was in the Marine Corps, I noticed that the drill instructor invariably picked on the guys who stood on the ends of the rows and in the front of the platoon, so I always tried to position myself in the middle of the middle row. Those of us who stood quietly in the middle were like ants, and we escaped harassment.

Now what? I asked myself later that night. My search was over. After traveling halfway around the world, I had found wisdom right in my own back yard. I remembered the dream I had in Bangalore of the small man with the childlike face, dressed in white. Bawa clearly was that man, the one I had speculated might be my teacher. Yes, I had come home.

As soon as I could, I arranged to speak to Bawa personally. "I have been looking for the truth for a long time, and I feel I have found it in Bawa and his teachings." I said to the translator, who conveyed my words to Bawa in Tamil. "Will Bawa accept me and take me into his heart as one of his children?"

"Of course my child, but the important thing is for *God* to take you to His heart," Bawa replied, looking at me intently. He paused a few seconds, gazing inward, and added, "I think He will."

It was the perfect thing to say, because if he had said, "God will accept you," I would have stopped working. If he had said, "God will not accept you," then what would I have done? I don't know.

His answer, unlike those of the gurus I had encountered before, had none of the 'I can help you, I will bring you along' flavor. Bawa deferred to the Higher Power: God will have to do this, not I. It reminded me of an AA saying, "When God is gone, I am here. When I am gone, God is here." The 'I,' of course, referred to the ego, and I could detect no ego in Bawa. Every discourse began with, "In the name of God, most merciful, most compassionate." Bawa made it simple: whatever your dilemma, turn it over to God, do your duty, and the rest will take care of itself. How different this was from my previous unsuccessful and frustrating attempts to 'storm the gates' of enlightenment by doing zazen or by 'getting shakti' from a guru, which is supposed to be your key to enlightenment.

"This is the right path," Bawa said. "There is no book for it. It originates from that one point as a vibration, and in it are many, many wonders. It is a learning that originates from a source that has no form or shadow. As those vibrations impact you, there is a thing that you can see through, a thing that is the final power. That power has the name of God. God's beautiful qualities are His form. His actions and His compassion, love, patience, and tolerance are His form. These qualities are His form. Any person who can become small enough to slip inside that form and that beauty and that resonance and that sound is God's child.

"I will adopt you in God's qualities. I will show you His beauties and point out what you need to know. Finally, I will say to God, 'Here, this is Your child. Please accept him.' That is the point. All right?"

I asked Bawa to show me how to practice the *Zikr*. "Of course, I will. When I bring up a child, I teach him whatever he needs to know. But not now." He asked someone the time and said, "Come back at twelve o'clock. I will do it then."

When I came back, Bawa was lying on his bed. Dr. Markar, a physician from Sri Lanka, was there to translate.

Bawa looked at me intently. "What I am giving you is not a mantra or a secret. It is not something you can buy. It is the word of God, which God himself recites. It is a powerful thing. You must store it in a safe place. It might burn off if you expose it to the air of satanic qualities. You must preserve it within the qualities of God. Do you understand?"

I nodded. Bawa told me to come closer. He sat up and sat cross-legged on the edge of his bed. "All praise belongs to God, the Creator, the Sustainer, the Protector. O God, my Father, may You accept me, all my body, my life, and my soul. I surrender all my intentions to You. Please accept them. O the One for whom all worship is due, You are the only one who has no form. There is no other God but You. You are God. *La ilaha*, there is no other God but You. *Ill-Allahu*, You are the one God. *La ilaha, Ill-Allahu. La ilaha, Ill-Allahu.*

"When you say *La ilaha*, the realization must be within you that there is no other God but God. When you say *Ill-Allahu*, you must draw in the breath from Him. Your intention and your concentration must be on that one point. Draw it in, draw in the breath, and focus it in your heart. *La ilaha, Ill-Allahu.*

"When you say *La ilaha*, breathe out with the left nostril. Then, as you say *Ill-Allahu*, just twinkle the right eye a little as you focus there and draw in the light through the right nostril. *La ilaha, Ill-Allahu. La ilaha, Ill-Allahu.* In the beginning, just recite it. After a while, you will be able to wiggle the tip of your tongue as if you were playing a flute. The movement of the tip of the tongue will say the prayer and regulate the breath, and the meaning will resonate.

"At some stage, you will feel it resonate. All the hairs on your body will resonate with that sound. Like mouths, each hair will recite this word. His note, His sound, will resound, and at that point, He will be looking at your kingdom and you will be looking at His kingdom.

"As you say *La ilaha*, the awareness will come in through your feet and travel up to your head, and from your head it comes down and out through the left nostril. *Ill-Allahu.*"

For some minutes, Bawa did the *Zikr* silently. The room was quiet. Then Bawa said something in Tamil, and Dr. Markar said,

"Put your right hand on the left side of Bawa's chest. Now, put your left hand on the right side of Bawa's chest." I did as I had been instructed.

"This is the way it is done. *La ilaha,*" he said, breathing out. I saw and felt Bawa's left pectoral move down. "*Ill-Allahu,*" he prayed, breathing in, and I saw and felt his right pectoral move up. It seemed quite natural at the time. I felt the movement of the pectorals distinctly, but I realized later that it is impossible to move the chest the way he did. Even yogis can't do that. The sides of the chest don't work separately.

Bawa continued doing the *Zikr* in this fashion for several minutes, allowing me to feel the motion. It was an initiation. Before we had begun, Bawa had said to the other people in the room, "Anyone who wants this, please listen and please be part of this." Everyone in the room received contact with that direct current, and I also received the physical experience of it.

Receiving the Zikr was not just a spiritual catharsis but a physical one as well. I knew Bawa could connect me with that current without the physical contact, but I had so much junk in me and so much toxicity of mind and spirit that physical contact with him may have been the only way to clear it. Why else would he have done it? It was a gift. I felt uplifted for several days after our session.

Over the next few months I had several talks with Bawa. I quickly grew accustomed to the presence of the translator. Also, even without translation I could understand Bawa by the tone of his voice and his body language. I am convinced that people who were close to Bawa could understand him, even without the translation. Bawa himself said we didn't need to understand his words because the vibration of his meaning was strong enough to come through. The words I heard were interesting, but the vibration of his voice and the melody of his language conveyed what needed to be conveyed. Although I recognize this may sound kind of silly, that's how it was. As to the content of what he said, I had heard or read many of these truths before, but they sounded quite different coming from him. Bawa's words had the ring of authenticity.

People who use brandy, wine, and other kinds of alcohol, or opium, marijuana, and other drugs become intoxicated, and their lives are destroyed by that. Other people become intoxicated by their love for land...Others drink the alcohol of arrogance and karma...the alcohol of illusion and illusory things...the alcohol of sex, or of gold and wealth.

So many intoxicants exist, and everybody is drunk...on one thing or another...No one is living in a state of clarity except that One, my God...So who can correct whom?

— M.R. Bawa Muhaiyaddeen,
Questions of Life,
Answers of Wisdom, Volume 1

–15–

WHO CAN CORRECT WHOM?

Now that my spiritual compass was pointing in the right direction, I turned my free attention to the matter of making a living. Bawa was not a teacher who cosseted his disciples.

Instead of returning to the field of counseling psychology after I left Muktananda, I had bought a large greenhouse in Paoli and started a company called Solar Grow with my childhood friend, Sandy MacFarlane. We raised organic vegetables and sold them to supermarkets and directly to the public. Bawa told me that farming was very good work, but I wasn't so sure. It was fun, to a certain extent, and it certainly helped me understand why Bawa valued the work of a farmer, but farming is tedious and backbreaking work without a lot of glory attached to it. A farmer is totally at the mercy of God and the elements. It is quite possible and happens frequently that a farmer will put in a tremendous amount of hard work only to have his crops dashed to the ground before the end of the season. Still, he picks himself up and goes through it all again.

Farming provides a good analogy for the intention and effort required to benefit from a spiritual path. Two days ago I gathered sixty pounds of tomatoes in one picking from a garden plot that is six feet by ten feet and has only twelve plants in it. Why? Because I dug the garden two feet deep and layered it with a mixture of mulch and topsoil, organic fertilizer, and biodynamic field spray. I tilled the area to a level of four inches and planted carefully. From the time the plants were two inches tall, I sprayed them every week with an organic enzyme solution. I never dreamed I would get clusters of tomatoes so big and delicious. The point is that bringing the crop to a successful harvest took constant attention. Some days, I had to force myself to spray and clip and cut and weed, but the rewards were great.

Progressing on the path and developing good qualities also take constant attention and effort. If I understand Bawa correctly, it is not possible to know God directly, but we can know Him through cultivating His qualities. To bring the seed of patience to fruition, for example, you have to dig impatience out by the roots. You have to weed out anger so that peacefulness will grow. Practice the qualities of God, Bawa told us, and you will become close to God.

A year or so after I met Bawa, I realized that Solar Grow was not going to make it as a business. We produced really tasty tomatoes, but we were dreamers and we were ahead of our time. I could have folded the business right then and saved money, but I stayed until all my creditors had been paid back and every penny was gone. The last thing I did was write checks for the two people working for me and give them two weeks' notice. Seeing the venture through to an honorable end symbolized for me building my masculine side, taking risks, and standing up for myself.

I found a new job in Baltimore at a private psychiatric hospital as director of their small alcoholism unit, which was the only position available there. Although it was the last thing I wanted to do, it was a job, and I had bills to pay. It was a traditional psychiatric hospital. Psychiatry at that time decried alternative modes of treatment. Nutrition, spiritual methodologies, and client-oriented therapy were ignored. We were supposed to discover the underlying problem and deal with it chemically or psychoanalytically, and the client was supposed to get better. This was the approach I was expected to use with alcoholics.

At first, I didn't even have an office of my own. I met with patients wherever I could find a quiet place. Alcoholic patients saw a psychiatrist daily or several times a week, took medication, and sometimes attended a weekly AA meeting, which was held on the grounds of the hospital by a senile man who often didn't show up and had little interest in group interaction. Understandably, morale was low, and most of the alcoholics were only marking time until their insurance ran out and they had to leave. A few had been at the hospital for more than a year, and one of these, who had permission to leave the hospital grounds, frequently strolled down to the local town, had a few drinks, and sauntered tipsily back up the hill to the hospital. The staff was oblivious to his behavior.

Perhaps because of what was happening in my spiritual life, I became fascinated with the human ability to change. I suspect it was because I still drank and was vicariously involved in the attempts of my alcoholic patients to change themselves and their lives. To change requires faith that there is a better way and certitude in your ability to change. It also takes determination to find the right path and stick to it when you have been going the other direction for most of your life. In the Bible, Paul says: *"Forgive me, Lord, for I do the things I ought not and do not do the things I ought."* Whether or not we are alcoholics, this is our human condition. We are all alike. Some are further along on the path than others, but we all strive for some kind of peace. The challenge with alcoholics is that they have learned to depend on a quick-fix peace, which only compounds their problems.

In the mid-seventies, the typical alcoholic seeking treatment was male, middle-aged, married, had three children, and went off to work every day. After work, he stopped at the local bar to have a few quick ones, staggered home to berate his wife and children for not being perfect, ate dinner, and passed out in front of the TV. This was the daily pattern, with more drinking on weekends, week after week, year after year, just like his father before him. If he were to change, he would have to learn to see beyond his small world.

The chief benefit of inpatient treatment is that it removes alcoholics from their cycle, sobers them up, and points out their self-destructive behavior. In itself, however, no treatment is enough to make alcoholics stop drinking for good. They question why they should give up a habit and a way of life that provides some pleasure and change to another way of life that is unfamiliar and uncomfortable. They can trust getting drunk. They don't trust getting sober. This is why, even after proper treatment, the majority of alcoholics return to their old habits.

As I learned more about alcoholism, I discovered that addiction to alcohol is not unlike addiction to cream cheese, candy, or a way of behaving. A member of the Fellowship once brought a group from an alcoholism treatment center to visit Bawa, presenting them as alcoholics who needed help. After greeting the visitors, Bawa paused, looked out at the other people gathered in the room, and said, "You are all alcoholics." He spoke of people addicted to things besides alcohol, like cars or sex or leisure, and even to qualities such as anger.

"Who does more harm," he asked, "a person who drinks liquor and falls asleep or a person who drinks anger and lashes out at his family and those with whom he works? Who does more damage?"

All of us have an addiction to something, sometimes to something as subtle as getting our way or judging others or backbiting—anything we need to do to feel good. These addictions form layers over our inner soul that obscure any true light or peace that exists within us. The addictions also maintain and strengthen our ego. An alcoholic is someone who wants what he wants when he wants it and how he wants it. Welcome to the world! We are all in it together, whether we are addicted to alcohol, anger, lust, or jealousy. Our addictions, chemical or emotional, effectively bar us from what we all desperately seek at the deepest level—peace.

Any change for the better must involve a third point that transcends the horizontal interaction between the world and us. If we postulate a third point above, we create a triangle with Self and World at the base and Wisdom at the apex. Instead of bouncing an issue back and forth between the self and the world and getting nowhere, we can toss the issue to wisdom and receive it back again, purified and enlightened. This changes our reactions. The bad qualities and wrong thinking that polluted the problem are scrubbed away by the catalyst of wisdom so that we can make real progress. This process is not as esoteric as it may sound. It is quite simple and natural.

Patrick, a young man who was a recovering alcoholic, told me that when he was six months' sober, he felt an incredible urge to drink. He walked out of his house and down to the corner where a bus would take him five miles to the nearest bar. The bus was late. As he waited, a very clear voice spoke in his ear. "Patrick," it said, "you have to do what is right, not what you want to do." This voice from nowhere so shocked him that he turned around and walked back to his house. He didn't take a drink that day and, last I heard, he was happily married, a proud father, and still sober.

Well, we all know what is right, so why don't we do it? We don't do it because we have been conditioned and we need to deprogram. Before we can deprogram, our lives have to come to a point where we realize that we are not heading in the right direction. That is the point at which we become open to change.

One success story was an Irish dockworker who had been drinking since he was sixteen years old. Every day, Pete went to the bar after work, had five or six beers with his buddies, and arrived home drunk and irritable. Concern over his job brought him into treatment for his alcoholism. When his wife came for her first visit, she was shocked over the change in Pete. They had been married for forty years and she had never seen him sober. She said it was like meeting her husband and finding someone else inside, someone far more human.

Pete was one of the patients who stayed sober. A lot of people who came in for treatment didn't, but he had what I call OTT: old time toughness. I noticed that many old timers took pride in their determination to kick their habit. Pete eventually was diagnosed with cancer of the liver. It was a perfect set up for going back to drinking. Most people would. But I went to visit Pete just a few weeks before his death and he said, "Doc? I haven't had a drink." It was very important to him that he die sober, and he did.

What is it that enables a person to become sober? Nancy Reagan's 'Just say no' policy may have had some truth to it, but it always made me think of the futility of telling a child not to eat candy because it's not good for him: something more is needed. We are ruled by our habits. Bawa referred to these as old tapes we play over and over and said we must erase the old tapes and record new ones. He talked about all the things that have to be reworked for us to get on the right path to God. When we first set out to do the right thing and make positive changes like giving up alcohol, a voice whispers in our ear, "You can handle it. Look, you've had three weeks' sober! Just have one, that's all." A lot of alcoholics listen to that voice.

The right kind of support is crucial. It is important that the alcoholic be able to talk regularly with someone who will reinforce positive qualities. The founders of AA, Bill W and Doctor Bob, got the idea for the organization one night in a kitchen in Ohio. All night they talked about how difficult it is to stay sober. By the time dawn came, they had gone through two quarts of coffee and they were still sober. Bill W realized that they had hit upon a solution: talk, mutual support, keeping busy, and drinking coffee instead of alcohol. He realized that if they could do it for one day, they could do it for three days.

If you go to an AA meeting every day, you are not likely to drink. That's why people who go into treatment are told to do ninety meetings in ninety days. If you miss a day, you do two the next day, and at the end of three months, you should have gone to ninety meetings. Most relapses take place in the first ninety days. Very few people who do a meeting a day will take a drink during that time, which allows room for a new pattern to become established.

Alina Lodge, a treatment center in the Northeast, specializes in treating hard-core alcoholics. They don't have an involved program. The minimum treatment period is one year, and some people stay for three years. That may seem like a long time, but it isn't when you weigh the time against losing your family or dying of alcoholism. The idea behind the one-year minimum is to get clients through four seasons. They discover the thrills of spring without a bottle of wine, the joy of a hot August and a baseball game without a six-pack, autumn weekends without spiked cider, and snowy nights warmed by friendship instead of hot toddies. They realize they can do it. The tape of old habits is recorded over by new and healthier habits.

Most fancy treatment centers have a rich and structured program. Alina Lodge keeps it simple. They don't have any fancy programs. Their one hard and fast rule, other than not leaving the grounds, is that you have to stay in the lunchroom for an hour after lunch. Why? Because alcoholics hate to talk when they are sober. They get bored or critical and impatient. They'll talk a blue streak when they've had a few beers or a couple of shots, but not when they are sober. Whiskey courage. At Alina Lodge, that hour after lunch eventually gets them accustomed to communicating without alcohol. Their recovery rate is very high.

Not all of my patients were alcoholics. One patient was so phobic about radioactivity that she wouldn't even pick up a newspaper published near the Three Mile Island nuclear power plant for fear of contamination.

Since I didn't have an office, I coaxed her to sit with me at a table just inside the huge formal dining room. She was terrified at first because she knew there was a microwave in the adjoining kitchen. I soothed her, and she learned to trust me. I worked with her twice a week for six months, and every time we met I selected a table just a tiny bit closer to the kitchen. She got much better. In fact, she recovered enough that she agreed to cook something in the microwave shortly before she was discharged.

It takes a long while, but if you meet regularly and if you soothe patients and give them love, many get well. This is very different from the approach used in most psychiatric hospitals.

Always looking to try out new approaches, I brought in Renee, a psychodramatist, as a regular weekly consultant for my unit. She used role-playing and other psychodrama techniques to open up patients to their pain and their weaknesses. I drummed up some interest and asked Renee to start a psychodrama group for the professionals in the hospital as well. Ten of us attended Renee's first session: two social workers, three psychologists, and five psychiatrists.

Very shortly into the session, one of the social workers was on the floor, sobbing uncontrollably. Renee had touched an open nerve relating to the holocaust experiences of the woman's parents. The psychiatrists looked at one another in amazement and some fear. We were all astonished at how quickly the social worker had entered this area of hurt, especially because she herself was a therapist. We gained respect for the power of psychodrama handled by a wise practitioner.

Only three people showed up for the next session—and none of the psychiatrists. It was clear to me that the psychiatrists were afraid of what might come up for them. They weren't ready to deal with their own issues, yet they were more than willing to take on the issues of others and be well paid for it.

Renee convinced me, as director of the alcoholism unit, to climb in the same boat as my patients. I became one of them during their weekly psychodrama sessions until I had dealt honestly with my own issues. It was embarrassing and fear provoking to abdicate my authority. Yet I did, and I emerged a much better counselor and a humbler and more compassionate listener.

This story reminds me of a conversation I read about that took place between Freud and Jung. It went something like this:

Freud said, "I had a very, very powerful dream, Carl."

"Sigmund, tell me."

"No, I dare not tell you, Carl."

"Why?"

"It would risk my authority."

That is when Jung started to go his own way. He could not study with someone under those conditions.

Who in the field of psychotherapy talks about his own process? You never hear a therapist venturing anything personal, particularly if it shows fragility. I do it all the time and I don't get embarrassed anymore. I find that self-disclosure can be extremely helpful; it places the client and I together on the same playing field. And that, in fact, is the truth of the situation: we are all part of this big movement of humanity through life, some a little ahead and some a little behind, but we are all here and we are all facing the same challenges.

It can help clients feel comfortable and give them hope when someone they are coming to see professionally is willing to be open in an appropriate way. One client said, "Well, if you can open up about it, I guess I can." Also, when others know that you have faced a similar challenge and found a way to cope, it gives them hope. People need hope.

Psychology is my field, but I hold many reservations about the benefits of most psychotherapeutic approaches. I know there are good practitioners out there, but after being with Bawa, I feel strongly that the answers lie in the spiritual realms. I had some problems, like all of us, and the answers I found did not come from psychology but from the loving guidance of a truly wise person along with my own efforts to do the things that were hard to do.

If we analyze each point within us, we will find that the faults we see in others are really within ourselves… those [are the] faults we have to correct, not the faults of others…That is the path to becoming true human beings.

We must wash away the dirt from our own garments. We should not try to remove the dirt from another person's garments. If we do, we will only get kicked.

— **M.R. Bawa Muhaiyaddeen,**
    Questions of Life,
    Answers of Wisdom, Volume 1

-16-

WASHING MY OWN GARMENTS

Because I worked in Baltimore, I could visit Bawa only on the weekends. I came up to Philadelphia nearly every Friday night, stayed at my mother's home in Paoli, and spent as much time as I could at the Fellowship.

One morning, I peeked in and saw that Bawa was alone in his bedroom except for one of his translators. Considering I had never seen fewer than ten people around him, I recognized that a rare opportunity for privacy had presented itself. I went in, greeted Bawa, and asked if I could talk to him about sexual desire. I told him it had been a big problem for me. Embarrassed to expose this blemish on my spiritual life, I glanced around again and was glad to see that the room was still empty. Bawa spoke two words in English, "SEXUAL DESIRE." As if by command, the door to his bedroom swung wide and in came more than a dozen women. To this day I don't know how it happened, but strange things frequently happened around Bawa.

"Little brother," he began. "God doesn't like this kind of life. It is like eating in a different restaurant every night. You keep sampling new dishes and smacking your lips, but the waiters don't eat the food; not even the chef does." He paused. "It is like this, my child," he continued. "You should have one woman, and then you will begin to find peace. God doesn't like this other way of life," he said again, "and many new diseases will come to man in the next decade, bringing much illness and many deaths." This was in 1976, several years before the AIDS epidemic came to light.

Bawa's words set something in motion. My only solid relationship at that time was with a woman named Jackie. She was beautiful and sexy and I could talk to her about the things that were most important to me.

Jackie had been raised in the same social fabric as I—the interconnected world of society, the Social Register, the Blue Book, known in Washington as the Green Book. If you are in it, you are 'in,' and if you are not in it, you are 'out.' The snobs had a term for this: OCD. The worst thing that could happen in that milieu was to have it whispered that you were 'not OCD,' which meant, 'not our class, dear.' *Our Class, Dear* meant that you went to an Ivy League college or your parents had lots of money or you knew the right people. Whatever it was, once you got on the list, you were definitely OCD and were invited to all the right social events. For the young people, that meant debutante balls, where parents introduced their daughters to society and made sure they found husbands of the right sort: OCD.

Since my family was a very old Philadelphia family and since I went to Andover and then on to Princeton, I was OCD. I got invited to parties and debutante balls all over the Northeast: Philadelphia, Long Island, New York, Baltimore, Washington, Boston.

Jackie was OCD. I first met Jackie at a debutante ball when I was in my late teens. Later, she dated my brother's college roommate, so we ran into each other from time to time and she heard about some of my escapades. Jackie's recollection of me was pretty bad: on a scale of 0 to 10, I had rated only a 1 or a 2. She saw me accurately as a playboy who drank too much and partied too much, so she would not have considered me for anything, let alone as a suitor.

We met again when I was teaching at University of Massachusetts at Amherst. My old love Mary and I had seen each other socially and talked after I returned from my travels, and she invited me to her home in Washington for lunch. She was happily married, and we were good friends. She said she wanted to introduce me to someone.

That someone turned out to be Jackie—She remembered me. She had been doubtful about our arranged lunch but finally decided to come anyway. Mary thought that we would enjoy talking. Jackie was a sincere spiritual seeker, too, although her explorations had been very different from mine—Ouija boards and the like.

I was very attracted to Jackie and she to me. Still, we went our own ways again, and neither of us thought much more about it for a while.

Some months later, an old friend, Peter, invited me to meet him at the Explorer's Club in New York. A third person was with us, Peter's friend Arthur, and Arthur was Jackie's husband. We had a nice time. Much later, Jackie told me that when Arthur came home that evening, he said, "I've met the man you are going to marry after we divorce. He's the person you've been looking for."

"Who is it?" she asked.

When Arthur mentioned my name, Jackie said, "Not on your life."

More months passed. Then, at a party in Washington, I was standing at the piano listening to someone play when Jackie joined me. We stood there talking. Jackie and I formed a bond that night. We had deep talks from time to time. Eventually, she and her husband divorced, and we began to see each other, although not exclusively.

We explored the spiritual scene together. I took her to meet Swami Muktananda early on in our relationship. It was an exotic scene: drums playing, incense wafting in the air, peacock feather fans keeping the swami comfortable, disciples running around talking about his miracles. Jackie got *shaktipat* and said it was like a lightning bolt going through her, so strong that she fell over. Still, she hadn't been overly impressed. There was nothing spiritual about it, she told me later.

After my talk with Bawa about settling on one woman, I gradually stopped seeing other people and established an exclusive relationship with Jackie. When the time was right, we took a big leap forward, and I moved into Jackie's house in Washington, DC. I had no idea then that I would be committed to her for life because I had never been really committed to any relationship. However, something very strong inside made me want this relationship to work. Whenever the idea of leaving crossed my mind, I thought, "Where else would I go?" I had been with enough women to know that there is no such thing as the one perfect mate. I realized I had been like a man in a supermarket, taking a bite here and a bite there but never getting any real nourishment. Bawa was right: I needed to choose one woman and make a commitment.

It was a difficult adjustment. I had been a bachelor for over forty years. When I wanted to do something, I did it. I went wherever I wanted to go, wore what I wanted to wear, combed my hair the way I wanted to comb it, and slept in whatever position I wanted to sleep in. Now someone else was there, sharing intimate time and space with me, and getting in the way of what I wanted to do. We were polishing off each other's rough spots, and it was often painful. I was emotionally immature about what nourishes a relationship. When I look back now I am amazed that our relationship lasted. I was an adolescent in many respects.

Jackie had two children. One had a serious problem with epilepsy and was living in a home where she could receive the medical and custodial attention she needed. Jackie had tried to care for her daughter at home for nine years, but it was virtually impossible, even with the help of a maid. So only her thirteen-year-old daughter Tania lived at home, and she gave me a very hard time.

Tania laughs about it now because she has come to love me. She also loves her father and he loves her, but he was not always there for her, and I don't think he understood what she needed. He left a lot of space for me to fill. As was the custom in our social circle, Tania was away at boarding school for much of the year, but she was very possessive of her mother when she was home and very feisty and abrasive with me.

I could see why she was angry and upset: I too had been a child of divorce. I knew where the pain came from, and so it was easy for me to let it go by. I knew that I could not make any inroads at that point, so I just tried not to ruffle her feathers. Besides, I wasn't placed in a leadership position with Tania. Her father still saw her.

She had her mother and her friends. She didn't really need me.

Eventually, several things changed. I knew she was artistic, so I gave her a very nice camera. She flipped. She loved it. She saw that I recognized her talents. I also taught her how to drive on an old stick shift car I had. She nearly broke the transmission learning to shift gears, but she learned. She was grateful to me, and the tide of our relationship turned. She became more chummy. We accepted each other, slowly became friends, and eventually she sought my advice on important matters. When she was considering marriage, she talked to me about her husband to be and asked me if I thought she should marry him.

When Tania was a teenager, I can remember telling Jackie on several occasions that I thought Tania was out of line. Jackie was defensive about it, and it was natural for her to defend her daughter. Sometimes I was right, though, and eventually Jackie even suggested that I talk to Tania about specific issues. That is when I became a second father to her.

And so, although it was not always easy, I did begin to find some peace as I tried to follow Bawa's advice.

I had taken Jackie to meet Bawa before we moved in together. She really loved Bawa, but she was afraid of him and always sat in the back of the room behind someone. Bawa knew she was there. During his talks, he addressed things she was thinking about or struggling with, and his messages got through to her. Now she wishes she had made more effort to push beyond her fear and get closer to Bawa, but it doesn't really matter because the bond between them was there.

I also invited my mother to meet Bawa. She was a good sport about it.

During my Muktananda phase, I had taken Mother to meet the swami. "You've got to meet Muktananda," I had enthused. "Yes, dear," she said indulgently. My mother was a society lady and very polite, with a heart of gold and a will of steel. In those days, Muktananda's followers were renting a space in New York City. Everyone crowded in, filling the aisles. The scent of Jean Nate cologne prevailed, sprayed into the air by devotees. The custom was to shuffle up the aisle on your knees until you reached the feet of the guru and his interpreter. Amazingly, Mother was willing to do this. Perhaps she did not want to be impolite.

Muktananda looked at my mother and then at me and said, "Mother?"

"Yes," I said. "This is my mother."

"Aah," he said. "A good child. A very good child."

My mother was pleased, of course. "Oh, yes, he is! He *is* a good child."

"You see how much better he is now that he has been here?"

After our turn in the spotlight, Mother leaned over to me and said, very quietly, "I need a drink. Let's get out of here."

This is why I say that my mother was a good sport to brave the guru ordeal again.

Fast-forward a couple of years. "Ma," I said. "You really have to come and meet Bawa. He is not like anyone else."

"Oh, yes, dear. Of course."

When we arrived at the Fellowship, Bawa was sitting in the alcove outside his room, an interpreter next to him. He looked at my mother and then at me. "Mother? Son?"

"Yes."

"Get your mother some tea."

I went to fetch the tea. I realized the tea was very hot, so I blew on it for about two minutes." I carried it in to my mother and handed it to her.

Bawa looked at me sternly and said, "Don't ever give your mother hot tea. Are you sure that tea is cool enough?"

I assured him that it was indeed cool enough.

Again Bawa looked from one of us to the other. "Mother. Son."

"Yes," I said. "Mother. Son."

"A very good child," Bawa said.

"Yes," my mother said, picking right up on her cue. She had been through this before. She knew her lines. "He *is* a good child."

"No, no, no," Bawa said. "Not him. You. You are a very good

child. He has been very naughty. You are a very good child, my daughter."

My mother had never believed in gurus or spiritual teachers, so it was remarkable to me that soon Bawa's picture was hanging on the wall outside her bedroom. "He said I was a very good child!" my mother told me, somewhat surprised and very moved by the experience.

When my mother died many years later, I had her tombstone engraved with her name, the dates of her birth and death, and this phrase: *A very good child.*

My father never met Bawa. He had made it very clear to me over the years that he did not understand my life choices. When I was staying in London during my early days abroad, he asked several people to look me up on their travels. I put a stop to this after a particularly unpleasant dinner with two old friends of his in London, a man and his wife whom I had known for years. Appropriately enough, the woman was nicknamed Tiger.

"What are you doing over here?" Tiger asked, almost shouting at me as we sat at our table. "You are just making a mess of your life. What do you think you're doing? You should be getting back to the States. You're killing your father, you know." It went on like this off and on throughout our dinner.

Tiger drank quite a bit that night, and her husband finally had to take her to their room. "Please excuse me," he said, obviously embarrassed by the whole scene.

I wrote a firm letter to my father. "You're my father. I love you and respect you, but you have to understand that this is my life and I am doing what has meaning for me. It is not your position now that I am an adult to criticize me and to send people over here to 'set me straight.' If you ever again subject me to an ordeal like the one I just went through, you can forget about any further communication between us, because I don't want it on that basis." I received a nice letter from him in reply, telling me he understood how I felt.

When I came back from Japan for my brother's funeral, my father invited me to spend a few days at his home in New York State. He met me at the airport in Rochester. During the hour-long drive to his house, he asked me about my life abroad. "What is it like? What are you doing?"

"Well, you know I spent a year in a monastery in Japan, and now I'm living on my own there, studying Zen Buddhism." I should have realized that this concept was entirely foreign to him. That a son of his was not working nine to five and making a lot of money was something he couldn't accept. In his mind, I was not doing what normal people do. I was just doing a lot of crazy things.

I wanted him to understand. With great enthusiasm, I said, "Dad, you really should try meditation. It's just amazing."

He recoiled as if I had slapped him and shot back at me, "Why in God's name should I do that?" I don't think he meant to hurt me, but his tone cut me like a sword. I had offered him a chance to share something that was very meaningful to me. I gave him a gift, and he stabbed me with his voice. Apparently, he had neither the interest nor the inclination to discover what his son was doing with his life and why. On the contrary, he appeared insulted and demeaned by my question. It seemed there was no further reason to be close. The rest of the visit was merely cordial, and I returned to Japan a few days later.

My father died on Christmas Day of 1981. His death did not affect me much, and I wondered about that. I asked Bawa about it, and he said that it was because I was so accustomed to dealing with tragedy and death and grief in my work. I think, too, that I had already processed much of my grief over the loss of my father when I was very young. In a sense, he had already died for me several times. The first death took place when he went away to war, which was not his fault, although I think the war gave him a good excuse to get away from us. When he left the second time to marry someone else, that really finished it for me. By the time my father actually died, I had already grieved for him twice.

I loved and respected many things about my father. He was a good man, but it wasn't his style to be emotionally close with his children. His father was a real taskmaster, and my father, in turn, was very strict with us when we were little. He took us fishing a few times, but otherwise he just wasn't good with kids. When he left my mother after World War II, he may as well have abandoned us. Except for a few visits a year, he cut ties not just with my mother, but with all of us, and in so doing he cut off any chance of further emotional involvement. He cut off the possibility of the bonding that can happen during the teenage years.

He had been living in California for years, and when I heard that he was dying of cancer, I went to see him for a few days. I had a long list of things I hoped we could iron out as father and son before he passed away: why he left me, why he didn't talk to me when I was growing up, why there was such a gulf between us, how he felt about this and that. When I got there, I told his third wife, Jean Marie, what I hoped to accomplish.

"Oh, Locke, you can't do this. You just cannot do it."

"But why?"

"It will kill him if you bring up all those things. He's not going to understand it, and it will just worry him. It won't resolve anything because he just doesn't know how to deal with those kinds of things. He is in a somewhat weakened state. If you bring a big load of stuff for the two of you to work through, he's not going to know what you want. He won't know how to answer, and it's just going to be a disaster. Please don't."

I thought about it and decided she was probably right. So Dad and I talked about other things. Before I left, I gave him a big hug.

"See you next time," he said, knowing that he would not be here for a 'next time.'

Although the weeks leading up to his death were quite difficult for him, Jean Marie told me that my father was peaceful during his last moments. That meant a lot to me. Despite his faults, my father was a fine man. He never said a bad word about my mother. He was a man of great integrity, a man of honor. He read the Bible faithfully. He was kind to many people and took care of them. He was congenial. In some ways he was a good role model, but he was emotionally distant, at least with his children.

...Lay your heart open. Unlock your mind. Unlock your life. Unlock it all and you will be able to look inside and make it clear. Open the door and look inside.

— M.R. Bawa Muhaiyaddeen

-17-

OPENING THE DOOR, LOOKING INSIDE

In 1982, I went to spend a few weeks with Bawa while he was in Sri Lanka, where he had been discovered many years before. Much about Bawa's origins and especially his age, which was a constant topic of speculation, remain mysterious even to this day. However, the following is one of the accounts of early encounters with Bawa in the jungles of Sri Lanka, and it has been verified by several credible sources.

In the early part of the 1900s at a riverside shrine in the south of Sri Lanka, Bawa called out to some pilgrims. He spoke with them for a while about their lives and about God. Deeply stirred by this unusual man, one of the group invited him to come to Jaffna and teach them. He promised that he would meet them there in forty days. After he had departed, they realized that they had not given him an address or directions for reaching their home. They were therefore elated when, forty days later, the small man in white appeared on the doorstep of the man who had invited him. They called him Bawa, or Father. For many years in Jaffna, he fed and cared for the poor, and his advice was sought on every conceivable practical and spiritual matter. Later, in the capitol city of Colombo, he was frequently the honored guest of the Macan-Markar family. People of every faith and social stratum, including the highest government officials, came to him for advice and wisdom. His teaching cut across all established lines of religion and belief. He spoke straight to the heart with pure understanding of this life and the path to God.

In 1971, Bawa accepted an invitation to visit the United States, where he began to gather his 'children from the West.' He returned with some of them to Sri Lanka at regular intervals, and, with their help, he rebuilt the ashram in Jaffna and built a House of God on the tiny peninsula of Mankumban, near Jaffna, where people of all faiths are invited to pray together.

Disciples who had made the trip to Sri Lanka told me that the time I spent there with Bawa would be different from the time I spent with him here in the United States. They were correct. My time there was intense. As a visitor to Sri Lanka, the worldly distractions of my normal day-to-day life were absent. It was a spiritual retreat. My sole reason for going was to steep myself in Bawa's presence. I hoped to understand myself better and to clear away the emotional debris that stood between Bawa and me.

I arrived in Colombo, where Bawa was staying at the home of Dr. Ajwad Macan-Markar and his wife, Ameen. Eager to see Bawa, I did not focus much on the locale when I arrived. Besides, I had traveled in many Eastern countries, and, except for the presence of Bawa, Sri Lanka did not seem much different. Three-wheeled motorcycles putted along the streets in the midst of rickshaws, trucks, cars, and an odd assortment of other vehicles. Horns blared, vendors called out their wares, and people in bright clothes hurried about their business. It was hot and steamy. It reminded me of India and somewhat of Thailand.

Dr. Ajwad's house was situated in a small compound. It was big and solid and had teakwood floors, but otherwise it was not particularly luxurious. The kitchen showed signs of constant use, which was inevitable since twenty or thirty people were being fed several times a day.

The entire household focused on Bawa, who was staying upstairs in the master bedroom. I slept downstairs in the living room with nine other guys. The first night I was there, I got up to go to the bathroom in the middle of the night and saw a gigantic, flying cockroach, the kind of nightlife that flourishes in a tropical climate.

I hit it with a broom, verified that it was dead, then came back an hour later to discover that it had revived itself and disappeared.

When I greeted Bawa upon my arrival, he said, "You have traveled a lot and you have learned a lot of things about the world but you haven't learned anything about God." I was happy for at least that much recognition, but my ego rose up, wanting to say, "I'm here, Bawa. I've done some pretty interesting things—more than some of these other guys. Won't you throw me a bone, please?" I never did get the bone.

I consoled myself that at least I had found Bawa and was in Sri Lanka with him. I had hoped that being in close proximity with Bawa over several weeks would finally make it possible for me to gain more access to him. Not being able to crack the inner circle had always made me envious. I wanted to come and go from his room freely, like the people who seemed to be by his side day and night or those who could walk right in whenever they were able to be there, people who seemed to have more chutzpah. Instead, I just hung in the background, waiting for that special recognition. This longing to be singled out by the father was a theme that arose over and over again in my relationship with Bawa.

The more I talk with Bawa's children, the more I discover that almost everyone was struggling with the desire to be the favored child and with old feelings of unworthiness or jealousy or competition that had not been resolved in childhood. Bawa gave us what we needed, and that was not always what we wanted. What we needed was spiritual insight, a good spiritual path, good qualities, true insight, and unconditional love. That's what we got. Special recognition could not be won by lobbying for it. It was given according to some design that no one could successfully manipulate. Bawa recognized our projections, and he was wise enough to know that it's not good to give a child candy every time it reaches for it.

After all, why should he have given me special recognition? For my spiritual yearning and accomplishments? I hadn't gained anything significant spiritually. I had possessed the wherewithal and certainly the desire to taste different spiritual paths, but everyone with Bawa was a serious seeker. The real truth was that, despite all the meditation and dream analysis and LSD therapy that I had hoped would resolve my emotional conflicts, I still craved attention and affection. When I was a kid, I had a lot of social grace and coordination that served me well even when my studies and athletics became a challenge. I was confident in my ability to get what I wanted, and there wasn't much I couldn't work out. But those things didn't count with Bawa. He showed me my place in the mass of humanity. Although I would have said that I was part of the mass of humanity, I secretly felt I was a little better because I had gone to Japan and India and the Black Forest and explored so many interesting disciplines. Bawa didn't focus on the past. He focused on the present and guided me to see the attitudes, beliefs, and actions that were blocking my spiritual growth.

I settled into the daily experience of living in close proximity to Bawa. We got up before dawn to recite the names of God downstairs. We'd have some breakfast. Whenever Bawa's room was open, I sat with him. He gave discourses every day when he was well, and sometimes I just sat and watched him while he talked with local people about their affairs or was engaged in some other work.

Bawa himself cooked frequently on a large hot plate by his bed and served the food out of big pots. I always had trouble with constipation, especially when I was traveling, so when I arrived in Sri Lanka, my time schedule was off and I was bloated. Some people said that if Bawa Muhaiyaddeen cooked, you had to eat every bit of it. I didn't feel up to eating much, so I tried to hide somewhere in the house when he was serving. Those were the only times I actually prayed to be overlooked. It didn't work. Soon enough, Bawa would send someone to look for me, "Psychology doctor? Psychology doctor? Come and get." Every single time, Bawa heaped vast quantities of food onto my plate. The first few times I ate it all, obviously in discomfort.

Thank God, someone noticed my plight. "Oh, no, you don't have to eat it all if it's too much. Scrape some of it into this container before you eat, if you like. We give the extra food to the poor people outside."

The food was delicious. Bawa said that food prepared with love has a power that is beyond our understanding. So I ate as much as I could. Even if I wasn't hungry, I ate a little bit.

As I had hoped, I found much more opportunity to interact with Bawa. While I was there, it seemed that everybody was getting a *dua*. *Duas* are special supplications written on paper then wound tightly, sealed with paraffin, and affixed to a specially knotted cotton string. Bawa would place these around a disciple's neck to be worn day and night. People got them for their health or their studies or to ward off evil, and so forth. For me, the point was that everyone seemed to be getting one, everyone but me, that is. I thought about it. Although I didn't feel I could just baldly ask Bawa for his attention and affection, I could ask him for a *dua*. One day I approached him.

"Bawa?"

"Yes, *thambi* (little brother)?"

"Can I have a *dua*?"

He looked at me with an expression of incredulity and perhaps a hint of skepticism and said, "A *dua*! What do *you* need a *dua* for? You don't need a *dua*."

I thought that was good. I felt pretty good about that.

Sometimes I was swayed by the world instead of the Spirit. A few of us would sneak off when we were supposed to be somewhere else doing something else, imagining that Bawa didn't know. I might have been sitting in Bawa's room all morning, waiting for him to give a discourse or listening to the flow of Tamil as he conversed with Sri Lankan visitors about what appeared to be worldly matters. Or I would hear he was sick and wouldn't be talking that morning. Whatever the reason, I would be persuaded to go on a shopping expedition or out to the Galle Face, an old fashioned hotel on the sea where we would enjoy a sumptuous tea served by Ceylonese waiters in turbans while we sat gazing out over a beautiful lawn and the sea beyond. It was quite wonderful, like turning back time a hundred years. Almost invariably, though, I'd return to discover I had missed something really good.

I had a dream about this one night. In the dream, I was torn between wanting to see Bawa and not wanting to hurt someone else's feelings. I knew the dream was trying to tell me that I couldn't let myself be swayed by others, that I had to keep my eye on the point and always be ready to receive. I had to ask myself what was most important, to defer to another person or to my own restlessness or to spend time with Bawa.

I watched for an opportunity to talk with Bawa about Jackie. She and I had been living together for several years by then, but there were difficulties in our relationship. When I put these matters to Bawa, the first thing he asked was where Jackie was. I told him that she had not come because she was afraid Bawa would see all her bad qualities. Bawa laughed good-naturedly, and then replied in his sweet voice, "Does she really think she needs to be here for me to see her?"

He gazed at me knowingly. "Thambi," he said, "you have made the wrong list."

I was taken aback by his words. Before leaving the United States, I was so frustrated with Jackie that I had made a list of all the things that were 'wrong' with her. I firmly believed that our life would be paradise if only she would change these things. Bawa's comment surprised me and also made me feel a bit exposed: I had not told him or anyone else about the list.

"You need to make a list on yourself and the qualities *you* need to correct. That's the way to improve your life."

This attitude adjustment was the beginning of my understanding about relationships and what makes them work. It also formed the basis for the marriage counseling I did later in my career.

I changed the subject to my major concern, which was whether to go ahead with my plan to open an alcoholism treatment center. I had serious doubts about modern psychology's effectiveness in dealing with the ills of my clients.

"Bawa, I'm about to start on a new venture, working with alcoholics, and I have many doubts about it."

"A psychologist is bound to have doubts. The field of psychology is an artificial kind of learning. It is not based on knowledge that develops out of one's own wisdom. It is based on knowledge that has been learned by rote from books or other external sources. It is copied and then played back, like an old tape recording.

"A therapist will never be able to cure anyone's illness unless he has developed sufficient wisdom, no matter how many books, drug therapies, and techniques he has studied. Unless he has wisdom, he will fall in love with his clients or identify with them to the extent that his own problems are compounded. Soon he may be as troubled as those who are looking to him for help.

"Beyond what the world presents as psychological knowledge is another kind of knowledge that is truly wondrous. A person who wants to study psychology needs divine wisdom above all else. Divine wisdom enables a therapist to look into a person's nature, his mind, his life, and his actions to discover the reason for the illness and find the appropriate remedy. There is no need to ask a lot of questions. With insight, it is relatively easy to help a person find some peace.

"In some countries there is no good, clear water. Even filtering doesn't help enough. Since water is necessary to maintain life, something has to be done, but what? There is a seed called tay-tan. If the inside of a vessel is rubbed with tay-tan, any dirt in the water that is poured inside will sink to the bottom immediately, leaving the water as clear as glass.

"In the same way, a heart that is murky must be rubbed with wisdom, comfort, and love. All the dirt will settle to the bottom and the heart will clear. This is not a matter of applying some preset formula or echoing what the person has brought.

"It takes wisdom to heal people, to restore their peace of mind, and to inspire faith in God. A person who has self-understanding and wisdom is like a mirror. His insight and understanding enable those who come before him to see their own reflections.

"Faith in God and the study of divine wisdom are essential for a psychologist or psychiatrist. Psychology needs to understand the energies of the mind. Only God's consciousness and the state of divine wisdom can truly know another person's mental state and know which treatment will achieve lasting results.

"God's psychology is true psychology; anything else is artificial and detrimental, both to the patient and to the therapist."

I felt inadequate to the task Bawa had set before me and pressed him to suggest another line of work, something simpler.

"You can do this kind of work. Study what needs to be studied and you will be able to do it."

"I don't have that kind of wisdom. I try to use the wisdom I have found in your books and teachings."

"Learn from someone who has real wisdom. That is the best university. Stay there and study. Develop certitude.

"You will need to be patient," he continued. "Think how much patience it takes to catch a fish. The fisherman lowers bait into the water and may have to stand there for hours, watching, waiting, and hoping that a fish will come along, notice the bait, and take the hook. Experienced fish, of course, will try to take the food without taking the hook. When the fisherman finally does hook a fish, the fish will not give up easily, but will swim back and forth, trying to escape. So you can see why a fisherman needs to be so patient.

"When we come to a wise man, we must be like fishermen, waiting patiently, watching, and learning. We must not be impatient and fret because we haven't caught any fish. After all, the fish's life is at stake; naturally it is going to do everything it can to escape. We cannot be in a hurry."

I wanted to be certain that I understood what Bawa was advising me to do about my work. "Meanwhile, do you feel it is all right for me to continue practicing psychology?"

"All work is like this, not just psychology. A medical doctor faces the same situation, and so does a farmer. Love, wisdom, and the qualities that can calm and subdue are needed to control a cow, a horse, or a goat. These qualities are necessary for success in any work we do. These good qualities are what cure illness, not just medication or injections. Genuine affection eases a person's mind, instills confidence, and encourages the growth of faith. The most valuable curative is within the heart. Medicine plays a very small part. It serves as an example of the real medicine within the heart, which should be able to touch and comfort a troubled heart.

"Doctor, my brother, we can cure only with God's qualities, God's love, God's wisdom, and faith in God. Whatever work we do, this is the point. This is what we must learn."

"How can I change and become better at doing what you have just said? How can I learn to show that kind of love more than I have during the last few years?"

"First, you must correct everything you copied in the past and inscribe on your heart God's wisdom, good qualities, true peacefulness, and patience. Take into your heart outer patience, inner patience, contentment, and trust in God. As you do this, the artificial things that were recorded earlier gradually will be corrected and overlaid by this new and genuine learning.

"If you keep changing yourself in this way, everything will turn out all right in the end. Bring what you have learned to the good path and the right point, and the old material will be refined and transformed."

"Does that mean I have not been refining for the past few years?"

"Yes. When water is clear, you have no doubt about whether you can drink it. Muddy water is not suitable for human beings, only for animals. You must filter it before you can consider it good water.

"All that you have learned is certainly knowledge, but it is knowledge muddied up with many other things. Everything is part of your learning, but it is muddy learning, suitable only for animals and demons. If you can bring it to the good state where truth and human beings can drink of it, learning can be called wisdom."

"Would it be easier to carry out this process in another line of work, or does it make any difference?"

"My brother, this is the world, is it not? No matter what kind of food we eat, we always end up in the bathroom. It all goes out the same way, and it all stinks. It is the same with our studies and our work. We may switch from one thing to another that seems more worthy, but unless we change the place where it comes out, it will smell just as bad. We need to transform our qualities, actions, behavior, and what we have copied. Until we do, all of it will have a bad odor to wisdom and to truth.

"The *kancheram* tree bears fruits that are very pretty and alluring, but they are deadly. None of the birds or animals will feed on them, because they know they would die if they did. However, before the fruits have formed, when that same tree is in blossom, honeybees sit on the flowers and extract the nectar. By itself, the nectar from *kancheram* blossoms is poisonous, but honeybees know how to extract it and mix it with nectar from other flowers so as to neutralize its poison and transform it into very tasty honey. So can you call the *kancheram* tree useless? No, it can be made into something beneficial, can it not? Honeybees do not avoid it; they transform it.

"We human beings are like *kancheram* trees. All of our qualities are poisonous. We must give up what the truth will not eat and learn to be like honeybees, extracting what is potentially good out of all of this poison and transforming it into something useful. To goodness, nothing in this life is useful unless wisdom has extracted the truth, mixed it with the essence of all that is good, and matured it until it has become delicious honey. With its poison neutralized, it is useful to us and to everyone else as well. This is true gnostic wisdom. Nothing is rejected totally; we can draw something useful from everything if we take the point, the essence, and leave the rest aside. Do you understand?"

"Yes." I said I understood, but I knew that I would have to chew on his words for a long time. Meanwhile, he was clear that I should proceed with my plans for the clinic.

"This is a very important point. What is your name?"

"Locke."

"Locke? Yes, many things are locked inside you. Psychology doctor, my brother, when you lock it up, it certainly is locked. Open it out; lay your heart open. Unlock your mind. Unlock your life. Unlock it all and you will be able to look inside and make it clear. Open the door and look inside.

"If we throw away everything that is unnecessary and transform what remains, then we will be clear, our houses will be clear, and we will be able to clear those who come to us. Everything will be good.

"What has been said is sufficient for now. Think about it. Take it in. After you have reflected on it, if you have anything more to ask, we can talk about it then."

Once again he had said that everything I had already recorded had to be erased and replaced by real learning. I thought of all the years I had spent traveling and studying, all the wondrous mystical experiences, all the 'knowledge' I had gained, and here I was being told to erase it all! He had said it when I first met him, but perhaps I had not fully grasped what he was asking me to do. I was devastated. I still had hoped to hear him say, "My, my, you're such a wise young man." But Bawa always went to the heart of an issue quickly. And of course it made sense. The psychology I was practicing really didn't help people very much. They paid a lot of money to tell me their problems. I struggled to understand, and I did understand on a worldly level, but I was a stranger to the inner heart, which is where change in a person truly takes place.

After I had been in Sri Lanka for about two weeks, Bawa encouraged me to visit Mankumban with a few other disciples. Mankumban is a tiny peninsula not far from Jaffna where Bawa had organized the building of a House of God that welcomed people of all faiths. I was intrigued: Bawa had said that he built the House of God to fulfill a promise he had made to Mary, the mother of Jesus.

On the way there and back, we stayed overnight at the Jaffna ashram. Jaffna is very different from Colombo. Poorer. The streets are not paved. The ashram there was very simple and small, made of cinderblocks. Bawa's room was austere but also had a sweetness about it. That first night, I stood at an upstairs window of the ashram. I could see across the street into a basement where a tailor was mending clothes. Every few minutes, he stopped his work and gazed upwards for a few moments, as if in prayer. It was very moving. This man, dutiful, quietly pursuing his trade into the night without complaint—this seemed to me the height of patience.

Next day, we traveled to Mankumban: sea, sand, palm trees, a simple house for prayer. I was really looking forward to sleeping in that holy place for a few nights and doing prayers.

I did not have the peaceful retreat I had envisioned. I endured. It was very hot. The mosquitoes nearly ate us alive. The man leading the prayers was either too fast or too loud or both. I was glad to leave.

When we got back to Colombo, Bawa asked us about our trip. I thought I would score a few points by being honest about the experience, so I said, "Well, Bawa, I had a difficult time. I didn't see the Virgin Mary or have any spiritual experiences. It was hot and there were lots of mosquitoes."

Bawa said, "Child, if you put feces in a bowl of punch, no one can drink it."

As I had heard, being in Sri Lanka with Bawa was like being in a furnace. Bawa didn't waste any time. He worked very hard and fast with people. He just cut to the point. I had been trying to gain favor. Worse, I had brought all my impatience and all my desires and all the parts of me that were accustomed to being spoiled to a beautiful, spiritual place, and all I experienced were the inconveniences.

I was really down because I had traveled so far to be with the teacher and, number one, he hadn't remembered my name and, number two, whenever he spoke to me, he beat me. I talked with Dr. Ganesan, a physician who translated for Bawa. I confessed that I was depressed about my life because I had wasted so much time. Dr. Ganesan told me a story about a goat.

"A goat was tethered to a stake in the middle of a field. The owner, who really loved the goat, had placed a delicious ambrosia-like food at the base of the stake. The goat sniffed the delicacy and then moved to the end of its tether and began munching on the weeds and refuse at the edge of the field instead.

As it grazed, the goat walked in circles, beginning at the perimeter of the field and slowly moving inward in smaller and smaller circles as the rope wound around the stake. Eventually the goat came back to the delicious food again, as if stumbling upon it for the first time, and devoured it gratefully. The goat never again left the stake to search for other food."

It was an apt story. I could see that I was like the goat. The ambrosia was right there in front of me, and all I could say was, "I want something else."

I pondered the meaning of the story. Like all of us, I had come into the world fresh, innocent, and pure. Apart from my basic needs, I was at peace with myself and everything around me. As I grew, I moved farther and farther away from my delicious inner sense of contentment, reaching out for the pleasures of my senses, my intellect, and the external world. Eventually, after exhausting the possibilities, I came to understand the shortcomings of these distractions and began the journey back to my center, back to the peace of the true self.

The Bible says, "Except ye become as little children, ye shall not enter the kingdom of God." The point is purity and coming back to the pure food. I saw that I needed to come to grips with the difference between childish and childlike. My pouting over not getting the attention I wanted in the way I wanted it was childish. My irritation with the mosquitoes and the fellow leading the prayers at Mankumban were childish. I was acting out the petulance of my 'inner child' and missing completely the true childlike state of wonder, awe, and connection to God.

The trip to Sri Lanka deepened my commitment to my work with Bawa. Previously, I had considered myself a true disciple, but, as they say in AA, there's a big difference between talking the talk and walking the walk. I recognized that some of Bawa's disciples seemed to have more spiritual focus—they saw on every level what they had found in Bawa and were willing to turn their lives over to him completely. If Bawa suggested they marry someone, they did it, even if they had barely noticed the person before. I don't think I could have done that. Of course, I was with Jackie, so I had neatly sidestepped that issue. I had always prided myself on picking the cream of the crop, and I wasn't ready to leave that selection to someone else, even Bawa. I knew he arranged marriages, but I never went to him, surrendering everything, and said, "I'm a blank piece of paper. Please do with me what you will." I could appreciate the opportunity such a stance presented for breaking karmic patterns, but I held back. I did not have the commitment level of some of the people closest to Bawa.

Instead, I hung around on the outskirts, saying by my actions, "I'm pretty good, I've already got a girlfriend, and I want to be your disciple." That's a very different position.

When I brought up my difficulties with Jackie again just before I left Sri Lanka, Bawa mentioned that he was aware of some of Jackie's spikier characteristics and the problems they were causing.

He didn't say it, but I sensed he was thinking, *If you had come to me, you would have been married and in a situation different from this.* What he did say was, "Don't blame her." He was right. I knew I had only myself to blame. He also said that if I continued to conduct myself in the right way, my marriage could be a very good marriage by the time I was in my late sixties, very sweet and peaceful.

"Don't misunderstand me," he continued. "Don't think that what I am saying is solely related to her. These things I am saying you have to apply to yourself."

Another significant thing happened before I left Sri Lanka. Bawa looked at me one day and said, seemingly out of nowhere, "A man who drinks is like a cook with a knife. With alcohol in him, he might cut himself or even kill someone. A wise man doesn't drink.

Come up on the bed," Bawa said, and he held me and talked with me. Time passed in the dream and again I came to him and was trying to get up on the bed with him. "No, no," he said. "Not this time. You had that. Now you have to do some work.

—Locke Rush, Dream Journal

−18−

Now You Have To Do Some Work

Fortified by Bawa's encouragement to continue with my career plans, I started Mainstream, the first intensive outpatient treatment clinic for chemically dependent people in the Baltimore area. It was a gamble, but having seen the success of similar centers in Minnesota, I felt certain it would succeed, especially since Bawa had advised me that if I did this work with the proper intention and qualities, it would turn out well. It was 1982. I lived in Washington with Jackie and commuted to Baltimore to run the clinic.

Most treatment for chemically dependent people at that time was done on an inpatient basis, with stays of twenty-eight days to several months. Observation of people coming out of treatment and good old common sense had shown that inpatient treatment had a big downside, and most people didn't need it. People who entered inpatient care for weeks or months were branded, they had no salary coming in, some were in danger of having no job to return to, and the dollar cost was extremely high. For example, most inpatient treatment plans call for at least one psychiatrist attached to a unit, and every patient may be seen by a psychiatrist several times a week. In my opinion, that is completely unnecessary and makes the cost prohibitive for most people.

Since the nucleus of what you get in inpatient treatment requires only three or four hours a day at the most, someone realized that an addiction treatment program designed around the work week and augmented by attendance at AA meetings on weekends could provide the benefits of treatment without the downside. I visited a number of these centers in Minnesota and found that the recovery rates were equal to inpatient treatment at about one-third the cost.

I was impressed. Only one such center existed on the East Coast, and that was near Washington, DC. Its founder, George Kolodner, MD, helped me set up my clinic, and several of the centers I visited in Minneapolis also helped by giving me copies of their treatment plans. I found an ideal property situated on a river that ran through a woods in an old neighborhood community that was technically inside the Baltimore city limits but had a real country feel. A top medical doctor in Baltimore came on as my medical director and chief of staff. I couldn't have asked for a more auspicious beginning.

The old timers in AA laughed at me. "You can't do it on an outpatient basis." But we did.

My trip to Sri Lanka had enlivened my path, and I tried harder than ever to make use of the wisdom I had learned from Bawa as I conducted my daily affairs, both personal and professional.

I had been working in the field of alcoholism for several years, but I was still drinking socially. I no longer saw my drinking as a serious problem, but Bawa's words kept ringing in my ears: "A wise man doesn't drink." I could not help but remember the damage I had done to my life and be painfully aware that alcohol problems were common in my family. My bother John had died of alcoholism, and although my father had not been an alcoholic, I felt that alcohol was partly responsible for the distance between us.

As my father and I had both grown older, I had made attempts to get to know him better, but the only time he could be warm or communicative was when he had been drinking. So, although the alcohol had made him more communicative, it also had negatively affected his clarity. Under those circumstances, I could have one or the other, and never both at the same time.

Because I was running an alcoholism center, people assumed I did not drink. I was becoming increasingly uncomfortable about it. I never said I was a recovering alcoholic, but they assumed I was. I wasn't actually lying, but I was being dishonest. I should have said,

"No, actually, I do drink," but I didn't. By my silence, I was leading them to believe I did not drink. When I went to conferences, Jackie and I chose restaurants as far away from the hotel as possible so that I could have a beer with dinner. I was living a lie, and it really bothered me.

Within a year after my trip to Sri Lanka, I had my last drink, and the decision didn't seem to be born out of great resolve. It happened quite naturally. I realized that alcohol just didn't taste so good to me anymore, and it wasn't getting me high, either. The main reason I had started drinking in the first place was to feel mellow, and drinking wasn't making me feel mellow. I was just drinking out of habit.

Jackie and I were in Sicily at the time, vacationing. We were enjoying a romantic evening at a hotel overlooking the ocean. The waves were dashing against the cliffs below as we sat on the balcony, finishing a gourmet dinner. A bottle of wine sat on the table, about two-thirds full. I had just finished a glass. There was nothing unusual about the evening that would have brought it on, but something subtle must have shifted within me. I looked at my glass, I looked at the bottle, and I looked at Jackie. "I'm not going to drink anymore," I said, and I never did.

Bawa had returned to the States in late 1982, a few months after my trip to Sri Lanka. His health had become even more fragile. He was suffering from chronic bronchitis, emphysema, and frequent bouts of pneumonia. I took a room in the home of a Fellowship couple who lived down the street from the Fellowship so that Jackie and I could be nearby when we came to Philadelphia on the weekends.

When I was at the Fellowship, like almost everyone else, I waited eagerly for Bawa's room to 'open.' Weekends at the Fellowship were busy. Bawa spoke two or three times a day when he was well enough. Occasionally, I asked him about matters that were troubling me, but mostly I drank in his words and basked in his presence. I knew what I needed to work on.

Once I had stopped drinking, I felt so good about it that I was struggling with the reforming spirit of the 'saved.' I turned to Bawa for guidance, "Bawa, if people are creating their own problems and making a mess of their lives, shouldn't we tell them? Shouldn't we let them know? And why should we help them if they are just digging their own graves?"

He jumped on me. "Correcting people is not your role. You have to treat people like that kindly. You have to try and bring them peace and serve them. It is not your role to tell them that what they are doing is wrong and is causing their problems."

On a rational level, it seems appropriate to tell a person who is drinking to excess, "You can't drink alcohol. Look at what is happening. You are losing your bank account. You are losing your health." Eventually, however, I came to understand the wisdom in Bawa's words. I have worked in the addiction field for twenty more years since then, and I know that telling alcoholics they should not drink is probably the worst thing you can do. Encouraging them to keep coming to meetings and speaking of your own experience is best. Support and encouragement, rather than admonition, are more likely to open people's hearts to the possibility of change.

When Bawa was not available, I helped out a little in the kitchen with food preparation or cleanup. Since my time there was limited, I was limited in how much I could contribute in the way of work. I still felt like an 'auslander' as I watched people come and go freely from Bawa's room, busy with the duties they had taken on. This cadre surrounding any important person is inevitable, but I still think some people hung around just to be there. I remember Bawa once telling someone who wanted to spend more time with him, "Fleas on a dog don't get enlightenment." If that was a hint, it didn't change anything.

More and more frequently Bawa spoke from his bed. The space around the bed would fill up quickly, taken up by people who acted as if they had priority—the presidents and executive committee and whatnot—so it was hard to get up close.

There was a pecking order. I felt two ways about it. When you are on the outside, the in- and out-group thing is not pleasant, but perhaps it was appropriate. Some people took on a lot of duty and stayed physically very close to Bawa, and maybe the closeness was necessary for their growth. On the other hand, wanting to be close probably had a lot to do with our insecurities. Like children, we thought that 'Daddy' would love us more if he saw more of us.

I wanted to be sure Bawa knew I was there. I wanted a father. I wanted that connection of the heart. I wanted to be recognized and singled out. I wanted to be in the inner circle. It was an issue that frequently showed up in my dreams.

This seems a good time to talk about wisdom dreams. If you gather any two or three of Bawa's disciples together, talk is sure to turn to wisdom dreams in which Bawa's presence is palpably felt. Many of us had extraordinary dreams of Bawa when he was alive and continue to have them now. Even more astonishing, since Bawa's death, some people who did not know of Bawa when he was alive have developed a relationship with him in the dream state or in visions. The dreams don't come to me very often. They come when I need them. Now that I know what I need to do on my path and how to do it, I don't need them as much, but I wish I had more because they are wonderful and elevating.

There is a big difference between the wisdom dreams I am describing here and an ordinary dream. Having experienced six months of intense Jungian dream analysis, I am fairly familiar with dreams and their interpretation. In all dreams, the unconscious provides characters and places and objects and in other ways fleshes out the scene. Everything in a dream is an aspect of the dreamer's conscious or subconscious mind. This is the case in both regular dreams and wisdom dreams of Bawa, except that in wisdom dreams of Bawa, Bawa is actually there.

The difference between a wisdom dream of Bawa and an ordinary dream is that wisdom dreams do not feel like dreams. They feel like experiences. And they are. In a Bawa dream, Bawa is inside talking, and no imitation or mental image has the same properties. In ordinary dreams, people and objects change from one thing to another and do things they would never do in real life. In a Bawa dream, Bawa is always Bawa, and although he may indeed do or say something surprising, it is never out of character with his good qualities and deep wisdom.

Bawa dreams register on my consciousness in a very different way. Ordinary dreams seem a bit fuzzy in places and hard to hang onto. Bawa dreams are not fuzzy. They linger in the consciousness for years, almost like tailor-made koans.

Soon after I met Bawa, I dreamed I was sitting with him in a gathering of disciples. He surprised us by asking a woman to tell her story. She did so, warming to the task. I listened to everything but felt more an observer than part of the gathering. I felt unworthy and deeply desirous of being one with the spirit of love and unity. Bawa looked at me. "You think you are greater than your Master." I reacted strongly. "No! No! You have misjudged me."

In the dream, Bawa showed me what he was. He demonstrated in a humble but clear manner the power and simplicity of God by His miracles, and I knew that I was blessed to be in the same room. The dream had the flavor of sanctity, real, but unreal. The experience was lifelike, but much purer, with less of the mundane, worldly taste.

The following dream illustrates how I was projecting my father issues onto Bawa. He provided the steadying, paternal influence that I had missed when I was growing up, and I longed for his attention and approval.

> Bawa was getting ready to leave. Everyone was bustling about, preparing for his departure. He asked me to come and read from a book. The book contained the names of some Fellowship members. I tried to focus on the print, but it was too difficult. My eyes were weak.
>
> Finally, Bawa called out the names anyway, as if he had known them all along. My heart was full. I was preoccupied with Bawa and his departure. I did not know whether it meant death, the final departure, or whether it meant another trip to Sri Lanka. It seemed odd that I was dreaming of a departure when he had returned from Sri Lanka only a few months before.

> In the beginning of the dream, Bawa was calling the
> names of different Fellowship families and talking about
> their states and progress. I felt quietly upset that I was not
> good enough to be singled out.

I wanted to be recognized and singled out or wanted at least to
have my presence acknowledged. I wanted him to say I was a good
child. Only twice in the time I knew Bawa did he ever say anything
about me, once when I was out of the room, and I was desperate
to find out what he had said! The other time, he said, referring to
me, "He doesn't cause any problems. He just comes and sits quietly.
He doesn't cause any problems." I wanted him to say, "Oh, he's
wonderful, he's enlightened," but no. All he said was, "He doesn't
cause any problems."

Another dream was especially pertinent to the desire for
recognition that haunted me.

> Bawa was well and loving all his children. He embraced
> them, one by one. Some he held for a long time. I felt
> separate. I was not one of the people he was embracing. I
> wanted it so much.
>
> Bawa jumped up and walked quickly through a hall into
> another room and then returned to his bed. Finally I looked
> at him from a short distance. I felt tears in my eyes for my
> love and need of him. He saw me and fixed my eyes with his.
> He had tears in his eyes, and the look said, "You have not
> come to embrace me, but nevertheless I embrace you from
> this distance. I love you and understand you."

The dream showed me that I came to Bawa not with a heart full
of giving but with a desperate wanting to be loved and pampered
and stroked and told I was a good child. Instead of giving up my
ego and surrendering to my teacher, I wanted my teacher to come
to me.

In my pain of longing, I went again to Dr. Ganesan. "Bawa
doesn't notice me. He doesn't know I am here. It's killing me."

"Yes, he does."

"How can I make sure he does? How can I get some attention? What should I do?"

Dr. Ganesan told me to show Bawa I was there. "Make a dent," he encouraged me, his eyes twinkling.

How was I to make a dent? I watched how other people handled the situation. One fellow, nicknamed Gold Leaf Howard because he was supervising the gold leaf work on a House of God that Bawa was building as an addition to the Fellowship house, plowed through all the barriers with his humor and wit. He was loud and flamboyant and quite lovable. He'd walk right in and sit down and say to Bawa, "How you doin', Pussycat?" People would say, "You can't call Bawa Pussycat!"

Bawa just laughed. "This child has a very good heart. He has a sweet heart. It makes no difference what he calls me." It was always fun to listen to Gold Leaf Howard's conversations with Bawa. People like Gold Leaf Howard brushed right past the guardians at the gate. That just wasn't my style. I didn't want to make trouble by challenging anyone's authority. I needed another solution.

Soon I hit upon an idea. I would bring Bawa Tamil films! I found a special store in Washington that carried all the latest releases, so they were sure to be films he had not seen. I was optimistic. Now the people who surrounded Bawa during his non-public times couldn't turn me away. I had created a practical reason to gain access to his room.

The first time I brought the films, I tapped on Bawa's door. Someone opened the door an inch or two and said, "Bawa is resting."

I indicated the video cartridges. "I've brought Bawa some Tamil films," I said, keeping a firm grip on them. After a moment's hesitation, the door opened to admit me. They had to let me in. Every weekend I brought films. Although Bawa acknowledged my presence, he never singled me out, and I was afraid he still didn't remember my name.

I thought back to my time in Sri Lanka when he had asked my name. I remembered the sound of my name as he repeated it.

"Locke." He told me I had to lay my heart open. "Unlock your mind. Unlock your life." He gazed at me and said my name again. "Locke." I knew what he meant. When you are working with other people, as I was, you have to be open. You can't be open if your heart is locked. I needed to learn humility. As Bawa often said, the more you make yourself humble and ask forgiveness, the more your true exaltedness is seen. To do that, you have to let go, open up, and admit that your puffed up ego is not worth very much. In admitting that, your heart opens and you receive a great deal.

As a result of my father going away to war, my trials at boarding school, and my parents' divorce, I had locked my doors, one by one, shutting away a big part of who I am, including my nameless trust in God. Bawa saw that and addressed it. I had used defense mechanisms to get through life, and I needed to start unlocking them.

We human beings are strange. Miracles surround us, but we don't have the eyes to see them. Babies know. Full of wonder and knowing no limitations, babies reach for the moon shining in the window,. Babies are totally sensitive. They love others unconditionally. When you bring a baby into a roomful of noisy people, the energy shifts. Everyone quiets down. A speechless, three-week-old baby draws everyone's attention. Why? Because infants are pure. You can almost see the light that streams from them. It is the closest thing to God we can see.

Bawa was an adult with an infant's purity and light. Fused with it were a mature intellect, a conscious and continuous link with God, and vast knowledge that came not from books or scriptures but from experience and inner knowing. All the things I had only dreamed about were present in this tiny but fully mature human being, and they revealed themselves as they needed to be revealed. This is why when Bawa said certain things to me, even things I may have heard or thought and dismissed before, they made a big impact. There is no way for me to prove this to anyone, but I have never experienced anything like it with anyone else I have encountered.

As Bawa became more frail and unable to physically embrace his children, people lined up after his discourses to greet him and kiss his hand. Usually, he held out his hand, palm down, but I had noticed that occasionally Bawa would turn his hand and open his palm to someone.

He had never offered me the palm of his hand. It seemed to me that he barely acknowledged me. He would hold out the back of his hand, perhaps nodding in my direction while apparently focused on making sure the little children got their chocolates, observing others in the room, or conversing with someone else. His action may have been designed to push my ego buttons. If so, it worked.

One day, just as I was about to kiss the back of his hand, he turned it palm up. There is something very auspicious about the open hand. It is a symbol of the open heart and the giving of bounty. The inside of the palm is very tender. I believe that Bawa recognized that the disciple in me was ready. I was ready to say that I needed his love, and I was ready to receive it. I had recognized my need for him as a true father and, instead of waiting for him to come to me, I was coming to him without reservation.

I kissed his palm and lingered there for a moment. He put his other hand around the back of my neck, stroked it, and patted me. I melted. He had seen into my heart and given me what I needed most. It brings tears to my eyes to remember that moment now, and the memory has satisfied my longing for years. He knew exactly what to give. Bawa knew that I was very much bound up with ego and very willful. Having been born with a charming personality, I was accustomed to getting my own way. Charm didn't work with Bawa. The way he dealt with me was perfect. If he had given me the attention and praise I craved when I was silently demanding it, you see, it would have been just another triumph.

Such are the miracles and the power of goodness that come from a person who is totally good and close to God. Bawa told us that if we would do the practices he told us about and cultivate our good qualities, we would come closer and closer to God, and eventually God would bestow His treasures upon us.

Although being in Bawa's presence was important, it would have meant nothing if I had not tried to apply the wisdom I learned from him to my daily life. He continually exhorted us to develop the qualities of God: patience, compassion, tolerance, and peacefulness. I strove to do this in my work at Mainstream.

My biggest challenge, however, was my relationship with Jackie. I was impatient. I wanted constant affection, and Jackie didn't want to give it. I pitied myself: *what did I do to deserve this?* After I spoke with Bawa in Sri Lanka, I began to see that maybe it was my fault. I was overreaching and too needy or too dependent. When I started correcting those things, everything started to change for the better. The work to be done in a relationship is always work on ourselves, never on the other person, although the individual work we do often has a positive effect on the other person. When I stopped reacting in the old way, I could see Jackie watching me very carefully and making an effort because of it. When I gave in and let go and did what I knew she wanted me to do even when I didn't want to, she really appreciated it.

An interesting thing happened about a year after I returned from Sri Lanka. I found that old list I had made of Jackie's faults. As I read it over, I saw that almost miraculously all of her 'faults' had disappeared or had at least dramatically improved. My life was better, our relationship was better, and I was better. This great improvement had come about because I had worked on changing myself instead of trying to change Jackie. The process had been quite simple. There had been no need for long, purging sessions with a therapist. I was pleasantly surprised, and I hoped that I could be a catalyst for change in the lives of my patients as they coped with addiction and their own difficult relationships.

In any good therapeutic process, the issues arise fairly quickly: my mother doesn't understand me, my husband yells at me, my wife doesn't understand my schedule, and so forth. The traditional way of dealing with these issues is to encourage the parties involved to open their hearts to each other. When a conflict surfaces, everyone works to sort out who is right and find compromises and adjustments so that the marriage can continue with less friction. Even so, the old ways reappear. We tend to revert to our old habits of dealing with each other. That is why, I have found, that of ten couples who come for counseling only two or three are really willing to work at their marriages; of those two or three, maybe one couple will have the courage and spiritual strength to persevere with the work it requires to bring about real change.

When Jackie and I decided to get married, we had been together for seven years. Before we made definite plans, however, we wanted Bawa's blessing and guidance, especially since for three years Bawa had been putting me off whenever I brought up the subject. "No. It's too soon. You have to spend more time together."

Now we really did feel ready to make a lifetime commitment, but getting in to see Bawa in 1985 was not easy. He was quite ill, and his energy was rationed out to giving discourses when he could and to other important matters. Since Jackie and I were in Philadelphia together only on weekends, we were often frustrated in our attempts to speak with him.

One afternoon I asked Dr. Ganesan if we could meet with Bawa to request his blessing for our marriage. Through the open door, I saw that Bawa had just sat up after a rest. He motioned for us to enter the room. As Doctor Ganesan translated to Bawa in Tamil our request for his blessing, Bawa took our hands and placed his, mine, and Jackie's together, one on top of the other. Looking at us with great compassion, he said a prayer asking God for His blessing that Jackie and I would have a long and bountiful life together. All the while I was breathing in a fragrance that was lovely, a combination of sandalwood and musk. This was most unusual since neither Bawa nor any of the people who attended him wore fragrance because of Bawa's delicate lungs.

He told us that we were married. "Now," he said, "go do it legally." Bawa had looked into our hearts and seen that we were ready for the next step, and so he had proceeded.

Somewhat in shock, Jackie and I withdrew from his room as man and wife. That night we had a small and quiet celebration at my mother's home, and a few weeks later we had a legal Quaker wedding.

Sufi Master M. R. Bawa Muhaiyaddeen

What has to die will die, and what has to remain will remain. Just because the well went dry, you cannot say that there is no water there. …those who have real thirst will dig a little deeper, and they will find water there. That which dies is dead and gone, but that which is will always be..

—M.R. Bawa Muhaiyaddeen,
Questions of Life,
Answers of Wisdom, Volume 1

-19-

WHAT IS WILL ALWAYS BE

Bawa died on December 8, 1986, peacefully slipping away. Many of his disciples were devastated. What would they do now? they wondered. Who would teach them? But Bawa had explained this situation while he was alive: he was in our hearts, and he would always be in our hearts. We needed only to turn inward for his guidance.

I always feel guilty saying this, but when Bawa passed away, I experienced a curious lightness. I did not feel he was gone. I felt he was closer to me than ever. A piece of Bawa had gone inside me, a little vibrating heart that gave me a sense of well-being. That vibrating piece of Bawa inside me was like the hug a child gets from his father that makes it possible for him to go outside on his own and explore.

Bawa also left his words for us and for generations to come. Quite a few books of Bawa's discourses have been published, and a vast audiovisual library of his work has been archived. What Bawa told me and the qualities he exemplified are imprinted on my heart. My link to these qualities and to God is my conscience. This inner guidance is free. There is no down payment, but like a good fruit, you have to eat it when it is ripe or it will rot.

Essentially, Bawa's message was that God exists and life has meaning. He suggested that we should inquire into the nature of our lives: Where did we come from? What is the purpose of life? Is this life all there is? Is there some existence after death and, if so, what? Where is justice if I can be mistreated and not get even? Why should I change if someone else is at fault? Why is life so unfair? Why did God do this to us?

Bawa Muhaiyaddeen understood these problems well, and his answers were simple:

> *We come from God, Who is eternal.*
>
> *Inside us is a tiny piece of flesh that is of God.*
>
> *We come here to understand our true heritage and nature.*
>
> *Life is a university and everything that*
> *happens to us is a teaching.*
>
> *How well we learn from the things around*
> *us in life determines our progress.*
>
> *Our innermost being is composed of the 99 beautiful qualities*
> *of God, among them compassion, patience, tolerance,*
> *forgiveness, understanding, wisdom, peacefulness, justice,*
> *forbearance, truthfulness, generosity, and love for all beings.*
>
> *Our Godly qualities are obscured by illusion, mind, and*
> *desire, and by the base inclinations arising out of our*
> *connection to the elements from which we are formed.*
> *These veils are inescapable; we all have them.*
>
> *Our life task is to clear away these veils and find the*
> *true self. This is the path to peace here and forever. If we*
> *can die to the world before we die, there is no death.*

These understandings unfold as part of the growth process of becoming fully human beings. This, I see now, is really the spiritual path of which I had intimations early in my life. Many opportunities to grow are afforded us. If we have wisdom, we make the best use of them.

I haven't followed Bawa's advice at all well, maybe only fifty percent of the time, but even that low percentage has brought many, many good changes. And what have I lost? Only a little bit of ego. That's the only thing you can lose.

There is a great power in changing just one little thing. If you can change just one little thing, it is amazing what comes from that. It is hard to do, but the more difficult it is, the more valuable it is. We can go as far as we want to go. And if we really want to walk the path, we can change everything.

Repeatedly, Bawa said, "Little by little, bit by bit. Just keep at it." He also said, "Don't try to drink an ocean of water in a single gulp. Take tiny sips." This is a challenge, because it's hard to maintain the faith that little tiny sips will quench our thirst before we die. We are impatient, and impatience leads to hastiness which leads to anger which leads to sin.

In addition to his words and the lasting effect of his presence upon us, Bawa left us something else: Islam. Not long after Bawa returned to the United States from a visit to Sri Lanka in 1982, he announced that we were going to build a God's house, a mosque.

Although even Bawa's earliest manuscripts, like *The Resonance of Allah*, had a strong Islamic focus, Bawa did not introduce his Western disciples to five-times prayer and fasting until the early eighties. He did, however, introduce silent *Zikr*, which I have described earlier in the book. Later, he said that no one was doing it correctly. Dr. Ajwad told me, "It was too soon. People had not done the necessary work on themselves to be able to utilize the *Zikr*. Everyone wanted the *Ill-Allahu*, the filling. No one was doing the *La ilaha*, the voiding." Because we were bringing God's name into a space that had not been cleared, Bawa gave us recitations for clearing. One was *Allahu Akbar, al-hamdu lillah* (God is great, all praise belongs to God), which we were to recite one hour a day for forty days. I completed this practice a few times.

Some of Bawa's disciples were resistant to following the practices of Islam; they had been drawn to Bawa because the rigid confines of formal religion had not satisfied them. I had no reaction. By that time, I had drunk at least a few draughts from the cups of a number of religions. I had been a baptized and confirmed Episcopalian, a Zen Buddhist, a Tibetan Buddhist, a serious practitioner of yoga, and a devotee of an Indian guru. I was not turned on or off by any religion; I was just looking for truth. I was looking for the right person to guide me, and that person was Bawa. None of the spiritual guides I met before Bawa had resonated with me. Bawa was the one who had resonated, and if he wanted us to practice Islam, then I would do that. I could learn Arabic prayers just as comfortably as I had learned Buddhist chants and Hindu mantras.

I understood why some people were resistant, but I remember Bawa telling us that we needed a boat to get across the river because the currents are rapid and dangerous in many spots. "If you don't have a boat," he told us, "you can't get across the river." He went on to say that the boat often has aspects of different religious practices. I remember very well that Bawa paused and looked around the room. "Of course," he said, "if any of you think that you have already gotten across, then you don't need the boat." No one said anything.

I had the following wisdom dream during those early days of Islam in the Fellowship. It reflects my deep level of acceptance.

> We were in a chamber, and I was talking to a cat, large and tawny. The cat understood me. All of us in that area were waiting. We were stuck. Someone with a long staff pushed open two large metal gates, and someone else said it was St. Peter. In front of us was a long, bright, golden esplanade.
>
> I entered a large building. I was with a brother and sister from the Fellowship. The building was somewhat like a cathedral with many chambers. I wasn't sure what it was. Then I saw a mosque, trimmed in gold and shining, with blue edges, and I knew that the place was Islam. People were explaining the wonders to be found there. The rooms were full of manuscripts and mosques and ancient books and miniature temples.
>
> I was with Fatimah, a Fellowship friend. I read her a date: 1323. I forget the actual day. I believe it was January something, 1323. The words had to do with her. She had been alive then and somehow knew it. It was a medieval time. I hugged two gold and red brocaded cushions and started to cry silently.

I walked from room to room. Others were standing
and gazing at the different mosques and religious items. I
was thrilled in my heart that the mosque was there, and
I wandered around and felt relief and a growing sense of
realization that I had stumbled across something of value.
Fatimah seemed to feel the same. I read to her from a
manuscript. It pleased her and made her wonder.

The dream was not so much a dream of great joy and light but
of a door being opened to reveal recognizable things of Islam in the
large space beyond. Splendor and silence filled the place. We had to
see and read what was there, absorb it. The dream symbolized a shift
from waiting to finding.

It was a great mercy that Bawa left us with the mosque and the
practices of Islam. His presence had been an anchor for us all. After
his death, Islam served as my anchor. Caramanli Dawn, the palm
reader I met in India, had been correct in her prophecy: as far-fetched
as it had seemed at the time, I had become a student of Islam.

Even after Bawa's death, I continued to struggle with the childish
desire to be given my place beside him without having to work for
it. One night I had the following dream:

I was talking to Bawa, seeing him, sitting at his feet. It
was bittersweet: sweet to be near him, bitter to know that I
am not. Every day, I went through a field to a small, raised
platform where Bawa sat so that I could listen to him talk.
I was the only one there. One day when I went, something
was different. Bawa asked me to get up on the platform with
him. The locale changed as I started to climb up, and we
were on another platform somewhere else.

I wanted to enter where others had entered, and I wanted
to climb up on the platform again, but Bawa wouldn't allow
it. "No. You cannot earn this here. You must earn it while
you are on the earth." I asked several times, pleading, but he
was firm—not discouraging, but firm.

It was a powerful dream. In one part I was able to climb up on the platform; later I could not. When I was in a state of childlike purity, I could do it. As soon as I demanded to do it, he let me know that he had taken me into his heart, but it was time for me to mature. I had to do the work.

Sometimes people ask me if I have found another teacher. I have no need for another teacher. Bawa is with me always in my heart. His words live in his books and in the hearts of all of his children.

I have also learned that everything around us provides a teaching. A dog's affection and obedience to its master show us the meaning of loyalty. A lioness suckling eight cubs that are constantly tugging and biting is an example of patience. A root seeking water is an example of perseverance. A good mother dealing with three young children at the supermarket provides a humbling example of tolerance and forbearance. The eyes of a baby show us our connection to God. The school of life is filled with teachers who show us how to use our wisdom and provide examples of the qualities that will help us grow into evolved human beings.

My parents were good teachers. Now that I have resolved my childhood disappointment in my father, I think only good of him. I never, ever heard my father say anything bad about another person. I never heard him gossip or speak ill of anyone. I never heard him be spiteful. These qualities are the most beautiful treasures he gave me. I have stopped blaming my father for the divorce. I imagine my parents were equally at fault, and it is clear that World War II strained their marriage to the breaking point.

My mother taught me generosity and thoughtfulness. If someone was coming to visit and she knew the person liked peanut butter ice cream, she would travel thirty-five miles to buy peanut butter ice cream. When people crossed the threshold of our home, she treated them like royalty.

Nothing was too much effort. If they were spending the night, she prepared the room with great care, put fresh flowers by the bedside, and laid out books that matched their interests. When I was younger, I thought things like these were silly, but I don't think that anymore. She was caring and thoughtful, and I love her for it. She filled her life with service to others, and it flowed from her quite naturally. It was a great teaching.

I have had many teachers in my life, only a few of whom have been mentioned here. Most of them are unaware of how they have influenced my life. All are examples of God's power working in people who make an effort. If we can develop good qualities, good things will happen. Our good qualities are the unspoken wisdom we give to others.

Wisdom calms your worries, and lovingly teaches the mind how to be peaceful. Then your qualities become peaceful, and your thoughts and intentions become peaceful. The wisdom you have inside yourself is the very best psychology. It will never abandon you. It will be there to teach you what you need to know. Please reflect on this.

—M.R. Bawa Muhaiyaddeen

–20–

Wisdom Psychology

Mainstream prospered and grew from a staff of two to more than twelve. We saw over one hundred clients a week. Intensive outpatient care for chemically dependent people was well on its way to acceptance. Business was so good that my administrative duties left me no time for hands-on work with clients. Therefore I was somewhat relieved when I was offered a good price for the business. I sold it, agreeing to stay on as a consultant for two years.

I am convinced that my success in this endeavor—how I got the space, how I set up the clinic, and the ease with which it all unfolded—was due to Bawa. These things don't happen so easily in normal circumstances.

In 1988, through a friend's introduction, I met a psychiatrist from Philadelphia who was director of the alcoholism treatment program at the Institute of Pennsylvania Hospital, which was at that time the oldest and most prestigious psychiatric hospital in Philadelphia, perhaps in the United States. We hit it off very well; his interest in intensive outpatient care dovetailed nicely with my experience. He asked me to work part time at the Institute, and I accepted. Thus began a seven-year period of working at IPH, eventually on a full-time basis.

Two factors made this unexpected offer especially serendipitous. First, the opportunity to work in Philadelphia was an answer to a prayer. Although Bawa was no longer physically here, I wanted to live close to the Fellowship community. Jackie understood. She worked four days a week in Washington and came up for long weekends, which we spent together at my mother's home in Paoli and at the Fellowship. The second factor that made the offer especially serendipitous was revealed in an interesting coincidence.

As I was walking down the main corridor on my first day at IPH, I saw a familiar picture on the wall. It was a copy of a painting done in 1813 by the prominent portrait painter Edward Savage. The subject of the portrait was Dr. Benjamin Rush, my great, great, great grandfather! The original was hanging over the fireplace in my mother's home. Dr. Rush was a signer of the Declaration of Independence and Surgeon General to George Washington, but perhaps most important to me, he was known as the Father of American Psychiatry.

He was born in the mid-1700s when people believed that mental patients were either possessed by the devil or dammed by God. They were fed garbage or very meager rations and were left to rot in their own excrement in dimly lit basement cells. People paid admission fees to gape at 'the animals.'

Dr. Rush pioneered a new way to deal with these unfortunates. He saw their humanity and advocated a compassionate and more hopeful approach. He insisted that they be kept clean and properly clothed, and he moved them to better quarters. Although the Institute of Pennsylvania Hospital was not built until the 1840s, after Dr. Rush's death, it was located and designed according to his views on treating the mentally ill: a country setting and beautiful grounds with a little trolley going around it for the patients; large, airy, well-heated rooms; a recreation program; art and music therapy.

Moreover, Dr. Rush was the first person to treat alcoholism as a disease. Until he came along, the general view was that people who drank to excess were simply morally corrupt. There was no insight into the role of nutrition or into the possibility that a coexisting psychiatric problem, such as bipolar disorder, might cause people to self-medicate with alcohol.

What a strange and wonderful twist of fate. God is always at work. I had known that Dr. Rush played a prominent role in the early days of psychiatry, but I hadn't realized that his ideas had been the basis for the design and formation of the Institute. And now, nearly two hundred years later, I was working at the hospital he inspired, trying to understand as he did human nature and trying to find a better, wiser, more spiritual way to cope with the problems of my patients.

Like Dr. Rush, I understood that you have to take the soul into consideration when you are dealing with human beings, no matter what their state. You have to make a place for the invisible, for that which you can't see but which motivates and is a person's base and center.

Even now, traditional psychiatry is not very interested in the spiritual side of a human being. Psychiatric hospitals take a generally allopathic or symptomatic approach, usually chemical: find the problem, match it with a drug, and administer the dosage. This kind of psychiatry treats the result of the illness and not the cause.

Even talk therapy is dying out in the psychiatric field. The cognitive folk, who believed that talking out issues was a way of massaging the fear out, are retiring. The younger ones are not trained to rely on talk therapy. Because of the way the HMOs operate, you have to process people quickly to make a decent living. If you can find a medication that fits the condition, you don't have to spend so much time talking to clients. The downside is that the roots of the problem are not treated and most clients remain dependent on medication.

The psychiatrists I encountered in my work were ordinary people who went through standard medical training followed by some psychiatric training and a residency. Treatment was done by the book. I saw strange contradictions. Patients who could have benefited from talk therapy and the like were given antidepressants and anti-anxiety drugs and discharged, while schizophrenics and people with manic-depressive disorders who were not in much shape to benefit from it were seen three or four times a week in individual sessions at $150 an hour. Psychiatrists applied the classic Freudian technique: *What do you think? How do you feel?* They took notes, dictated them, and it all added up to money for time spent. The treatment plans were designed that way, and the psychiatrists were conditioned to believe that what they were doing was really important.

I am sure they meant well. I met a few psychiatrists who were quite good, but most were too young to have gathered much life experience and certainly had not evolved to a point of wisdom in their own lives. What is more, the suicide and alcoholism rate among psychiatrists is eye opening, for it is higher than that for the average person on the street.

My question is this: how can a twenty-eight-year-old person who has just finished a residency—no matter how intelligent and well-trained in medicine—effectively treat a sixty-year-old who is depressed, has little self-value, and is drinking too much? Young doctors have not lived long enough to understand such a patient, and I have observed that most don't feel comfortable getting into those waters. It's not surprising. It's much easier to find a medication that will control the symptoms, especially when many clients are looking for a quick fix themselves. Most of the psychiatrists I observed did not bring clients a spiritual outlook or even a proven, pragmatic, cognitive solution based on their own experience.

I was therefore relieved to note that at the 1994 Annual American Psychiatric Association Convention in Washington, DC, the most popular speaker was Scott Peck, MD, whose book *The Road Less Traveled* focuses on a spiritual approach to treating mental illness. I suspect that the interest was more intellectual than spiritual at first, but I am heartened to see that among the many approaches represented in the APA, spiritual psychiatry is now by far the fastest growing area.

I wonder, though, how serious the interest is. If you were to select a random sample of psychiatrists and ask, "What do you think about the power of God in a person?" my hunch is that only a small number would view the power of God as the catalyst for change.

In my opinion, psychologists and social workers, although they are not authorized to prescribe medication, are often a better choice for people who want talk therapy. But here, too, the focus is more on alleviating symptoms than on cultivating a spiritual approach to life. For example, modern psychology encourages us to express our anger, but venting our negative emotions on the people who frustrate us only compounds the problem: the target of our anger feels worse, and this leads to more anger and recrimination. Even confining the anger to beating pillows in the therapist's office only empties the anger bucket temporarily.

If you want to see an example of a really good therapist, watch the film *Good Will Hunting*. The therapist had total confidence in his approach. He was wiser than the kid but kind of a big kid himself. He had lived it all and was not afraid to share his experiences, but he also knew when to be quiet. He couldn't be bamboozled. He knew when to draw the boundaries. He was not worried about money or fame or his reputation. He was keenly interested in helping a young man learn about his soul.

Real change is not quick or easy. In the early days of my practice, I followed the approach of asking clients how they felt about the things that were going wrong in their lives. I could not fail to observe that there was rarely any lasting change. They were stuck in their reactions and their stories. Now I say, "Tell me what you don't want to tell me and you can save a lot of money." Surprisingly, they often do. I say, "Pardon me, but my experience tells me this: if you know you have difficulty with this thing, you are not going to change it by talking about it or writing it down. The only way to change it is to act the opposite to it."

God has given us antidotes for all the dark things within us. For anger, it's patience or tolerance or forgiveness. Feeling angry and acting just a little contrary to your anger—just a little—is worth ten sessions with a therapist. If you can refrain from acting out your anger and find a way to de-fuse it, the calm you achieve cannot help but have a positive effect on the situation. For fear, it's affirmative action, done in little bits and pieces. I find that the quickest way to break through a barrier of fear, for example, is to do what you fear doing. When I was working at the psychiatric hospital near Baltimore, I was afraid to ask for a salary increase; when I finally did it, I got more than a raise—I got past a lot of my old baggage.

Bawa taught me that love is what heals. Even when a medicine is administered, love is the healing factor. I am convinced this is true. Bawa's love is what healed me. Love helps you believe in yourself and trust that you can grow from any circumstances. Love is the support for change.

To be effective, a therapist must experience real empathy with a patient and feel the person's pain, not just see it intellectually. Empathy establishes a connection with the client, who can sense it immediately. Trust develops, and without trust, there can be no effective healing. First, however, a therapist must be able to look at his or her own problems objectively and resolve them, in much the same way that I worked on my own bad qualities to bring about change in my marriage.

When people consult with me, I try to make them comfortable. I look them in the eyes and embrace them lightly when they leave if it seems appropriate. This is what I learned from Bawa. Sometimes it surprises people a bit when I embrace them, but they like it. The ones who are open come back. I also follow many AA principles in my work, no matter what issues a client brings. The most valuable of these has been speaking from my own experience rather than giving advice. This is the method I use with my clients, and I don't think that talking or journaling or screaming or beating pillows works any faster, if at all.

One of my jobs at IPH was to serve as liaison and consultant to Mill Creek School, which was situated on the grounds of the hospital. In this capacity, I monitored the chemical dependency problems of students and facilitated group therapy sessions with the 'problem kids.' These kids also went to a group run by a psychiatrist. Once I asked them how their group was going.

They laughed and exchanged looks. "We pulled his chain for an hour and Marcia threw a fit."

"What are you saying?"

"Aw, Dr. Rush, that guy is so full of shit."

Later, when I talked to one of the girls, she told me that no trust had been established. "He comes in with his little notebook, all business, and we just play tricks on him or we don't say anything."

One of the students, seventeen-year-old Susan, was seeing a woman psychiatrist regularly, but they were making little headway. The psychiatrist wanted control, and the girl, reminded of her domineering and abusive mother, resisted.

The psychiatrist asked if I would sit in on a session, and next day we all met. After several minutes, the psychiatrist had lost control and was angry, and the girl was crying hysterically and shouting accusations at the psychiatrist. The girl had some trust in me because previously I had spent a little time getting to know her in a non-clinical mode. I knew how she felt and what she needed. I calmed her down and asked what was bothering her. Susan replied, "*She just doesn't listen.*" What she meant was that the psychiatrist didn't grasp the suffering underneath her words. When I asked Susan why she had said such hurtful, accusatory things to the psychiatrist, out tumbled, amidst a flood of tears, the real pain in her heart. The healing had begun.

Listening, really listening, is an essential quality for a therapist of any kind, and it is not something you can learn in a book. My mother instinctively knew the value of listening to others and nurturing them. When she was in her seventies, she 'cured' a distant relative, Fred, who had struggled with serious mental illness for many years. He had spent quite a while in a mental hospital where he had received countless electroshock treatments. Eventually, he calmed down enough to be released, and although he could function well enough to drive a car and write out checks, he was emotionally disadvantaged and quite eccentric. One day, he dropped by to see my mother, and soon he became a regular visitor.

On these visits, Mother and Fred would sit in the kitchen. She'd fix him a nice meal and sit near the stove, mending things, while he talked. She didn't say much. She'd just listen, even when he was talking gibberish. She knew he needed to talk. She'd nod and say, "Yes, dear," while she sewed. After a few weeks, everyone in the family noticed that Fred was doing a lot better. Since he wasn't receiving any treatment other than these weekly visits with my mother, we had to admit that she was the reason for his turnaround.

This is a perfect example of the power of listening. My mother had no training whatsoever as a therapist, but she knew how to listen and love unconditionally. Soon, Fred was well enough to set up a small baking business, and it was a success.

Bawa spoke of the need for a 'melting heart.' Without a melting heart we cannot be peaceful, and if we are not peaceful, we will not be able to guide anyone else to peace. How can we know another's heart unless we know our own? We need to dig deep down into ourselves so that we can discover and understand our own destructive qualities as well as the potential of our good qualities to heal any illness.

In my practice now, when someone is telling me a story I watch for clues—a faltering voice or something happening with the eyes. When I see it, I interrupt immediately. "What's happening? Something has changed." Usually the tears begin to flow. It is easy for people to get stuck in their stories, but their stories are far less important than their reactions to those stories.

Bawa's approach of God Psychology drastically changed my way of dealing with my problems and the problems of my clients. Book psychology addresses the developmental issues; the effects of emotional, physical, and sexual abuse; the effects of the unfairness, injustice, and punishment that inevitably are part of a child's conditioning; and so on. These factors certainly create problems that must be resolved. However, there is something a priori to all of that. We have physical bodies, and our physical bodies are made up of physical elements that have the potential to destroy each other when they are out of balance: earth, fire, water, air, and ether. Associated with the elements are certain base inclinations toward that which is lowest in our nature, toward that which is not part of our humanity but part of our animal nature. Bawa called these the *nafs*. The *nafs* can also be described as desires that incite us toward what is evil. The *nafs* were there when we were formed in the womb, and they are part of what we are. The developmental issues surely add on to the problem by stirring up the *nafs*, but the original sin is mistaking these base desires for who we are and letting them run our lives unchecked. One way we do this is by justifying our mistreatment of others with the excuse that someone else is responsible for our actions: *He made me do it!*

According to Bawa, the *nafs* incite a specific cluster of negative qualities associated with each element: fear (earth), anger (fire), lust (water), desire (air), illusion (ether). It is impossible to get rid of the *nafs*. Even people who are spiritually advanced feel anger and the other negative qualities from time to time. The difference is that they have learned to restrain themselves from acting on the negativity, which neutralizes its potential to harm others or themselves. The practice of restraint develops outer patience. According to Bawa, outer patience is the first step in developing good qualities, followed by inner patience, contentment, trust in God and, finally, gratitude to God for everything that happens. He also said that the enlightened person can command the cells of the body to purify themselves.

To bring this discussion from the esoteric to the practical, I must speak from my experience. When I can suspend my reactions for even two seconds, which is hard enough to do, that is often the whole battle. Even two seconds of outer patience gives inner patience a chance to take over. Whenever I exercise outer patience, my overall impatience shrinks just a little bit. This is an example of the true meaning of *jihad*. The real holy war is fought inside us, and the *nafs* are the unbelievers.

If the concept of *nafs* or base desires sounds strange, suspend your disbelief for just a bit and consider it. All religions address the tendency to evil in our nature. Most of us agree with the sages who have said that we live in a world of illusion, but I don't think we understand what that means. We act as if we are only what we appear to be, but underneath the skin of the homeliest or most beautiful face and body, we are all the same: flesh, blood, bones, sinew. Saints and sinners are made of the same physical stuff. People with wisdom are not taken in by the allure of the body because they see that it is only flesh and blood and bone and sinew. What makes it hard for us to accept this evidence of the animal side of our nature is that we don't usually see it for what it really is; we see only the outer shell and the social graces and the pretenses and all the illusions we project upon the forms of the world. Some people glorify their evil tendencies: *It's a dog eat dog world.* Others refuse to accept their evil tendencies: *I'm not like that!*

Psychiatry and psychology often fail because they do not address the original *nafs.* We were born to discover who we are. We have two sides to our nature, animal and divine, and it is the conflict between these two opposing forces within us that causes our pain. Inside the elemental form is the essence of God, which is our highest potential, but how can we find the essence of God? We can't. We can, however, find the qualities that are the formless form of God. We can practice the qualities of God, starting with outer patience and gradually developing inner patience, contentment, surrender, and gratitude. Through this practice, the base desires are controlled by our developing wisdom, and the Godly qualities eventually become who we are. Moving with the actions of the qualities is what will bring us peace. With peace comes understanding and with understanding comes the fulfillment of our lives.

We can change our lives if we make the effort. Someone asked Bawa about the role of destiny in determining our lives. He replied, "If our destiny was already decided, then why did God send the prophets and why am I here talking to you now?" Everyone laughed. "Parents do many things that affect us, but those influences can be washed away, just like dirt can be washed out of a fabric."

Psychology can help us see the dirt we gathered while we were developing, and, practiced correctly, it can help us wash it out. The original stuff, however, the original anger or fire arising out of the belly, the original lust arising out of the water, the original fear arising out of the earth, the original desire arising out of the air, the original illusion arising out of the ether—these can be controlled only by wisdom and by practicing the qualities of God.

Practicing the divine qualities brings peace even to those who are emotionally troubled or mentally ill. For severe disorders like schizophrenia or manic depression, of course, drug therapy is necessary. The majority of people seeking help, however, are struggling with ordinary anxieties and depression and don't need to rely on drugs. Therapy that addresses both our base desires and our highest human potential is usually enough.

Recognizing both our animal nature and our human nature is crucial. I hear so many people say, "Why can't I get my life together? Why do I feel so terrible? Should I do this or should I do that?" These are questions I have asked myself. I knew I was supposed to 'do good.' The Bible told me that. I knew I wasn't supposed to have sex with a different person every night. I knew I shouldn't go out and get drunk. I knew these things, but somehow I never made a clear connection between these behaviors and my mental and emotional unrest. Now I know that when I do good, I feel good. The more balanced and wholesome my lifestyle is, the more peaceful I am. When I was unaware that something inside was dragging me toward what is lowest in my nature, I did not feel good about myself. I didn't feel good about myself until I became aware of my *nafs* and began to do things that made me feel good about myself.

The reason for doing good is not to keep from being a drunk or a whoremaster, and it's not to avoid eternal damnation and win a place in heaven. The reason for doing good is that we can never be happy if we don't do the right thing. We won't feel good about ourselves. When we are following our *nafs*, something inside us knows it, and the tension between what we are doing and what we know to be true is what makes us unhappy and sick.

Why does non-clinical work like AA succeed beyond anything that psychiatrists can do for the disease of alcoholism? In AA, no one pontificates. The wisest ones say, "I can't tell you what you ought to do, but this is what I did and this is how I felt." Eventually, the active alcoholic hears that often enough to try a new way of life. AA keeps it simple: Don't take the first drink and keep coming back. People start doing the right thing, like Patrick from back in my days at the psychiatric hospital in Baltimore whose inner voice told him, "You have to do what is right, not what you want to do." After you do what is right (and in the case of alcoholism, what is right usually is essential for maintaining your health and your life), something inside begins to rouse itself, begins to notice the sunrise and the sunset. That something is called self-value. If the alcoholic seeks first sobriety, which is part of the kingdom of heaven in Christian terms and which is right action in the Buddhist sense, then everything else is added on.

While I was working with alcoholics, I heard many miraculous stories. One fellow who had stayed sober for several months walked into a company right off the street. "I don't have any experience in this field yet," he said, "but I'd like to work here."

The interviewer looked him over and liked what he saw. "Well, you look like a nice guy. Let's give it a try. You can have the job." Good things happen when we get on a good path and make an effort.

You don't have to abuse alcohol or drugs to be an addict. Our *nafs* drag us into every conceivable addiction: people are addicted to food, clothes, television, anger, fear, being in love, watching sports, being alone or being with people, lying, doing nothing—there's no end to the list. It's not other people but our *nafs* that stir up desire, lust, fear, illusions, and anger.

The other day I was in a hurry and I dropped a brand new container of organic raisins, $4.80 worth of raisins spilled all over the floor. I got furious, and at what? Myself. It is a perfect example of the *nafs* in action. All the negativity was inside me. The raisins didn't do anything wrong. Jackie wasn't there to take the blame for 'making me' move too fast. Nothing was there except Locke and his impatience and the raisins. My negative impulses, my *nafs*, have nothing to do with anyone else. They have only to do with me.

One story I believe offers external proof of the connection between the physical elements of the body and negative qualities comes from a medical textbook case. Decades ago, a farmer I will call Bill was climbing over a fence when he tripped and his shotgun went off, blowing away all the external flesh of his belly. Eventually his wound healed, all except for the skin. He had no skin covering the mucous membrane of his intestines. For the rest of his life, he had to keep the area covered with a sterile dressing that he changed every night. It didn't seem to bother him. He had no pain. Since his was such a strange case, every few years the medical staff would bring him in, feed him well, and run experiments. One experiment tested the effect of his emotions on his mucosa. They would send in a nurse whose job it was to get him angry. She would change the bed brusquely and aggravate him in various ways until he got angry, then they'd test his mucosa. A test with litmus paper showed that anger increased Bill's bile acids. I was told that this was when doctors first discovered that the chemistry of the body is changed by anger. Perhaps this is an example of how the *nafs* affect us.

If it is not stretching things too far to say this, when I put my hands on Bawa's chest, it had a permanent calming effect on my *nafs*. I can't prove that, but I know that it did. I sensed a current, for want of a better word, perhaps a God current. I know that when I left his room that day, I was different. I felt recognized. I had been the recipient of a mystical and powerful act.

God is great, God is great.

I bear witness that there is one God.

I bear witness that Muhammad is His Messenger.

Come to prayer; come to victory.

God is great.

There is no God but God.

—Translation of The Call to Prayer

-21-

COME TO PRAYER

Pilgrimage to Mecca is an adventure. It's a journey to the Promised Land, a trip to Shangri-La. I didn't know what I was getting into, but I had seen the pictures and heard the stories of little miracles. One was the coming together of a group of Turkish Sufis and a group from the Fellowship. The Turks had heard about Bawa Muhaiyaddeen from their sheikh, who had also passed away. They had been trying to find out more about him, and somehow in the multitude, these two groups found each other and formed an alliance of brotherly love that has endured for several years.

My expectation mounted as I prepared for the journey. It staggered me to know I was going to the place where Prophet Muhammad, may peace be upon him, once lived and breathed. I was going to the place where Abraham's footprints are, the place where Abraham built the first house of God, the place where Hagar cried out to God for water when she was banished to the desert with her son Ishmael, the place where the miraculous *zumzum* water, which is said to pour forth from the spring of abundance in paradise, still flows. Every day, hundreds of thousands of pilgrims from all over the world gather to pray in the sacred cities of Mecca and Medina.

I first went to Mecca for two weeks in 1991 with four other people from the Fellowship. It was a spontaneous decision: the group had room for an extra person and I was able to get away, so I got a visa and joined them.

To enter Mecca, I had to officially become a Muslim. Fulfilling the basic requirement is not complicated: you profess faith that there is one God and that Muhammad is His Prophet. In addition to belief in God, a Muslim accepts the obligations of prayer to God, charity, fasting, and pilgrimage to Mecca. Even learning to do the prayers is fairly easy because you can just observe what others are doing and follow along.

I also needed to choose an Arabic name. I had always wanted one, but I had never asked Bawa to choose one for me. Instead, a little boy chose my name. At the time, I was running a branch of the Fellowship in Washington that met at our house and sometimes at the home of Dennis and Julie Dougherty. One day, as I was walking to the Dougherty's door, their two-year-old son, Michael Raheem, started jumping up and down and trying to say my name. "It's Locke," his parents told him. "Haqq! Haqq!" he called to me. In Arabic, *haqq* is the word for truth. I had always loved the word's sharp, clean sound, which seemed to me the sound of truth. So when it came time to choose an Arabic name, I did not hesitate. "My name is Muhammad Abd al-Haqq," I said, which means slave of the Truth.

We spent our first night in Saudi Arabia in a hotel near the airport in Riyadh. Next day, we did some necessary shopping, climbed on a bus for the trip from Riyadh to Mecca, and arrived just after night had fallen.

The holy city was dazzling. The minarets of the giant, open-air mosque surrounding the Ka'bah were lit up. It was like *The Arabian Nights!* Despite the heat, I shivered. In Islam, the Ka'bah is the most important place of worship, for it is where Muhammad and the earlier prophets gathered in prayer.

At our hotel, we changed into white clothes. As is the custom, the women wore one-piece white garments and we men wrapped ourselves in the *ihram*, the white burial shroud. The garments are a symbol of being dead to the material world.

We went to evening prayers and did a circumambulation, which consists of walking seven times around the Ka'bah, reciting prayers. Next we went to Saffa and Marwa, the two little hills between which Hagar ran back and forth, crying out to God for water. Once these rituals had been performed, we settled into our hotel. Except for a visit to Mt. Arafat, where Adam and Eve asked God's forgiveness and where Prophet Muhammad gave his last sermon, and a four-day trip to Medina where the Prophet and his family are buried, the rest of the time was free time.

At three o'clock the next morning, the call to prayer rang out, an unbelievably beautiful sound. I had laid out a simple white robe and kufi* the night before, so all I had to do was wash and dress, and I was on my way to prayer in less than five minutes.

After dawn prayers, the people who live in the city begin their daily routines. Some of the pilgrims do circumambulations around the Ka'bah, some stay in the mosque to pray quietly, and some return to take breakfast or a nap or perhaps to do some shopping.

You can buy anything you want in Mecca. The latest camera. The latest watch. Incense. Tailored apparel. In many ways, Mecca is not different from other cities. It is very busy. People hawk their wares in myriad little shops. But when prayer time comes at midday, afternoon, sunset, and evening, the shopkeepers shut down their shops and everyone in the city hurries to the Ka'bah for prayers.

I was floored by the unity. No one is forced to go to prayers, but that's what everyone does, five times a day at least. Up to three-quarters of a million people pray together in circles, shoulder to shoulder, facing the Ka'bah, the center point: men, women, and children of every race and color, and all are Muslims. I have never seen anything like it. Humanity really is one family. The differences of nationality and race and social class that create so much trouble in the world are wiped away. The pilgrims mingle and accept each other. You cannot tell the princes and the millionaires from people who don't have two pennies to rub together. Everyone is wearing white, barefoot, and devoid of jewelry. This unified devotion gives Mecca a magical quality, but I reminded myself not to idealize the place. Bawa had said that the people who live in Mecca are not going to go to heaven before everyone else simply because of their proximity to a holy place.

When Bawa first introduced us to the practices of Islam, I wondered about the obligation of the faithful to make at least one pilgrimage to Mecca in their lifetime, aware that many people don't have the resources. As always, Bawa stressed the inner meaning of the scriptures and traditions of all religions. He often said that the real *hajj*, the real pilgrimage, is the pilgrimage to the inner heart, but it took me a few years to understand the truth in those words. My strict Protestant upbringing had conditioned me to focus on the letter of scriptural law, but it is now quite clear to me that Bawa was right. Also, I have experienced that going to the Fellowship mosque here or to the mazaar where Bawa is buried can be as profound an experience as going to Mecca.

Everything is symbolic. Bawa often related the traditional story of the man who saved money all his life to make the pilgrimage to Mecca and then gave it away to someone who had no other hope of going. This, Bawa said, was an act of selfless giving that was equivalent to making the pilgrimage to Mecca.

My first visit to Mecca was a profound, reassuring, and enlightening experience. As I flew home, I prayed that I would be able to sustain the openhearted love I had felt there and the easy connection to prayer and contemplation. Bawa often said it is not enough to go on pilgrimage and get a certain feeling and focus. The trick is to keep it when you return to your normal life.

I thought, *Wouldn't it be wonderful if Jackie would go? Wouldn't that be wonderful?*

I mentioned it to her soon after my return. Well, I may as well have asked if she wanted to run down Broadway naked. There was no way she was thinking about it. She just cut me off at the pass, and I tried not to bring it up again. But I prayed that she would open her heart and decide to go because I knew it would be good for our marriage. I wanted to share the experience with her.

Whenever I found myself wishing that Jackie would become a Muslim, I thought of Bawa's words. A reporter once asked Bawa, gesturing to the crowd of people in the room, many of whom were Westerners, "So, these people here are all Muslims?"

"I don't see any Muslims here," Bawa replied. In fact, none of us can be called Muslim in the true sense of the word, which means "one who has surrendered his will to God." We can only *try* to be Muslims.

It was a few years later, when I was planning my second trip to Mecca, that Jackie decided she would accompany me. I was overjoyed. I'd had no hint that she had been considering the possibility. She told me she wanted to see what Mecca was like and what I had experienced. She also thought it was important to go because Bawa had encouraged all his children to make the trip if there was any possible way to do so. Her decision fulfilled my deepest heart's desire. To tell you the truth, I hadn't expected her to change her mind. I saw it as God's work.

So we went to Mecca, and Jackie participated fully. Later, when a friend expressed amazement that she had made the pilgrimage, Jackie said, "Where else could you ever go in all the world and be with God alone for two weeks?" She said it was wonderful to see people from all over the world and the colorful clothes and especially the many kindnesses expressed, regardless of language barriers.

That particular trip to Mecca was an intense experience for me for another reason. There I was, storming the gates of enlightenment yet again, doing up to fifty circumambulations of the Ka'bah a day while I recited prayers. I was nearly walking off the ground. Good things were happening internally. And then I got sick, so sick, the three-way runs. I was so sick that Jackie was alarmed.

For a day or so that seemed an eternity, I was in real agony. Then Andrew, a Fellowship brother, brought me some coriander tea and made me force it down. It may have been the sweetest thing he ever did. He had gone to the hotel chef and instructed him on how to make coriander tea; the chef got confused and threw out the liquid instead of the leaves, so Andrew had to go through the whole process again. God bless him for his persistence.

Shortly after I had the tea, the fever broke, and I wrote the following:

Crying, sobbing, choking with gratitude. Some understanding. Great relief and gratitude for that relief, and somehow the knowledge, intuitive, deep down in the wellspring of my being, that there was great and singular meaning for this whole experience: the sickness, the suffering, the dark night, and then the dawn. God lifted the illness and brought me out of suffering into light. Why? What was the meaning of it all? I was sobbing, praying to God, asking Him to help me to be more serving to others, to use this gratitude, to make use of this relief, this miracle, this bounty—not just to enjoy it. Like a man who finds a treasure in his backyard, I have two options: I can delight in having it all to myself, or I can share it with others.

Have I been sharing my treasures? Yes, somewhat. But I need to share what I have much more than before.

What is our role, our purpose in life? Why are we here? Bawa Muhaiyaddeen gave a beautiful, powerful, intensely practical answer to this question: while we are alive, we need to strive to know our true identity, our true being. If we can touch this, then we have achieved our goal here on earth—true peace and love that surpasses all understanding. This center of our being can be reached by practicing God's qualities. This will enable us to find true love.

I had been doing all that circumanbulation and praying and then, just when I was really getting good at it, the worst thing happened: I got sick. It wasn't in my script. Out of that sickness, when the fever broke, my heart opened. I cried for half an hour. And then I realized: that's the way we learn. Sometimes we learn in the craziest ways. God had made me very sick and very grateful for my health when the dawn came. I had been grateful before, but it took the sickness to polish my gratitude and bring out the shine.

The first day or so after the illness, I didn't talk as much. I listened and empathized. I didn't hurry. I walked more slowly; I was patient, more tolerant, and less egotistical.

Getting sick was the greatest spiritual gift I received on my second pilgrimage to Mecca.

Time is moving fast. When will you have your provisions for the journey properly packed? How long can your body last? Would you thus spend your life in vain? Time is precious and must be well-employed.

—Sri Anandamayi Ma,
Mother as Seen by Her Devotees

–22–

TIME IS MOVING FAST

Once again I awoke from the terrors of a dream I had been having periodically since my college days. In the dream, I was about to sit for my final exam. For some reason, I had let things go. I had not studied. Anxiety and dread pervaded my consciousness. There was nothing I could do. It was too late. I knew I would fail.

As I lay in bed reflecting on the dream, I realized that the final examination of my nightmares was more than a bad memory. It was a premonition of the questioning in the grave, the final life review we all will take when we die. My homework is to clear away the veils of illusion that separate me from God. Whether I pass or fail will be determined by the choices I make, moment by moment: my wise and unwise actions, my selfish and unselfish thoughts, my good and bad qualities, and my effort and lack of effort.

The dream was deeply disturbing because it always felt absolutely real. I was back at Princeton, alive and awake and saying to myself, *I'm not going to sit for the exam. I'm just not going.* It was obstinacy, but underneath was a belief that the dilemma would vanish if I could just keep looking the other way.

I recall someone asking Bawa what was needed to succeed both in life and in the spiritual realm. Bawa's answer was simple, "Intention and effort." Intention without effort has very little value. As the saying goes, "The road to hell is paved with good intentions." If I want a good harvest, I need to make an effort. Likewise, effort without a clear intention behind it is scattered and largely wasted.

My intentions and the effort I make will determine my state after my body dies. Right at this moment, I am building my house in the hereafter.

Bawa has given me everything I need to prepare for my final life exam: *Zikr*, prayer, fasting, the example of what it means to develop the beautiful qualities of God, and an abundance of wisdom to draw on. He made it very clear that we will get into hell or heaven not as a result of what anyone else does, but as a result of our own actions and qualities.

The last time I had the final exam dream, I was not doing my spiritual practices consistently, which is a common experience for many of us who follow a spiritual path. I would do a practice for a while, start congratulating myself, and eventually slack off. Over the years, the dream kept pointing me toward the nagging feeling that something was wrong in my life, like a cancer I was trying to ignore, hoping it would go away. The desire to make the problem go away, I finally realized, was the essential problem. I saw that as long as I kept looking the other way and telling myself I could do it tomorrow, I would never do it. That very morning, I made a firm commitment to get up every day for dawn prayers and recitation of the names of God. Even when I can't do anything more, I now spend the first two hours of my day focusing on God.

My marriage was suffering from the same sporadic lack of attention. As I have said before, my marriage is the most important barometer of my spiritual progress. At any given moment, what is going on in my marriage tells me exactly how patient, how tolerant, how understanding, how gentle, and how kind I really am. It is so easy to take your partner for granted and fail to focus on developing good qualities in context of the relationship. Bawa often said that if you lose your temper even once, you are not making progress. I hold that up as a powerful ideal. The final exam dream made me aware that I had to increase my efforts to build a harmonious relationship with Jackie.

I conducted myself poorly for the first few years we were together. I filled yellow legal pads by the dozens, analyzing my wife, our marriage, and what she needed to do to correct it. I understood intimately why she did what she did and why I reacted as I did. Although I was quite smitten by how cleverly I had worded them, all those brilliant observations on the psychology of a man and a woman in marriage had produced virtually no positive change in me, in her, or in our relationship. They were just slick intellectualisms. I was an expert on marriage, but our marriage was stuck.

Finally I got it. The tone of my analysis had leaned heavily toward the changes *Jackie* should make, which Bawa had tried to nip in the bud at the outset of our relationship. However, *I* was the one who had to change and let go. *I* had to forgive, understand, and serve my spouse. *I* had to learn to surrender, to defer, to say, "It's okay" and "You are right." I had to refrain from taking exception. I had to refrain from holding out. I had to refrain from giving vent to my anger and hastiness. I had not been doing any of those things consistently.

A few years have passed since then, and I can say that my conduct in marriage has improved considerably. This accomplishment is certainly due to Bawa's influence. Most important was what I learned from him about commitment and the intention to succeed. You do not have to find the perfect person to have a good marriage partner. Certainly I am not the perfect person for Jackie, nor is she the perfect person for me.

When we first settled in together, the hardest part for me was just staying involved and accepting that I was no longer a bachelor. Most single people, and particularly single men, do exactly what they want to do. When you get married, you can no longer do exactly what you want to do if you expect your marriage to be even moderately successful. Marriage requires a 180-degree turnaround. You have to compromise on all things.

Compromise was difficult for me, particularly at subconscious levels. I found myself outraged at times, as in "How dare she do this!" or "How dare she do that!" I had to learn to forgive Jackie. I had to learn to forgive myself. I had to learn to let go of things quickly to keep them from festering. I had to learn that anger could poison the well of our marriage for days. I knew I could no longer allow myself to act out in anger, or, if I did, I had to apologize quickly for my own faults and let the matter go.

Insisting on getting my own way stood between peace and me. Everything must be surrendered. The only way to get to God is to stop hanging on to willfulness. Except for what is life threatening or financially stupid, it is best to let go of everything, even the things we hold most sacred. It has been difficult but more than worth the effort.

For a long time, it was easier to talk the talk and stop at that. I knew about projection. I knew that the faults I saw in others were faults I had in myself. It was easier to recite this truth to myself than it was to actually examine my motivations and change my behavior. More than enough psychological and spiritual wisdom was floating around in my brain, but I hadn't really understood it. I knew I shouldn't find fault with others, but I told myself that sometimes the other person really *is* wrong and I thought that gave me the right, perhaps even the obligation, to point it out. This was another quality that Bawa had addressed when he told me that correcting people is not my role. To underscore the lesson, which obviously I had not fully absorbed, a few small incidents occurred with my wife that showed me quite clearly that I was wrong when I had been certain I was right. I am still amazed at how convinced I was that I was right when I was one hundred percent wrong.

I have always prided myself on my map-reading skills and sense of direction and criticized my wife for being a poor navigator. I had the evidence: more than once over the years she had informed me of highway exits just as we were passing them, taking us miles out of our way. That kind of thing. It infuriated me. I was The Navigator. I was the one who knew how to scope out a city and find the best way to a good restaurant. I was the one who selected the point of reference. "See? There's the tower, so the restaurant is in this direction." I always knew how to do it right.

Once, when Jackie and I were en route to Asheville, North Carolina, I tapped at a point on the map. "You see here? This is the way we go."

Jackie said no, that was not correct, and she was adamant

about it. "Okay," I said finally. "Do it your way." I was smug. I was condescending.

She was right! I never would have imagined that.

We got to Asheville and soon set off for the restaurant with my excellent directions. I knew exactly where it was because I had made a mental note of its location in relation to a specific building, which was quite tall.

"No, no, no," Jackie protested. "It's the other way."

"No," I said, sure of myself and testy with her. "It is not!"

She was right.

As we drove back to the hotel after dinner, we disagreed over another logistical detail and again I was convinced that I was right.

She was right.

The point I am trying to make is not that she was right. The point is that in all three instances I had been totally convinced that I was right and she was wrong, and I became very angry when she persisted. What dawned on me was, "My God! If this is happening with little things, how many other times has this happened in my life? Maybe I don't know anything!"

Everything that comes our way is either a lesson or a duty, and it is all homework to prepare us for our final life exam. The lesson I got on that trip to Asheville was vital to my spiritual path. It hit me over the head not once but three times. It took three times to make me understand that I really don't know everything. The incident forced upon me humility I thought I already had. I had no idea how arrogant I was. I used to resist pleasure trips with Jackie on the sanctimonious grounds that vacationing might interfere with 'my spiritual path.' I don't do that anymore. On what I had considered a frivolous little trip to Asheville, God showed me an important truth about myself.

In the early 1990s, Jackie and I bought a home in Chester County, Pennsylvania, only a short distance from Bawa's burial place. We are happier now than I ever could have imagined. Many years ago, Bawa told me, "Little brother, if you focus on changing yourself instead of your wife, and if you pray every day, your marriage could be very good. Toward the end of your sixties, your marriage could be very good, indeed." His words have come true. There is a new sweetness in our interaction. We have been together for twenty-three years, and just ten years ago I never dreamed that we could be as happy as we are now.

I see my own struggles mirrored in the struggles that my clients undergo. I have a small clientele, and most of them are working on marriage difficulties. So many things people argue about don't make any difference. What simple, wonderful advice it was when Bawa told me to correct my own faults instead of focusing on my wife's faults. It has worked beautifully for me and for some of my clients. But so many times over the years I have relapsed, forgetting my shortcomings and zeroing in on hers. Each time I start faultfinding, the situation gets worse; whenever I tend to the weeding in my own garden, I see good results.

Most of us with marital challenges find the work of staying focused on self-correction most difficult. The enemy within is not so easy to define as the one you can see on the outside. The inner enemy is elusive, deceitful, and clever beyond imagination. Ego's strength comes from illusion, the world of mind. Good action comes from the heart, that tiny piece of God inside. The power of God within our inner hearts is omnipotent, but when we neglect to turn to it or are blind to it, ego takes over, and our difficulties multiply and take over our lives. If we can begin to act toward others and ourselves with the kindness and understanding we would bring to dealing with a child's transgressions, in time our problems will vanish, one by one.

A tiny incident occurred last weekend. I had the impulse to react in a snappish way to something Jackie said and caught myself. It happened again, and this time I did not catch myself. What I said was not meant to be hurtful, but it was insensitive, and it affected her. As soon as I heard myself speak the words, I realized I was wrong and apologized. I am trying to hold to the truth of becoming as peaceful and undemanding and uncritical as I can be.

Little things like this are the wisdom microcosms on the road to enlightenment: seeing something wrong and correcting it to create more harmony; seeing something wrong and correcting it so the ego doesn't rule me.

Bawa said a husband and wife should share the journey of life, one person leading the camel and the other riding, and changing places from time to time. It should be like that, tremendous unity and looking out for each other, feeling each other's pain. For years, these were just words, but now I see that such a state is possible. In a good marriage, each person's heart should flower.

Jackie has her own path and her own way of following that path. She loves people and the goodness in people. She loves God. She prays a lot. She is very private about her spiritual life. If Jackie were to be asked whether she is a Muslim, I am certain that she would think of the formal religion of Islam with all its strictures and formalities and say that she is not that.

I guess it would be most fair to say that Jackie is ambivalent about Islam. I know that she would be most comfortable with a good Christian sermon on a Sunday morning, followed by a nice chat with someone who speaks her lingo. Without question, she saw the beauty and incredible wisdom and love in Bawa Muhaiyaddeen and is devoted to that, but she goes her own way. She is set in stone against anything that pushes her to pray a certain way or to follow specific practices.

For a long time, I tried to 'reform' her. I would say, "Look, can't you understand the connection between the incredible depth and wisdom of Bawa Muhaiyaddeen and what he has requested of his children? There's no missing the fact that nothing will get you there faster than five-times prayer and *Zikr*."

I struggled with my feelings about these differences between us for many years, and I finally gave it up. I remembered how many times people came to Bawa, critical of another person and looking for validation. "You know," I heard him say more than once, "this person you are speaking of has a very good heart. You can never know another person's heart."

Whenever I find myself getting judgmental I think about those words, and also about the time Bawa told me that I should have made a list of my own bad qualities, not Jackie's. His words eventually pushed away my resistance to Jackie living her life the way she wants to live it. He said on numerous occasions that if men had the qualities of women the world would be a better place.

Bawa could cut through all the awful stuff we were doing and see clear through to the center of goodness within us. He asked all of us to treat each other in the same way, and we don't do it. We get caught in thinking we can help others along by correcting them. However, the truth is that we do not know the nature of the veils covering another person's soul, so how could we possibly remove them? The only way to lead someone along is by your own actions and qualities. When I get overbearing with people, they run the other direction. When I am loving and listen to them, sometimes they ask for my advice. Then I have to say that I don't know. I try to follow the motto I learned from AA: "I can't tell you what is right for you, but I can tell you what happened with me." Bawa, too, advised us to speak from our own experience.

If we had the amazing capability to see into the hearts of others, clearly and without passing judgment, we would see that each person is a reflection of God. I think it must have been that way for Bawa. He always began his discourses with, "Precious jeweled lights of my eyes." Each of us, despite our faults, was a pleasant reminder of the existence of God.

I hope I finally have learned that it is fruitless to try to force people into my way of thinking. Greeting others with love and compassion creates a bond and makes people more receptive. When we surrender to God's will and step over the line between just talking about faith and genuinely believing that everything is in God's hands, trying to control others is not an issue. Surrender draws people closer.

No matter what happens, keeping the focus on changing ourselves instead of the other person is the most constructive thing we can do. "When someone wrongs you," Bawa told us, "apologize as soon as you can." I thought it was a weird idea at first. Apologize when someone has hurt you? Then a friend told me about her experience when she followed this advice. Someone had hurt her. After she had walked around in a funk for a day or two, she came across those words of Bawa's.

"It took a few days to work myself up to it," she told me, "but finally I sought out the person. I said, 'Please forgive me about the unpleasantness that took place the other day.' The minute the words were out of my mouth, I experienced something that must be close to an epiphany. All the weight slid off my shoulders. I felt as if I had been lifted off the ground. I felt light, cleansed, pure. I was no longer harboring resentment."

When we feel wronged, the resentment begins to form immediately. One molecule of resentment attracts all the other molecules of resentment that have been floating around, and soon a big ball of resentment has formed. Resentment is toxic. How can we find clarity or enlightenment if we have the toxin of resentment in us? The apology to the other is not a masochistic act; it is an apology for the resentment. At that point, it has nothing to do with the other person.

Bad qualities are contagious. Like viruses, they spread quickly from person to person, and good qualities are the only antidote.

An angry woman worked at the corner store near me for several years. She gave her coworkers a hard time and made sure a couple of them got fired when they told her off. One morning when I went in for a newspaper, I didn't have any change. "I'm sorry," I said. "I don't have anything smaller than a ten-dollar bill."

"If you were sorry," she barked, "you wouldn't do it again. Are you really sorry?"

In the old days, I would have said something sarcastic in return, and the toxin would have lingered in my system for a few hours. This time I paused and thought before I said anything. "That's a good point. I can't tell you I won't do it again, but I'll try my best."

I could see that my reaction surprised her. She stared at me for a moment, and then she smiled and made a joke.

These situations happen to us every day. God gives us many opportunities to practice restraint and good qualities, and these opportunities are part of the homework to prepare us for our final exam.

When I was a teenager, we'd say, "Don't sweat the small stuff."

Today I'd say exactly the opposite. The little things acted upon create habits, and habits slowly build character. Little things are important. If you leave out even a single character in an email address, you won't make the connection you intended to make—every little thing in the address has to be perfect.

The devil is in the details. Evil comes not only in the form of Hitlers who kill people but also in tiny sins of omission and commission: not saying *I'm sorry*, being impatient, rushing, holding little grudges. It's not as easy to walk the good path as it is to talk about it. The ego forces its way into our best intentions. It is relentless. It is fighting for its life.

A theme in Bawa's teaching that I found most meaningful and helpful in my own life was *jihad,* holy war. Today we frequently hear this word mentioned in context with war between ideologies, but the meaning of *jihad* has been twisted by the ego. The holy war is internal. Bawa's use of the word hearkened back to Prophet Muhammad's original teachings, which stressed that *jihad* is the internal war each of us wages against our base qualities. My searching had made me all too familiar with groups that placed great importance on 'blissing out,' singing, dancing, and the like, which were seen as the perks and rewards of the spiritual life. Bawa did not seem opposed to these experiences, but his virtual exclusion of their mention in his daily talks made it clear that when it comes to progressing on the spiritual path, washing dishes has far more value.

Bawa's teaching on *jihad* was a valuable gift. Whenever we complained about another person or what was going on in the outer world, Bawa turned us around and focused us inward, reminding us of the need for prayer and duty and of the immense rewards of persisting in the struggle against our own bad qualities. Here was mystical subtlety infused into my most mundane actions. I knew that if I accepted and understood the need to wage the inner *jihad,* every second of the day would be an opportunity to do good and make progress.

Marriage offers a grand opportunity to embrace *jihad,* or the struggle with the ego. When we live alone, we can fool ourselves about the progress we are making, but we can never fool a partner. Our marriage partner is our mirror, reflecting the consequence of our every thought and action.

I learned more about spirituality in my first year of living with Jackie than I learned while I was in the Zen Buddhist monastery. There was no more easy out. It really is not possible to change another person. The only person you can change is yourself, and herein lies the great difficulty and the great opportunity of marriage. Nowhere else can you work as effectively on your darker side. To bring harmony into any marriage, you have to struggle with your own anger, impatience, resentment, and intolerance. When you succeed, three things happen: you improve, your marriage improves, and you move forward on the spiritual path.

So Bawa always pointed us back to ourselves. This is not a strange concept, for he was simply saying what it says in the Bible, "The kingdom of Heaven is within." The real work is done on the inside; we don't have to travel around the world or delve into exotic practices or traditions or teachers. This work is available to everyone. I will be forever grateful to Bawa for showing me the true meaning of holy war. Only through true *jihad* will we reach the goal of understanding our true nature.

It is easy to get off track and to find support for a wrong way of thinking. Earlier in my life, after I had searched everywhere trying to find myself, I came to the conclusion that there was nothing to find. All I needed to do was to be myself. I loved to recite a Chinese proverb I had discovered:

> *The snow goose need not bathe to make itself white—*
> *neither need you do aught but be yourself.*

I loved those words. They were reassuring. I'm really okay, I thought. My true nature doesn't need cleansing. I was so enamored of this proverb that it took a while to see the real truth: snow geese are always preening. Their feathers stay white because they clean them. Just being yourself is not possible until you see and touch that

Self, which requires cleaning off the stuff that gets in the way. This is our work as human beings.

Just as imagining that a snow goose doesn't need to clean itself to stay white, merely thinking about good qualities doesn't mean we have them. We have to practice them, and that requires effort. What good is it to imagine ourselves helping an old man cross the street if we don't act on it? Unless we actually go to the old man and do what we can to help, we have not served and we have gained nothing. What good is it to talk about good qualities if we allow ourselves to give in to our irritation with others? Restraining the quick retort to another's unpleasantness can give just enough space for good qualities to prevail.

Just after I returned from Japan, I took a suit to a dry cleaner that advertised same-day service. I needed the suit for a formal engagement that same night. I got there as soon as the place opened and was the first customer of the day. The fellow working there had an angry face. I put the suit on the counter and asked, "What time today can I pick this up?"

He gave me a surly look. "I can't do it today."

"But it says on the sign outside that you have same-day service."

"I can't do this!" He shoved my suit aside brusquely as another customer came in the door.

I stepped to the side and waited. For some reason, I didn't get angry. Staying calm helped me see that the fellow was upset about something. I prayed a bit. A few other customers came and went, and soon the store was empty again except for the dry cleaner and me.

I stepped up to the counter again. I didn't say anything. I just looked at him. I wondered what was troubling him, and I think he could feel my concern. In a totally different voice, he said, "You come back at five o'clock and I have this for you."

Unless we make a firm intention to practice good qualities and make the effort, we will not reach the state of merging with God. The intention and the effort required to practice the divine qualities as best we can will gradually force out our negative qualities and establish the good qualities at deeper and truer levels. It's that simple.

I now realize with some surprise that before I met Bawa, I thought that doing a kind act for someone required abstinence or self-sacrifice on my part. In my mind, the bounty of my actions was solely for the recipient. Now I understand that I, too, receive the bounty of my actions in equal measure. When I do something kind for someone else, a drop of patience or tolerance or some other good quality falls quietly into the golden bowl of my soul, filling it ever so subtly with goodness. And, you know, the strange part is that I can feel it. I feel good when I do a kind or thoughtful thing.

I find that when I make an effort and treat a person "as if" he or she were the most important thing in my life at that instant, amazing things happen. People respond positively; sometimes they return the kindness. The effort it takes to be kind or thoughtful or patient or simply to listen is rewarded tenfold. It is triply blessed: it brings peace to the heart of the other, it brings peace into my heart, and it strengthens God's qualities inside me. The more these qualities gather and strengthen, the more peace I feel, and, imperceptible though it may be, the closer I am to God.

Developing good qualities may seem too simple and ordinary, but it is very mystical for me. For a long while, it seemed that goodness was not politically correct. We admired famous people and flashy gestures. Not many people emulated those who were humble and selfless. The destruction of the World Trade Center has changed all that. Just as I was wondering what had happened to goodness and why it was so underrated, I saw humble and selfless people risking their lives, first to dig out a few survivors and then to uncover whatever remained of the thousands of people who died. The rescue workers were so humble and selfless that most did not even question risking their own lives, often for people they did not know. They gave of themselves out of a sense of duty and a desire to serve. How beautiful! It made us blazingly aware of the purpose of life. Goodness for the sake of goodness is once again politically correct and is being seen for its true value in this life and the next. Finally, we are doing more than paying lip service to the goal of being a good person, which the scriptures of all religions hold as a goal of life.

Recently, I found an extraordinary description of Prophet Muhammad, who has been described as a person who was never judgmental and who never pointed out the faults of others. I do not know its origin, but it is most likely from the *Hadith*, which are traditional stories from the time of the Prophet.

> *His nature was very gentle. He was very considerate of everyone he associated with and employed such a gentle and easy manner that no one experienced any discomfort on his account. If he had to go outside at night, he would put on his shoes very softly, open the door panel very gingerly, and walk out very quietly.*
>
> *Hazrat Anas said, "I served him for ten years. In those ten years, no matter what I did, he never said, 'Why did you do this?' If I failed to do something, he never asked, 'Why didn't you do this?'"*
>
> *No useless word ever slipped from his tongue. He sought to know the wish of each person's heart. He never did anything to cause distress to another. He was prudent in defending himself against the mischief of oppressors and troublemakers, but he treated such people in turn with good cheer and good nature.*
>
> *In sum, he was the best-natured of all people. If someone did something unpleasant, he never admonished that person face-to-face. There was no harshness in his personality, nor did he ever affect a severe expression the way some people do...or speak angrily and threaten others. It was not his habit to shout. He did not requite evil with evil; rather, he forgave the offender and overlooked the deed.*

Although I am far from achieving my goal, I strive to emulate the qualities of the Prophet. I'm a little more self-aware these days. I catch myself sooner when I make a mistake. I remember to practice good qualities more often. These changes in self-awareness, along with making a proper meditation space and using it every day, are changing the quality of my life. Sometimes now I experience the melting heart state that Bawa spoke of. This is a direct result of effort. As Bawa said, intention and effort are all you need. Nothing fancy, just intention and effort.

I knew I would have to die. I was traveling in a car, and I knew my time had come. I heard beautiful, heavenly music. I checked the radio and the tape player; they were not on. The music was coming from somewhere else. I was not afraid. I knew I was going on a long trip to leave this world, and I didn't know whether I would return.

I started through the stages. My friend Chuck was there. Each stage was a test I had to go through, like a preview, and all were connected to moving on and dying, yet not dying. Faith and certitude were important. I had no power as I was moved from one place to the next. This was the world beyond, a void. It was momentary, yet eternal.

I moved up a level from a deeper space to a more conscious one. I began to sense I was still alive, still in this world. I was not sure I was alive, and I did not think I would see Chuck again. He thought I had gone on to the next world. But I came back.

—**Locke Rush, Dream Journal**

-23-

I Know I Have To Die

When we are in the womb, God's presence is constantly with us, preparing us for birth and for life in the world. He tells us we will encounter both good and evil and that our life's work will be to extract what is good and return to Him. God teaches us the importance of remembering Him with every breath, practicing the divine qualities, and serving others selflessly, for these actions will enable us to stay on the straight path and find our way back home. This is what Bawa Muhaiyaddeen taught the people who came to him for wisdom.

For a while after we are born, our hearts remember God's wisdom and goodness. It is quiet knowledge. We cannot speak, but we *live* our connection to God, as only one with a pure heart can live it. We remember the joy of His presence. We know what we need to do to complete our journey successfully. As we begin to absorb the world, the God knowledge hidden deep inside is gradually and almost imperceptibly covered by veil after veil after veil. Emotional reactions, desires, fears, and false concepts arise, forming layers around our inherent wisdom.

By the time we are adults, most of us have forgotten our true identity and why we are here. We plunge into the distractions of life eagerly. However, the difficulties we encounter soon teach us that marriage, children, career, wealth, titles, and power do not guarantee happiness. The seekers among us, hoping to find reasons and solutions for the unpredictability and chaos, turn to books, religion, philosophies, teachers, other cultures, and the like.

As I grew older and the golden days of early childhood faded, I turned to the pleasures of the world, looking for ways to regain the inner joy I once had felt. I tried to persuade myself that I was doing what was expected of me, and I hoped that worldly pursuits would fulfill me and give my life meaning. Soon, however, my conscience and self-honesty let me know I was way off track.

I delved into myself, looking for a truer direction. Quite unexpectedly, a new life opened up for me. My spiritual awakening as I struggled with my inner demons in New York City was the most momentous internal experience I have ever had. I was given a taste of the divine, and it changed me for the better. I saw it as a sign from God that it was time to walk a different path, a true path, a path that would answer my deepest questions and reveal the purpose of my existence.

And so my search for truth began in earnest. I opened and closed many doors on my journey. The time I spent in Europe with Benoit, Harding, Durckheim, and others was stimulating. I craved esoteric knowledge, and I explored their teachings wholeheartedly. Ultimately, what I found was not enough to sustain me. By then, however, I had fallen into an easy lifestyle that kept me distracted. It took the 'black cat episode' to shock me into action. I saw that I could die at any moment, like a cat in the street, without ever understanding why I had been born.

Japan beckoned, and I opened the door to an entirely new life of discipline and contemplation. I submitted myself fully to practicing the Zen way for three years. I cannot say I had any great revelations or *Aha!* experiences, however I did develop a more peaceful inner and outer countenance. Eventually, though, I began to question my guides and the nature of the enlightenment experience they were leading me toward and to yearn for a way to unlock my heart.

My travels in India deepened my skepticism about so-called enlightenment. I saw parallels to my experiences in Japan. The foundation of the practice of Zen Buddhism is to ground your presence in the belly. The belly is considered the cauldron, the vital center of being, the *hara* or field out of which everything grows. Theoretically, when you are grounded in the belly, the energy accumulates and rises up through all the chakras. In Hinduism, this phenomenon is called the awakening of the *kundalini* energy. In my experience, all the energy I concentrated in my belly did not rise to my heart center, which I have found to be an even more vital center. And even if the energy had risen to my heart center, energy is just energy, and it is very different from the peace that Bawa pointed me toward. Energy, shakti, prana—whatever you call it, it still belongs to the world and not to God.

While I was in India, I heard about hundreds of 'enlightened' gurus and their 'miraculous' feats. I marveled, but where was the wisdom? Where was the peace? What was the point of it all?

The fortuneteller I met in a Delhi marketplace may have offered me the wisest guidance of all. Although he performed psychic magic that astounded me, I certainly didn't feel I was in the presence of a saint, nor did he make any claims to that state. On the contrary, he informed me that the ability to see the future or leave your body or other such feats were skills that almost anyone could master given the right information and enough practice. I believe this is true. For example, I know that people can learn to separate their consciousness from their physical bodies. Bawa did it, but he advised his children to look much deeper. "That's easy!" he told us. "It's easy to be a swami. What is difficult is to be a true human being."

I have noticed that spiritual seekers tend to use the label 'spiritual' for anything that provides a bit of power or mystical insight. When Bill Moyers interviewed my friend Huston Smith, he asked him what constitutes a true conversion or spiritual experience. Smith's answer was clear and simple. No matter what is seen, heard, or felt, Huston contended, an experience cannot be classified as a real spiritual experience unless it results in the betterment of the person. Anything less may be called psychic, but not spiritual.

My own explorations have convinced me that Smith's view is accurate. A real spiritual experience should at least make a person noticeably more peaceful or compassionate. I thought I had learned that lesson by the time I closed the door on India, but it only returned in a different guise behind a different door when I saw before me the seductive wonders of drug-induced experiences.

Often over the years since taking LSD I have asked myself whether there was any redeeming factor, anything good that came of it? My answer is yes, but it was only the benefit of trying one more door and discovering that true self-knowledge lay elsewhere. I didn't gain any permanent knowledge through my experimentation with LSD or Ketalar, or with the transpersonal movement in general, but I did get an unforgettable intimation of the existence of levels of being beyond my normal experience. LSD may be a way to discover that life is not what it appears to be, but I certainly wouldn't recommend such a potentially dangerous method. LSD was alluring but artificial, like a beautiful car that goes three miles and falls to pieces.

What I have said about my LSD experiences applies to most of the exploration I did during the early to mid-seventies. As far as I know, the days of sanctioned (and funded!) LSD research in this country are over, but the LSD experience heavily influenced the New Age therapies that now abound. How could it be otherwise? Grof, Lilly, Elmer Green, and other pioneers of transpersonal psychology were fascinated by the implications of the drug. Grof's work with the stages of birth and their effects on the psyche continued sans-LSD in Holotropic Breathwork. Many routes to heightened awareness have entered the mainstream: yoga, countless meditation techniques, group therapy marathons, massage and healing touch, art and music and movement therapies, sex therapies. Some of these experiences may alter consciousness temporarily, but they are just that—temporary. Soen Roshi dismissed even my most profound Zen meditation experiences as illusory. He understood the traps of illusion. Yet oh how I cherished every enhanced moment! Despite my understanding of the illusory quality of experience, I spent most of my life stringing these moments together like pearls, trying to make a necklace of enlightenment.

Like an alcoholic, I was addicted to the feel-good feeling and whatever it took to sustain it. I was bouncing from one 'fix' to another, counting on each new exploration to bring me the happiness and peace I sought. Over and over I had to learn that reliance on substances and people and anything but God was bound to disappoint me._

Bill Wilson, the founder of Alcoholics Anonymous, wrote in the Big Book of AA:

> *I am beginning to see that all my troubles have their root in a habitual and absolute dependence upon my personal prestige, security, and romantic attachment. When these things go wrong there is depression. Now this absolute dependence upon people and situations for emotional security is, I think, the immense and devastating fallacy that makes us miserable.*
>
> *This craving for such dependencies, this utter dependence upon people and situations can only lead to conflict; both on the surface and at depth. We are making demands on circumstances and people that are bound to fail us. The only safe and sure channel of absolute dependence is upon God Himself.*

The purest and deepest of spiritual literature tells us that if we were to glimpse our true being for even an instant, we would know a permanent state of peace. Lesser experiences are illusory and misleading. They do not uncover the inner light; they skew it and warp it and layer it over with distraction. I am not saying that we cannot see or feel God reflected in great art or in unitive experiences, but we have a tendency to accept the reflection as real, and that gets in our way. To find peace and live in it requires that we probe deeper into the source of the reflection.

When the LSD trials ended, I let go of seeking for a while. I had reached a plateau and saw no reason to keep climbing when I had no indication that I was moving in the right direction. Although stimulating, exotic, and powerful, none of the forms of mystical endeavor I had examined had answered my longing for the truth.

None had resonated in my heart, put an end to my doubts, or pointed me directly to a goal that seemed truly satisfying.

When the student is ready the teacher appears. I believe this is true. Everything I had experienced up to then had shown me what I didn't want or didn't need, or it had been dangled in front of me by someone I could not trust. I needed a guide with real wisdom.

Some of Bawa's disciples had powerful and strange experiences when they met him. Not me. There were no flashing lights for me. My connection with Bawa happened at such a deep level that it was almost unconscious.

"You can't know God or see God," Bawa said to the people gathered around him on that first night. "But you *can* know the qualities of God." The moment I heard him speak, something clicked into place, explaining and easing my confusion. The knowledge that had been right before me like an open secret unfolded in a wonderful way: I didn't need some complicated spiritual technology to find God; I could be close to Him by recognizing and cultivating good qualities. Within just a few minutes of meeting me, Bawa had given me the key to the mystery of life.

Without my saying a word, Bawa looked directly into my eyes and summarized my life up to then. If I wanted to find the true answers I had set out to find, he said, I would have to start all over again. "All the tapes you have recorded must be erased. You have to record over them. The new recording comes from an entirely different place. Only God's teaching and God's wisdom and God's psychology will give you the peace you seek. But first," he repeated, "you must erase the old tapes."

Hearing these words was a shocking and transformative experience. I didn't want to throw out all those experiences. I had spent a lot of time, energy, and money on them. I had immersed myself in the wonders I found behind the countless doors of illusion. In retrospect, I don't believe that Bawa was telling me that all my earlier explorations were a complete waste of time. However, I already had extracted the essence of truth from each of them, so there was no point in hanging on. When I entered the monastery, Soen Roshi said essentially the same thing, that all the reading and talking about Zen I had done would be nothing compared to committing myself to the practices. The night I met Bawa, I recognized my powerful connection to him, and I understood that I would have to leave behind all that had come before to embrace a higher path. Although the elemental part of me did not welcome the idea of erasing years and years of study and practice, the truth in me recognized the truth when I heard it.

At first I judged myself harshly for spending so many years looking in the wrong direction, but I see it differently now. I had to seek. I had to open doors leading to nowhere until I found the door to somewhere I wanted to go.

Meeting Bawa Muhaiyaddeen and seeing incarnate the kind of person I had been reading about for thirty years was so powerful that I still scratch my head in amazement. Bawa was a spiritual alchemist of the highest order. He made the loftiest of my spiritual fantasies seem mundane. His sainthood was apparent to anyone who met him. I wondered what I had I done to deserve such grace. How ironic that after traveling throughout the world looking for a teacher with real wisdom and firsthand knowledge of the path to God, I had found Bawa twenty miles from my childhood home.

From our first encounter, I knew Bawa would never trick me or deceive me. I have never had that feeling with anyone else. His demeanor was impeccable and his purity so obvious that any doubt simply evaporated. I found his simplicity wonderfully refreshing.

I hadn't recognized it until then, but I had always known that the truth should be simple and straightforward. I had not found the answers I sought in the realm of the intellectual, the wealthy, or the influential. I had met many people like that on my journey. Like me, most were so entranced by their own point of view that they were blind to the plain truth in front of their eyes. A few of those I met stood out as truly good souls. Most of these people had little or no education and were doing simple jobs. All radiated a quality of goodness. They said little about themselves; they were much more interested in my life and how they might help me.

These people had qualities I trusted, respected, and admired.

Bawa was this kind of person, except that he had attained a level far beyond the good folk described above. He was mystical and compelling yet at the same time eminently practical and accessible. His goodness drew me to him. As a child I had been attracted to goodness. I felt a sense of unity within myself and with others. Doing things for people was a joy; I don't recall needing to be thanked. The joy was in the doing. My love and compassion for the people in my family was natural. I felt their pain as if it were my own.

The wholesome world of my childhood seemed totally removed from the awesome theology I was taught. My father had been strict. In a certain mood, he had sometimes punished even a minor infraction by making me memorize Bible verses. I got the idea that God was a fierce yet benevolent power that would punish me if I did wrong. Quite naturally, God took on an anthropomorphic form in my imagination. I was in awe of Him, and I knew that death was somehow connected to believing in Him.

Bawa's words and his qualities confirmed for me at last that God as goodness expressed through the human form is possible. I saw that the unconditional love I had felt for others when I was a child arose from a silent, abundant source deep inside me. As I grew older, however, I had pulled back and become more self-centered. I thought that the inner source of love had dried up. I forgot the purpose of my being all the while I was searching for it.

Finally I had found the wise guide I had been looking for, but I soon learned just exactly how cunning, baffling, powerful, and often invisible the ego is. My mind tried to play tricks on me. "Slow down," it whispered. "Relax. You're in! You've touched the hem of a saint's robe. The hard part is over. Now you can do the work at your leisure."

However, Bawa made it clear that finding the teacher is only the beginning, and that it would take real effort to reap the rewards. I had found the map to buried treasure, but I still had to follow where it pointed and do a lot of digging. As my real journey began, the focus shifted to extracting the essence of wisdom from Bawa's teachings and doing my best to put what I learned into practice.

I did not change instantly. Like the story I related previously of the goat tethered to a stake next to a feast of ambrosia, I sniffed at the delicate aroma of the ambrosia I had found then wandered out to the farthest perimeter of the field to browse for more familiar food. My stake was at Bawa's house in Philadelphia, but my rope extended all the way down to Washington, DC. I spent my weekdays there and lived a fairly worldly life, foraging among the tin cans and brambles. I continued to drink socially. I wasn't into prayer. I wasn't doing much *Zikr*. Thank God, my tether held fast. Every weekend when I came to visit Bawa, the rope would make another loop around the stake and bring me a little closer to the ambrosia. I read Bawa's books. I did the *Zikr* more often. I had more talks with Bawa and got to know people in the Fellowship. And gradually the extent of my tether grew shorter and shorter. Like the goat in the story, eventually I wound my way back to the ambrosia and stayed, giving it my full attention. Twenty-seven years have passed since then, and it still satisfies me.

Eventually, I did change. Bawa's words were not merely words, for I had read and listened to many words earlier in my life that had left me doubtful or unsatisfied. He did not speak from theory but as only someone who *knows* can speak, and his qualities and actions radiated the same truth. His impact on me was so powerful that when he said, "God doesn't like a promiscuous life," I soon followed his advice and settled down with one woman after years and years of indiscriminate sexual behavior. And when in Sri Lanka he told me, "A wise man doesn't drink," it wasn't long before I stopped drinking entirely, something I had not been able to do previously.

A characteristic I found unique in Bawa was his intense focus on the hidden truth in each of us, not on the ego identity that was obscuring the truth. Because of his state, Bawa could instantly see our spiritual station, what was blocking us, and what we needed to move forward on the path. While other masters I had met complimented their followers and praised their abilities and actions, Bawa would have little of this. When one of us reported an experience that suggested other-worldliness, although he might acknowledge it or say that it was a good sign, he never dwelt on it. He knew that the path to God required going way beyond the occasional glimpse of heaven.

Mostly, though, Bawa stressed the importance of practicing good qualities, serving others, and remembering God with every breath. He often said that we who call ourselves human beings don't contribute even as much as a tree does. A mature tree provides shade for anyone who comes to sit under it and hundreds of fruits for anyone who comes to eat. A tree doesn't eat of its own fruit, and it never asks to be thanked for what it is giving.

After Bawa's death, when I was on pilgrimage, I had the opportunity to talk with Razeen, a disciple of many years who had enjoyed many long and intimate discussions with Bawa.

One morning, as I was leaving the pre-dawn *fajr* prayers in the huge mosque in Medina and thousands of people were pouring into the streets, someone grabbed my arm. "Locke?" It was Razeen. I wondered at the miracle of our chance encounter in that sea of people. "Let's walk to the graveyard," he said, referring to the place where Prophet Muhammad's family was buried.

I took the opportunity to ask Razeen what Bawa had said about the purpose of life.

With no hesitation, Razeen answered, "Bawa said two things about that. He said that the purpose of life is to see the truth as goodness and to put goodness into action. Bawa also said that the purpose of life was to serve others with a melting heart."

Writing these words, my thoughts go back to my meeting with Sri Anandamayi Ma. When I asked her, "How do we love?" she replied that we learn to love by serving others with our bodies. It is not enough to know we have love inside; it is essential that we *use* that love. I firmly believe that this is why we are here in this life and that if we do not fulfill this purpose, we are no more than unplanted seeds. Nothing will grow from us; we will bear no fruit.

Acting from the heart is natural, but the inner heart is like an unused muscle, stiff and somewhat rigid, perhaps even frozen. As I persist in making an effort with others, the ice melts, bit by bit, and the pure water begins to flow. Even doing little things gradually melts the heart.

Practicing the qualities of God in service to others makes us purer and brings us closer to our true nature. When we finally see and experience who we really are at the center of our being, God will affirm our goodness and accept us as His *true* children. With this acceptance comes complete surrender to God's will and with that come the peace, understanding, and wisdom that are our birthright. This is the state out of which we can serve our fellow human beings at the highest level. If we need to know about another's pain or difficulty, the knowledge will appear as if on a page in our mind. Whenever we need to know something and can surrender our will to God's will, God will provide what is needed.

Although Bawa valued and praised formal prayer and readily encouraged his children in this practice, he cut through even the religious tenets of Islam. He spoke about formless prayer. Formless prayer may express itself in serving others, being kind, listening to others' problems, feeling their pain, and, ultimately, regarding each person's life as if it were our own. He told us that these actions were prayers of the highest order, and this truth hit home with me. Many times I had seen people somewhat pleased with their sanctity and expertise in prayer act in rude or hurtful ways to others. *What is the purpose of doing formal prayers,* I asked myself at those times, *if the result does not soften your heart toward others?*

A good example of this Sufi take on the formal aspects of Islam is Bawa's instruction regarding the practice of five-times prayer. Bawa told us repeatedly that the most important part of each prayer time is at the end, when each of us should turn toward the person next to us, look him in the eyes, say, *"A'salaam Alaikum* (peace be upon you)," and embrace him. He asked us to greet each person in this way before we left the prayer room. This simple act, Bawa assured us, was more valuable than reciting the prayers. Why? Because often we feel distant toward certain people or are angry with them because of something that has happened. Over time, the act of embracing others removes the barriers. Sometimes it is difficult to do, which brings me back to the true meaning of *jihad* and the opportunity to slay some of the demons of my psyche.

The first time I went to Mecca, I turned to my neighbor after the prayer had finished. I looked him in the eyes and lightly touched his shoulders to embrace him. He was quite surprised, even startled, and instinctively drew away a bit, but I persisted. *"A'salaam Alaikum,"* I said, embracing him. He allowed the embrace and returned the blessing, and it seemed to me that he was truly moved by my actions.

These are some of the truths I learned from Bawa. He described the loftiest of all spiritual paths. It was clear to those of us around him that he himself had reached the level of surrender to God and had been accepted as one of God's own true children. I had no doubt that he had merged with his Maker.

And so, as I sit here having just reread this manuscript, one thing is certain. Amidst the plethora of experiences, clarity and true faith came into my life the day I met Bawa Muhaiyaddeen. Before that, I had been gathering experiences, comparing and classifying them, and extracting whatever wisdom I could find. Now I know that to find wisdom, you must know what wisdom is and have it, for only wisdom recognizes wisdom. Bawa was the personification of the wisdom I had sought. Merely being in his presence enabled me to absorb his wisdom and feel its resonance.

Now that Bawa's body is gone—and the father and teacher who opened my heart is no longer in the physical world—I continue to hold the Fellowship in reverence, as if he were still physically present there. I will always love to spend time in his room. I find it a holy place.

Bawa came here, he brought the truth, he brought wisdom, he brought clarity, he brought the light. He brought the state of Muhaiyaddeen, which is the Nourisher and Strengthener of our faith. He showed us that life has meaning. The world is a university, a place in which we have the opportunity to find out who we really are and work out our destinies with real diligence. We were not born to rush through life and grab a handful of gold rings. Our time here is significant because our real life starts after this one, and what we do here is cf immense importance to us now as well as later. We are creating our heaven and our hell every day. I did not understand that before I met Bawa. Once I knew it in my heart, I had to act on it. I hope I do it well enough.

Finding out who you really are and coming closer to God are not dependent on getting into an organized religion and beating it to death. Wisdom is available to everyone. It is inside. Enlightened Buddhists may get there despite the religion of Buddhism, enlightened Hindus may get there despite the religion of Hinduism, enlightened Jews may get there despite the religion of Judaism, enlightened Christians may get there despite the religion of Christianity, and enlightened Muslims may get there despite the religion of Islam. Enlightenment is not about the dogma and ritual of any religion. It is something very personal and internal.

The Buddha sat in meditation for seven years and attained enlightenment, but I wonder how many of his followers came close to that state. The people who came after him developed techniques that have been successful in opening up certain levels of the mind, and these techniques, along with stories of the Buddha, were expounded upon by scholars. That is what came to be known as Buddhism. There is no doubt that if you sit in meditation for several years you will have some extraordinary experiences, but what is the source of those experiences, and where are they leading?

And how many people really understand what Jesus was saying? After his death, his disciples wrote about their experiences and a form was created. Inevitably things would have been added and dropped. The result became what we know today as Christianity, but how much does it have to do with what Christ taught? Certainly people who pray devoutly may experience miraculous interventions in their lives, but experiences are only experiences. Look what LSD can do, but is that the truth of God?

The mystical path is as common as the nose on your face. Whatever your religion, the mystical path is practicing the qualities of God. The mystical path is about becoming a child again, a child of God. It is about being generous and loving and not discriminating against others. If we as adults practice these qualities sincerely and step over that threshold to real faith, the gifts begin to flow.

After all the meditation practices I have explored, you might wonder what meditation I practice now. I consider myself a Sufi in the broadest sense of that word. I do silent *Zikr*, breathing out the world and breathing in God. The *Zikr* is a gift from God. I can practice it anywhere I am.

I think of my practice more as prayer than as meditation. Prayer nourishes me, opens me, satisfies me. I don't often get a high with prayer, and that is not why I pray. Zen and yoga meditation used to give me a rush, a pleasurable feeling. It was shakti—energy—and shakti is a wonderful thing to experience. *Zikr* and prayer bring me to a different state. They strengthen my faith and belief and bring me peace. I believe in the benefits of *Zikr* and so I do it, and doing the Zikr increases my faith in that belief and brings me peace, which is subtle but central. Prayer reaches beyond the desire to feel good and connects me to the Source of my being. Prayer reminds me that I am beholden to God for everything and that I cannot draw even a breath without His willing it to be so. When I meditated earlier in my life, it was only me meditating on this or that. Bawa frequently said that only God can meditate on God, and I have come to see that prayer is my connection to the God that exists everywhere and also in me.

My method is not particularly mystical; it is learned. The key is to let go of trying to control the meditation. Any spiritual practice works better when you are not focused on having some experience. The more you want the experience, the less likely you are to get it. Bawa said that the *Zikr* will teach you if you keep doing it. If you simply observe the breath process and allow it to unfold, the practice does itself. Peace descends upon you. The body relaxes. There's a sense of well-being.

You begin to realize that *you* are not breathing. You never have been the one who is breathing. You are *being breathed*. God is breathing you. If you can stay out of the way and watch the breath move of its own accord, already you are halfway there. You are joining with

God and watching a biological process that is inextricably bound up with your life.

One day, as I watched the breath, I was aware of a deep peace. I had no desire to move. I wanted only to remain in that state of peace. Wisdom seemed to instruct me: *This is a good state. Don't go to sleep in it. Keep practicing the Zikr. Keep being aware that nothing exists, that only God exists. Don't stop any part of the practice. The practice is what keeps you from blissing out. The practice keeps you on the edge of another state.*

There's a wonderful book called *The Way of the Pilgrim*, which was written by an anonymous monk in the nineteenth century. Left alone when his family died, he became a pilgrim. He desperately wanted to know God. A priest taught him the Prayer of the Heart: *Lord Jesus Christ*, said on the in breath, and *Have mercy on me*, said on the out breath. The priest instructed the pilgrim to begin by doing this prayer three thousand times a day. It was difficult, but soon he was able to do it. The priest then instructed him to increase the number of times a day to five thousand, and later, to ten thousand. Practicing this very simple prayer, the man became a walking saint. He began to have visions, and mysterious 'coincidences' guided his inner and outer life—all as a result of this simple practice.

The Prayer of the Heart is a Christian prayer, but it is essentially the same as the *Zikr*. If we reach out to God and say, "Please help me," God will hear our prayer. If God does not respond the way we want, it is for a reason, and part of faith and surrender is accepting God's will. This understanding is the heart of the Serenity Prayer:

> *God, grant me the serenity to accept the things I cannot change, the courage to change the things I can, and the wisdom to know the difference.*

No matter what practice you do, there are three magic words for success: *begin and continue*. The point is to keep renewing your connection to God and recharging until the practice is tightly woven into every breath you take. I haven't even come close to remembering God from morning until night, which was the ideal that Bawa inspired in me, but I am working on it, bit by bit.

I remember a story about a sage who was asked if it was difficult to pray every morning. His answer was, "Well, the first thirty years were hard."

It is difficult to follow a practice faithfully. Very difficult. And although *Zikr* is the master key for me, others may find a different approach more compatible. It is not for me to say. My wife is a good example of another approach. Jackie doesn't do the *Zikr* or go to morning prayers, but she has an intensely private and sweet area of serving and helping other people, and that is her prayer. I would not presume to say that my way is any better than that.

Sometimes I yearn for more of those world-changing Bawa dreams or for natural out-of-body experiences while doing *Zikr.* These things don't come to me as often as they do to some of Bawa's other children. I don't worry about that anymore. Even if such experiences never come to me, when I leave here they won't make any difference anyway.

Everything in life proceeds according to God's will. Every project I set out to do with the best-laid plans and preparation will go awry unless God wills it to succeed. All my efforts to better myself and to eradicate my bad qualities will only succeed with God's grace, which flows into me when all is right. Try as I may, without this wondrous grace I will not succeed. So I pray for grace. When I consistently do the things necessary to maintain my well-being—get up early, pray, serve others, give charity, try to understand the hearts of those around me and, above all, practice the qualities of God—I can feel my life changing. The feeling is subtle, as if there were a tiny but very accurate barometer deep inside me measuring the conditions of my internal climate.

I have many challenges to face in the short time I have left, challenges that involve becoming a better human being. Fortunately, God has given me good health and the wherewithal to explore these challenges and work at them. My duty is to try. When I let go of my attempts to control and surrender to God instead, my life unfolds effortlessly. I am still learning to let go and understand that "when God is not here, I am here; when I am not here, God is here." When I try my best to follow Bawa's guidance, I am walking the mystical path that I have been looking for all my life. It is not a flashy path. It is rather simple, and it is very difficult. It is easy to talk about and difficult to do. Keeping my intention strong and making an effort require absolute determination.

The words 'absolute determination' bring to mind an unusual story I heard when I was living in Corsica one summer. I had met a group of local skin divers, and I frequently dove with them. They knew the best areas, and they were experts. They could dive down ten meters without tanks, holding their breath for over three minutes. They knew where all the large grouper were, and could shoot forty or fifty pounds of fish each with their spear guns every day.

Over lunch, they bantered about their experiences, and that was how I heard the story of one of their heroes, Philippe. On the island, Philippe was a legend. He had been a resistance fighter in World War II and had single-handedly foiled some of the Nazi incursions on the island. But Philippe had a nemesis that he could not conquer. It was a grouper that weighed at least two hundred pounds. It hid in a cave and was wary of divers.

One day, Philippe managed to spear this monster of a fish. Perhaps he had a moment of exaltation (we can imagine that he did), but when he tried to bring the grouper to the surface, it retreated into its cave. Firmly ensconced, the giant fished opened its fins and wedged itself solidly behind the mouth of the cave. Philippe likewise planted himself at the entrance to the cave, and man and fish engaged in a tug of war.

I guess you could say that both won. Or perhaps both lost. Philippe's lifeless body floated to the surface and, some hours later, so did the body of the fish. Philippe was determined, and he gave up his life as he struggled to reach his goal.

When I think of Philippe's determination, I am in awe. It certainly seems stupid to die for a fish, but I imagine there are those who think me stupid to spend my life searching for God.

For me, Philippe's determination is the point of the story. He was so engaged in his endeavor that he didn't realize his air was gone, and he drowned. If I were to show just a small amount of this determination, think what I could accomplish! Although my story is not so dramatic as Philippe's, I have my own struggles: losing my temper, being impatient, being stubborn, being intolerant. So many fish to kill! But the interesting thing I find is that when I make mistakes, I learn, and the next time I do a little better. Occasionally I realize that a bad quality I have been struggling with hasn't surfaced for some time. I have made a little progress. My determination to fight this fight and to persevere is the *jihad* Bawa spoke of. It is the mother of wars for me.

It is a relief to know I don't have to keep searching and opening doors anymore. I don't have to run off to Timbuktu or find some other latest thing. Behind the one door I could never open until I met Bawa, I found the 99 beautiful qualities of God, and I found the way that will lead me home.

The circuitous route by which I came to Bawa is probably a route that others are taking now, bouncing from one set of experiences to another. I want to say by my life, "Look, you don't have to go through all that." I have tried to show the detours and wrong turns that can occur on the path to God, as well as to define the best, clearest, and most efficient way to know ourselves. What is the point of all the bouncing around? Where is it taking you, and what is the meaning of it? Before I met Bawa, I knew there must be a purpose to life. I knew what it was not, but I did not know exactly what it was. I knew I should try to be a good person, but I didn't know why, and I didn't really understand the consequences of my actions.

Now I have found that the learning available in everyday life comes through experiencing the boring, the unpleasant, and the frightening again and again and again and seeing that we always emerge from the struggle. There *is* a cycle. Trying to avoid the downs of the cycle only cultivates fear. By entering into the entire cycle, the ups as well as the downs, we build our faith in the order of things, in the rightful flow, the Tao, and every circumstance becomes an experiment in awareness rather than a blind struggle.

Embracing this more realistic view of the conditions of my life brightened and strengthened my self-esteem, as well as my esteem for others. Experiencing and understanding that we are all the same, that we all live and die, and that no human being is better than another freed me from much of my guilt, fear, and tension.

Soon, I will be seventy years old. I feel most blessed. I have found what I have been looking for all my life: the path to God. It is not God, but it leads me there, and I am grateful beyond words to have it.

So, now that this traveler has found the way that leads home, what do I do with myself every day?

I rise at 3:30 in the morning and make my morning tea, which I enjoy with crackers drizzled with olive oil. I drive ten minutes to the mazaar, Bawa's burial place, and there I participate in what we loosely refer to as the 'out-loud Zikr.' This 'out-loud Zikr' consists of singing the names of God and various phrases of worship in a particular cadence. It is most beautiful and powerful. Although in the daytime and at certain holy times, people travel hundreds, even thousands, of miles to visit this holy place and pay their respects to Bawa Muhaiyaddeen, at four in the morning, usually only a couple of people are there.

According to Bawa, recitation of the names of God cleanses our souls and gives us a powerful medicine to start our day. He even mentioned that many illnesses could be removed by these recitations and serious illness greatly lessened.

I can only report that my experience with this whole gestalt of rising early, gathering with others, and singing in remembrance of God has proved indispensable. The decisive moment comes every morning when the alarm rings. If I shut it off without sitting up, I am toast. Next thing I know, an hour has passed, and it is too late to go to prayers. Fortunately, this has only happened a few times. I do indeed 'sweat this little thing' of getting up for morning prayers. Getting out of bed when the alarm rings for prayers is my declaration that something is far more important to me than my senses and my comfort. It is the grand moment of conscience out of which I have the opportunity to grow a little or to slip a little.

On some mornings, I have had a cold or cough or congestion upon entering the mazaar, but by the time prayers are over, it is usually gone or hardly noticeable. As I walk the short path back to my car in the pre-dawn light, often I find myself praying, or singing aloud some portion of the holy words of praise. My day has begun well and is off to a glowing start. When good will and good qualities are circulating through my system, they crowd out any negativism or dark thoughts. I have an abundance of energy and well-being. With my day spread out before me, I look forward to spending this valuable currency.

A few minutes later when I stop at the local convenience store to pick up a newspaper, I meet other early risers —a jockey, a horse trainer, a retired fisherman, a retired professor, a salesman, and a World War II veteran who was a prisoner of war in Europe. Whoever is there, we share some banter about politics or the weather.

Back home, I read the papers with my breakfast, shower, and begin my day with ten minutes of yoga. The average day for me is punctuated by a midday visit to the YMCA and short afternoon and evening prayer breaks. In between these, I see counseling clients, work outside, and do errands or paperwork.

I have come to a better understanding of why it is vital to punctuate the day with short periods of prayer. Without it, life simply rolls on, unfolding itself into the next day and the next, day after day. The world offers many tasty tidbits along the way, but a central theme is missing. Without these intervals of remembering God and the reason for my existence, I am just driving along in the nice car that is my life with no destination. I'm putting in effort but without a clear intention.

Organizing my life around morning, afternoon, and evening prayer gives meaning and focus to whatever I am doing. Interaction with my wife and friends becomes not merely interaction but a measure of how well I listen and empathize. Instead of being irritating, inconveniences become opportunities to develop and strengthen my patience. Minor setbacks don't get blown out of proportion but become occasions to deepen my tolerance. Having a central theme of practicing restraint and expanding my good qualities endows even the simplest circumstance with deep significance. When seen through the filter of life's purpose, everything flows from that inner point of wisdom. The ancient Zen master was right when he said that Zen is "carrying water and chopping wood."

In today's world where this viewpoint of a simple spiritual path is most needed, it is also rarely found. The faster we move and the more our minds gyrate, the further we spin away from peace. A century ago, visiting a neighbor usually meant harnessing a horse, hitching up a carriage, and driving on a country lane for two hours. Slowly, in cadence with the horse's hooves, our ancestors would glide past valleys, streams, forests, and meadows filled with flowers and trees. Their minds would be at peace, gently absorbing nature and reminded of God's presence in everything. The drive by necessity provided ample time for pondering the meaning of life and seeking answers to life's mysteries.

How different is the world we live in today. It's not so much that the modern pace leaves no room for peace but that we tend to choose a way of life that makes inner harmony much more difficult to cultivate. Nowadays, we hop into the SUV, accelerate onto the fastest road that will get us where we want to go, turn on the radio, and dial up our broker to check stock prices—all while weaving in and out of traffic. We fill up the little spaces we have for peace with endless distractions.

Where are we going so fast? What is the hurry? Modern life programs us to hurry, and we continually reinforce the programming. Whenever I become aware that this has happened, I slow down immediately to a speed that is slower than normal. If the hurry has taken over while I am at home, I stop for a moment then recommence the chore I was doing at one-half the speed for at least five minutes. The results of practicing slowness are remarkable if you have faith in the practice and persevere.

I have searched everywhere for wisdom and finally had to see that what you know means very little; what is important is what the Buddhists call 'right action.' Right action requires us to slow down. Bawa said, "Hastiness is the guru of anger, and anger is the guru of sin." In Hinayana Buddhism, seekers spend entire days practicing *sattipana vipassana* meditation, where everything is done in slow motion. Lifting, lifting, lifting the spoon. Opening, opening, opening the mouth. Taking in, taking in, taking in the food. Chewing, chewing, chewing.

Slowness is a great aid to true peace of mind. It is impossible to maintain awareness when you are rushing around. The movements of an enlightened being are never hurried. All of us can learn to move more slowly no matter what we are doing: driving, eating, walking, talking. The practice of slowness is first experienced from the outside in, but soon it takes hold within us; we assimilate the slowness; we become the slowness. Slowness is a first cousin to patience, which is the mother of all good qualities.

I am most blessed to live in the country, surrounded by a meadow and nearby trees and singing birds. I do have the option of turning on the television or computer, but I am less inclined to do so these days. Walking, gardening, repairing, and cleaning all allow me the possibility of tuning into awareness of my own being, which lends a subtle, quiet sense of gratitude and meaning to all I do and touch. Granted, most people do not have the luxury of a quiet country life, but the point here is that wherever I am, I make an effort to create this calm space within.

I do a half-hour radio show on a local station in Philadelphia every Friday. It consists usually of taped interviews with people I know who I believe have some wisdom regarding t the purpose and conduct of their lives.

Not long ago, I interviewed a woman who had recently lost her twenty-year-old son. Her deep pain and shock led her to examine her life more closely and, ultimately, her loss strengthened her faith in God. We talked about these things. Her son had died indirectly as a result of alcohol consumption, and this led us to discuss alcoholism and addiction. She said, "People, as my son did, drink for many reasons, not the least of which is instant gratification. A glass of your favorite stuff can give you an instant glow or high." She smiled when she said this. "You know," she went on, "why would I want that high when I already have a much better (and non-toxic) one inside? All I have to do is turn to it."

She put her finger on the real point of wisdom in our lives. Most of us tend to run around, consciously seeking the highs: the best wine, the prettiest girl, the fastest car, the best job, the perfect vacation, the most inspiring book. These things become our idols. But the irony is, if we could move these attractions aside, look inside, and begin a serious journey to our center, we would find peace, joy, and a sense of oneness that would entirely eliminate the need for artificial highs. When I am able to touch this inner peace for even a few seconds, I need no other distractions. You could not tempt me away from that place with any gem you could offer.

Do I still have doubts and fears? Yes. But now I don't doubt the path, only my ability to walk it. And what I fear is that I may not walk it well enough or far enough to prove acceptable to my Maker. Every day I think of Bawa's words, "You will receive in the hereafter what you have earned as a result of your efforts." So now, all my efforts, no matter how distasteful, have taken on a new meaning. I know that they are little nuggets of gold even when their true value is not easy to discern.

I was most fortunate to come into contact with that rarest of rare beings—an *Insan Kamil*, a perfected being, a true child of God. Everything that Bawa gave to those of us who found our way to his door is still accessible after his death. The truths I have put forth in this book came from firsthand experience with a sage, and they are readily available to all who want them.

My brothers and sisters who read this book, forgive me for anything I have said that is wrong, or for anything that may have hurt you. I have written about my own life, trying to extract and give you something that may be of value. We are all together on this journey of life: black, white, red, yellow, brown; Jew, Christian, Muslim, Hindu, Buddhist; large, small, rich, poor, sick, healthy, old, young. We all came from God, and all of us will return to God.

It seems an age ago that I set out to become a monk in Japan and storm the gates of enlightenment. Now at least I know exactly where and how I need to do this work. My place is here in the ordinary world. For me, coping with the challenges and difficulties of everyday life and relationships requires all the wisdom, determination, and faith I can muster. My father, Bawa Muhaiyaddeen, made the task seem very simple, although, in truth, it is very difficult:

> *Have a melting heart and serve others with that heart.*
> *See the truth as goodness and put that goodness into action.*

May God grace us all, dear reader, with the courage and wisdom to pursue this amazing path, this path to our true home.

ACKNOWLEDGMENTS

I want to thank Sarah Aschenbach for her editing work on the book. She brought to the task not only her proficiency as a wordsmith but a rich background and familiarity with the realm of spiritual searching.

Thanks also to Phyllis Theroux for her editorial contribution to an earlier version of this book, and to Sally Green for her thoughtful comments on a final draft of the manuscript.

Lastly, deepest thanks to my wife Jackie, for her wisdom and advice thoughout the writing and editing of this book.

SUFI MASTER
M.R. BAWA MUHAIYADDEEN

Where could I go, my child, but into your heart?

True peace for human beings exists in only one place.

That place is not a meditation room,
not a church, not a temple.

That place cannot be found through psychology, science,
mantras, meditation, ritual, or spiritual practices.

That place is found only within the open space
of pure light, which is the human soul.

—M.R. Bawa Muhaiyaddeen

About the Author

Locke Rush has over 25 years of experience as a psychotherapist and marriage counselor. A graduate of Princeton University and a former officer in the United States Marine Corps, he also was co-author and co-producer of Rooftops of New York, an Academy Award nominated short subject film. He lived in Japan for four years, studying and practicing the disciplines of Zen Buddhism, and spent a year as a lay monk in the Ryutaku-ji Zen Monastery.

He received a PhD in Counseling Psychology in 1974 and went on to found the first intensive outpatient addiction treatment program in Maryland. From 1975 through 1986 he studied under the great Sufi Master M.R. Bawa Muhaiyaddeen. He lives happily in the Pennsylvania countryside with his wife, Jackie, and continues his counseling practice at his home.

285

If you practice patience, you become more patient.

If you become more patient, you become quieter.

If you become quieter, you become more aware.

*If you become more aware, you
become more compassionate.*

*If you become more compassionate,
you become more understanding.*

*If you become more understanding,
you become wiser.*

If you become wiser, you become more accepting.

*If you become more accepting, you
become more peaceful.*

*If you become more peaceful, you
see unity in all things.*

*If you see unity in all things,
you become more grateful.*

If you become more grateful, you thank God.

If you thank God, you will praise God.

*If you praise God, you have understood
Life and the meaning of your life,*

*And you have come to know that the
Kingdom of Heaven is indeed within.*